Cocos2d for iPhone 0.99 Beginner's Guide

Make mind-blowing 2D games for iPhone with this fast, flexible, and easy-to-use framework!

Pablo Ruiz

BIRMINGHAM - MUMBAI

Cocos2d for iPhone 0.99 Beginner's Guide

Copyright © 2010 Packt Publishing

All rights reserved. No part of this book may be reproduced, stored in a retrieval system, or transmitted in any form or by any means, without the prior written permission of the publisher, except in the case of brief quotations embedded in critical articles or reviews.

Every effort has been made in the preparation of this book to ensure the accuracy of the information presented. However, the information contained in this book is sold without warranty, either express or implied. Neither the author, nor Packt Publishing, and its dealers and distributors will be held liable for any damages caused or alleged to be caused directly or indirectly by this book.

Packt Publishing has endeavored to provide trademark information about all of the companies and products mentioned in this book by the appropriate use of capitals. However, Packt Publishing cannot guarantee the accuracy of this information.

First published: December 2010

Production Reference: 1081210

Published by Packt Publishing Ltd.
32 Lincoln Road
Olton
Birmingham, B27 6PA, UK.

ISBN 978-1-849513-16-6

www.packtpub.com

Cover Image by Charwak (charwak86@gmail.com)

Credits

Author
Pablo Ruiz

Reviewers
Chris Cockcroft
Hai "EvilJack" Nguyen
Mathieu Roy

Acquisition Editor
Usha Iyer

Development Editor
Susmita Panda

Technical Editor
Azharuddin Sheikh

Copy Editor
Neha Shetty

Indexer
Monica Ajmera Mehta
Rekha Nair
Hemangini Bari

Editorial Team Leader
Akshara Aware

Project Team Leader
Lata Basantani

Project Coordinator
Vishal Bodwani

Proofreader
Aaron Nash

Graphics
Nilesh Mohite

Production Coordinator
Alwin Roy

Cover Work
Alwin Roy

About the Author

Pablo Ruiz has six years of experience in software development and a lifetime of experience playing games. After years of programming in different languages, he started developing applications for iPhone and he did not look back. After making his first game, Aqua Rush for iPhone, he dedicated himself to working as a consultant. In 2010, he and his partner formed their own company, Infinix, Soft-Digital Solutions, offering other companies their expertise in Mobile software development.

> I would like to thank my family for their constant support, especially to my girlfriend, Tamara, for without her advice, support, and patience I wouldn't be where I am. I'd also like to thank Julieta Vicente for making such beautiful illustrations for the example games presented throughout the book. Finally, thanks to my cousin, Victor, for listening to me and encouraging me to do everything I do and my partner, Ivan, for working so hard that I have one less thing to worry about. Of course, this book wouldn't have been possible without Ricardo Quesada's huge effort into making this excellent framework.

About the Reviewers

Chris Cockcroft has over twelve years of experience in the graphic design and illustration industry. Chris Cockcroft has more recently become involved in iOS interactive entertainment in both design and development roles. In addition to self-publishing several titles built around the Cocos2d frameworks, Chris also worked with developer Andreas Ehnbom on the visual design of the popular Cocos2d-driven (and Apple-featured) title, Fuji Leaves. Chris's work can be viewed at www.chriscockcroft.com.

Hai "EvilJack" Nguyen fits your typical engineering stereotype: scrawny, loves to program, and scared to death of women. He spends his free time tinkering with gadgets and updating his Facebook status.

After finishing graduate school at the University of Florida, Jack moved to Taiwan in mid 2003. Shortly thereafter SARS hit the Asia pacific region (unrelated to Jack's arrival, of course). He then joined a software company that worked on mobile phones (Aplix) and got a chance to play with all the latest phones and gadgets.

Eventually, he left that awesome job and moved to Korea a few years later (to chase a girl) and spent the better part of a year studying Korean. Shortly after moving there, North Korea began conducting tests on their nuclear stockpile (unrelated to Jack's arrival, of course).

Eventually, he moved back to the USA and began working for a voice over IP startup creating mobile applications for them. Shortly after moving back to the US (2007), the greatest financial crisis in almost a century occurred (unrelated to Jack's arrival, of course).

Jack currently splits his time between California and Florida while trying to avoid getting kicked out of (yet) another country.

Mathieu Roy is a young programmer in his 20s, who started programming and doing some heavy PHP for various projects and contracts. As soon as iPhone came out, he went straight to Objective-C and OpenGL, wanting to make games. His first title, *Rocket Boy 2D*, is available on the application store. His blog is at www.qcmat.com. He is the partial owner and programmer of PowPowGames. They are a new company, developing games for iPhone, iPod, and iPad. PowPowGame's website is www.powpowgames.com.

> I'd like to thanks my family, especially my daughter, who encourage me and believe in me.

Table of Contents

Preface	**1**
Chapter 1: Getting Started with Cocos2d	**11**
Downloading Cocos2d for iPhone	12
Time for action – opening the samples project	12
Installing the templates	14
Time for action – installing the templates	14
Creating a new project from the templates	16
Time for action – creating a HelloCocos2d project	16
Managing the game with the CCDirector	17
Types of CCDirectors	18
Time for action – taking a first look at the HelloCocos2dAppDelegate	18
Scene management	21
Doing everything with CCNodes	22
Time for action – peeking at the HelloWorldScene class	22
CCNodes properties	25
Handling CCNodes	26
Checking your timing	27
Time for action – using timers to make units shoot each second	27
Delaying a method call	31
Time for action – destroying your units	31
Debugging cocos2d applications	33
Time for action – checking Cocos2d debug messages	33
Time for action – checking deallocing messages	34
Time for action – knowing your errors	35
Time for action – removing debug messages	35
Summary	36

Chapter 2: Playing with Sprites — 37
- Making a puzzle game — 38
- Beginning a new project — 38
- Time for action – creating a new project — 38
- Displaying images with CCSprites — 41
- Time for action – adding a background image to the game — 41
  - Creating CCSprites — 43
    - Pixel formats — 43
    - More ways of creating CCSprites — 44
- Time for action – creating the Stone class — 44
- Creating the game board — 48
- Time for action – placing stones in the grid — 49
- Interacting with sprites — 53
- Time for action – registering the stones for receiving touches — 54
- Time for action – handling touches for swapping stones — 55
- Time for action – swapping the stones around — 59
- Time for action – checking for matches — 62
- Making them fall! — 68
- Time for action – refilling the grid — 68
  - Analyzing the logic — 70
- Playing with CCSprite's properties — 73
- Time for action – making a time bar — 74
- Changing a sprite's texture at runtime — 76
- Time for action – changing textures on the fly — 77
  - The CCTextureCache — 78
- Using Spritesheets — 79
- Time for action – creating sprites from Spritesheets — 81
- Creating Spritesheets with zwoptex — 85
- Time for action – creating more colored stones — 86
- with Spritesheets — 86
- Preloading images — 88
- Time for action – preloading your images — 89
- Making OpenGl Calls — 90
- Time for action – selecting a stone for swapping — 90
- Summary — 92

Chapter 3: Let's Do Some Actions — 93
- Basic actions — 94
- Time for action – animating the stone falling — 94
  - Using other basic actions — 95
- Time for action – destroying stones with actions — 98
- Time for action – tinting the time bar — 99

Composition actions	101
Time for action – making a nice disappear effect	101
More composition actions	102
Time for action – making stones fall and grow	103
Time for action – animating the grid	103
Ease actions	105
Time for action – modifying animations with ease actions	106
Effect actions	107
Time for action – making the background shake when matching five stones	108 108
Applying a single action to multiple CCNodes	110
Special actions	111
Time for action – ready, set, go!	111
Using CCCallFuncND	114
Time for action – telling the player he lost	115
Animations	116
Time for action – animating the stones	117
CCSpriteFrame and the CCSpriteFrameCache	121
The CCAnimation class	123
Summary	124

Chapter 4: Pasting Labels — 125

Using CCLabels	126
Time for action – first time tutorials	126
Displaying texts with CCLabelAtlas	133
Time for action – displaying and updating scores with CCLabelAtlas	134 134
Creating texts with CCBitmapFontAtlas	136
Time for action – showing feedback	137
Time for action – running actions on texts	140
Making your own BitmapFontAtlas with BM Font tool	142
Time for action – creating your own Bitmap font	142
Wrapping up the game	148
Summary	148

Chapter 5: Surfing through Scenes — 149

Aerial Gun, a vertical shooter game	150
Creating new scenes	150
Time for action – creating the splash and main menu scene	151
Transitioning through scenes	158
Time for action – moving through scenes in a nice way	158
Implementing the game logic	159

Table of Contents

Preparing for the game	160
Making a hero	162
Time for action – creating the hero class	**162**
Making yourself some enemies	165
Time for action – throwing enemies at your hero	**165**
Forging some bullets	171
Time for action – creating and reusing bullets	**171**
Handling accelerometer input	**176**
Time for action – moving your hero with the accelerometer	**177**
Handling touches on layers	**179**
Time for action – firing the bullets	**180**
Detecting collisions	**184**
Time for action – shooting down your enemies	**184**
Time for action – losing your life	**188**
Adding more layers to scenes	**192**
Time for action – creating a HUD to display lives and the score	**192**
Time for action – creating a pause menu	**198**
Time for action – pausing the game while inactive	**204**
Summary	**206**
Chapter 6: Menu Design	**207**
Creating a simple menu	207
Time for action – adding a menu with texts to the main scene	**208**
Using image menu items	**212**
Time for action – adding a difficulty selection screen	**212**
Animating menu items	**216**
Time for action – animating the main menu	**216**
Using toggle menu items	**218**
Time for action – creating the options menu	**218**
Saving and loading preferences	**225**
Time for action – persisting options data	**225**
Summary	**227**
Chapter 7: Implementing Particle Systems	**229**
Taking a look at the prebuilt particle systems	230
Time for action – running the particle test	**231**
Time for action – analyzing the ParticleMeteor system	**231**
Particle system properties	232
Implementing particle systems in your game using Gravity mode	**234**
CCPointParticleSystem	234
CCQuadParticleSystem	234
Time for action – making bombs explode	**235**

[iv]

Using the radius mode	239
Time for action – hurting your enemies	240
Changing the way particle systems move	243
Using Particle Designer to create particle systems	244
Time for action – creating a smoke trail	245
Summary	249

Chapter 8: Familiarizing Yourself with Tilemaps — 251

Using tilemaps	251
Creating tilemaps with Tiled	253
Time for action – creating your first map	253
Loading tilemaps in Cocos2d	259
Time for action – using tilemaps in Cocos2d	260
Time for action – running actions on layers	261
Time for action – reaching the end of the level	262
Time for action – fixing black gaps and glitches	263
Using layers to hold objects	265
Time for action – adding object layers in tiled	265
Time for action – retrieving objects in Cocos2d	266
Summary	270

Chapter 9: Playing Sounds with CocosDenshion — 271

What is CocosDenshion?	271
Getting started with sounds	272
Time for action – using SimpleAudioEngine	272
Methods for handling sound effects	273
Time for action – playing background music with SimpleAudioEngine	274
	274
Methods for handling background music	274
Using CDSoundEngine	275
Time for action – setting it up	276
Time for action – playing sound effects for explosions	278
Time for action – loading effects asynchronously with CDSoundEngine	279
	279
Time for action – playing background music with CDAudioManager	280
	280
Summary	282

Chapter 10: Using Physics Engines — 283

A word about physics engines	284
Box2d	284
Chipmunk	284
So, which one should I use?	285

Totem balance, a physical game	**285**
Time for action –taking a look at the Chipmunk template	**286**
Understanding cpBodies and cpShapes	289
Preparing the game	**291**
Bringing objects to life	**292**
The Totem	292
Time for action – creating a poly-shaped object	**292**
Time for action – creating the goal platform	**296**
Removable blocks	299
Time for action – building blocks	**299**
Time for action – destroying shapes with touch	**306**
Collision callbacks	**309**
Time for action –losing the game	**310**
Time for action –winning the game	**312**
Placing static shapes	**314**
Summary	**316**
Chapter 11: Integrating OpenFeint	**317**
Signing up and downloading the SDK	**318**
Time for action – signing up and downloading the SDK	**318**
Integrating OpenFeint into your game	**320**
Time for action – making OpenFeint work	**320**
Time for action – displaying the OpenFeint dashboard	**322**
Adding leaderboards to your game	**326**
Time for action – creating a leaderboard	**326**
Adding achievements to your game	**329**
Time for action – creating an achievement	**330**
Submitting your game for OpenFeint approval	**333**
Summary	**333**
Appendix: Pop Quiz Answers	**335**
Chapter 2:	**335**
Playing with Sprites	335
Chapter 3:	**335**
Let's do some actions	335
Chapter 4:	**335**
Pasting labels	335
Chapter 5:	**336**
Surfing through scenes	336
Chapter 6:	**336**
Menu design	336

Chapter 7:	**336**
Implementing particle systems	**336**
Chapter 8:	**336**
Familiarizing yourself with tilemaps	336
Chapter 9:	**337**
Playing sounds with CocosDenshion	337
Chapter 10:	**337**
Using physics engine	337
Chapter 11:	**337**
Integrating OpenFeint	337
Index	**339**

Preface

Cocos2d for iPhone is a framework for building 2D games, applications, presentations, demos, and more. It was originally made for Python and then ported to IPhone by **Ricardo Quesada** as an open source project with the MIT license.

This book will teach you the fundamentals of how to write games with this framework. As this book is meant to give you a basic knowledge of the most important aspects of Cocos2d, it will cover a lot of subjects very quickly. However, do not worry! Almost every chapter will include tasks for you to complete and examples for you to practice. Throughout this book, we'll make three different games and each chapter will build on the previous one, but can also be considered independently, so feel free to skip to any chapter that interests you.

Learning to use Cocos2d is really easy and will allow you to start building your games in no time. It includes a lot of sample code full of comments explaining every little part of it.

One of the greatest key points of this framework is its big, active community. Every time you get stuck with something or find some bug, you can pay a visit to their forum where a lot of great people will surely help you. You will also find a lot of useful tips and code to enhance your game.

Cocos2d follows the 'copyleft' idea, so when you start making your own modifications to any core part of the framework, you should send them so that they can be added to the framework. You are not obligated to do so, but if you do, you will help the community and the framework itself a lot.

As of this writing, Cocos2d for iPhone is in its 0.99.5 version. I have been using it from Version 0.7x and the improvements made by its author and the community have been huge. Right now, it is one of the most used 2D game frameworks available for iPhone development.

Cocos2d can be used to build any kind of 2D game; from simple puzzle games to intensive physics simulations. Right now, there are more than 2000 applications made with it. Among all those applications, there are some bestsellers such as Trainyard, Farmville, and Stick Wars.

Preface

What this book covers

This book is designed to get you familiarized with Cocos2d for iPhone, allowing you to build your own games. To that end, the book is organized in easy-to-follow examples. Through the book, we'll be building three different types of games that exploit all the power that Cocos2d has.

Chapter 1, Getting Started with Cocos2d, starts by taking a look at the sample projects that are included in the source. Then you will learn how to install the templates to easily start a new project and then you'll make your first simple project. We'll also talk about some Cocos2d basic concepts. Finally, we'll take a look at the debugging features of Cocos2d.

Chapter 2, Playing with Sprites, allows you to learn all there is to Sprites. By the end of the chapter, you will be able to create and manage your own objects. We'll also start building the first of the three games that we'll make in the book. We'll take a look at how to begin developing a simple puzzle game.

Chapter 3, Let's Do Some Actions, allows you to move, scale, tint, and apply a lot more effects to objects over time. In this chapter, we'll continue enhancing the first game to make it look nicer.

Chapter 4, Pasting Labels, explains that every game needs to show some text at some point. It could be an instruction text, hints, scores, or a lot of other things. So, this chapter will take a look at all the ways Cocos2d has to place texts on the screen and modify them.

Chapter 5, Surfing Through Scenes, Layers, and Transitions, discusses how Scenes and Layers are where all the content of Cocos2d games is placed. Your game may consist of just one Scene with one Layer, or as many as you want! This chapter will get into the details of how to make the best use of them, switch between scenes with Transitions, and also how to handle accelerometer and touch input on the layers.

Chapter 6, Menu Design, highlights the importance of menus, which are a very important part of any game. Cocos2d comes with several ways to create them. It even let's you animate them like you would animate any other Sprite. This chapter will also talk about saving preferences and loading them back.

Chapter 7, Implementing Particle Systems, explains the importance of using flashy effects. This chapter explains how to implement the existing particle systems that are included in Cocos2d and you will even create your own.

Chapter 8, Familiarizing Yourself with Tilemaps, provides information about Tilemaps, which are used to create big levels while using small images to create the maps. You can use Tilemaps to create games such as Shrumps, platform games, or RPGs quite easily. This chapter will take a look at how to create these Tilemaps with Tiled and how to load and manipulate them with Cocos2d.

Chapter 9, Playing Sounds with CocosDenshion, covers topics related to playing sound and music in your game. Almost every game needs to play sound and music. Cocos2d includes a great sound engine for all your sound needs. You will be using background music and sound effects in no time after reading this chapter. Here we will also learn some preloading techniques.

Chapter 10, Using Physics Engines, explains the importance and role of physics engines. A lot of games that have come out lately make use of physics engines. These engines allow games to behave like they would in real life. Cocos2d can be integrated with Chipmunk and Box2d (two great physics engines). This chapter will explain how to use Chipmunk in any game you want.

Chapter 11, Integrating Cocos2d with Social Networks, tells us that once you have completed your game there is a lot to be done. You may want to monetize it by using Admob ads or add social aspects to it such as leaderboards or achievements, allowing users to post their scores to Facebook and Twitter. So, this chapter will take a look at the basics of making your game reach the entire world.

Appendix, Pop Quiz Answers, contains answers to all the Pop Quizzes in the book.

What you need for this book

You'll need the following things to get started with writing Cocos2d games (or any kind of application) for iPhone:

- An Intel-based Macintosh running Leopard(OS X 10.5.3 or later)
- Xcode
- You must be enrolled as an iPhone developer in order to test the example projects in your device
- Games require a lot of assets such as images, UI design, sounds, and music; this book comes with the resources that you'll need to build the example projects
- And of course, the latest Cocos2d for iPhone sources

For your own games, you will need some graphic design software to make your own images, and sound design software for your music and sounds. If you are not comfortable doing that, you should hire someone who can. There are lots of sites dedicated to help people meet with designers to work together. Alternatively, there are lots of sites where you can buy royalty-free images and sounds at a low rate; these are very useful for small projects or when you are low on budget.

Who is this book for?

This book is for anyone who wishes to get into game programming.

Game programming is one of the most difficult subjects for a beginner but it is a very rewarding experience, so you should have some patience if this is your first time! Fortunately, Cocos2d makes it very easy for you to start working and seeing some results.

Cocos2d-iPhone uses Objective-C as its main language, so some basic knowledge of Objective-C is a must. This book assumes that you understand the fundamentals of object-oriented programming and programming in general. Cocos2d includes two physics engines, Chipmunk and Box2d, which are programmed in C and C++ respectively, so you should have some basic understanding of those languages in order to be able to work with physics simulations.

Previous knowledge of game programming is not needed but it is a plus.

This book is designed to get you to make your own games for iOS, so you should be familiar with the iPhone/iPad itself. The iPhone is a great platform for programming. It looks nice and feels nice. I guess you already know that and you have already played a lot of games in it. Once you have started programming your own games, take a look at the ones you like. Play them and try to understand how they behave and what makes them great.

What games will you be making in this book?

Throughout this book, I will show you how to create three different games that explore a lot of Cocos2d topics and general game programming concepts.

Coloured Stones

This is a simple match three puzzle game. It will have a grid with stones and you will be able to match three or more of them by swapping their positions.

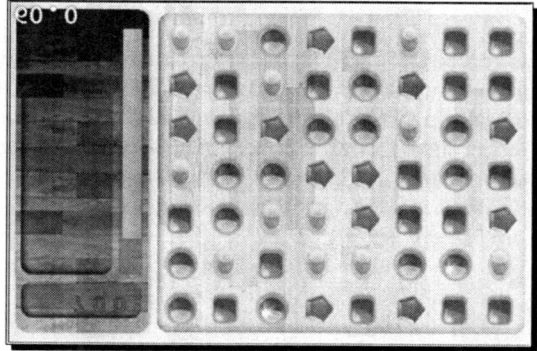

AerialGun

This is an action vertical shooter game. You will take the role of an accelerometer controlled plane taking out opposing forces by shooting and bombing them.

Totem balance

In this physics based game, you will have to remove elements from the screen while not letting the Totem fall to the ground.

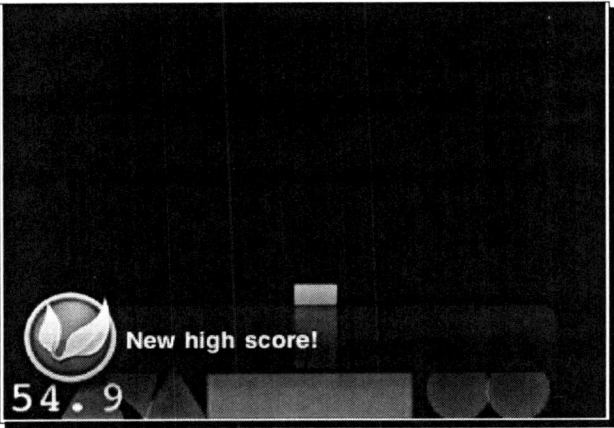

Cocos2d open source and commercial projects

This is a list of some Cocos2d projects made available by their authors. Take a look at them after you have learned the basics. They provide a lot of useful material that may help you make your own game better or learn some new concepts from real games.

Have in mind that most of them were made with older versions of Cocos2d, so they will most likely need some changes if you want to try them using the latest Cocos2d version.

 If you need to change or test these games using the latest Cocos2d version, visit http://www.cocos2d-iphone.org/wiki/doku.php/prog_guide:migrating_to_0_9 to migrate from the older version to 0.9x or newer.

ABC123

- Author: http://kwigbo.com
- Homepage: http://kwigbo.com/private/305272732/tumblr_kve45bK4RO1qav61q
- License: http://creativecommons.org/licenses/by-sa/3.0/us/

DeBlock

- Author: http://www.lhunath.com/
- Homepage: http://www.lhunath.com/
- License: Open Source (URL)

Gorillas

- Author: http://kwigbo.com
- Homepage: http://kwigbo.com/private/305272732/tumblr_kve45bK4RO1qav61q
- License: http://creativecommons.org/licenses/by-sa/3.0/us/

Grabbed

- Author: http://ortatherox.com/
- Homepage: http://ortatherox.com/grabbed/
- License: Open source

Pusher

- Author: http://kwigbo.com
- Homepage: http://kwigbo.com/post/335053103/pusher-source-code
- License: http://creativecommons.org/licenses/by/3.0/us/

Thrown

- Author: http://ortatherox.com/
- Homepage: http://ortatherox.com/thrown/
- License: Open source

Tweejump

- Author: http://iplayful.com
- Homepage: http://github.com/haqu/tweejump
- License: Open source

Sapus Tongue

- Author: http://www.sapusmedia.com/
- Homepage: http://www.sapusmedia.com/sources
- License: Commercial

Conventions

In this book, you will find a number of styles of text that distinguish between different kinds of information. Here are some examples of these styles, and an explanation of their meaning.

Code words in text are shown as follows: " In the GameScene.m file, find the checkGroups method and where we were checking if three or more stones matched."

A block of code is set as follows:

```
if([n count]>=3)
{
  for(Stone * c in n)
  {
     // not relevant code...
     [c.mySprite setTextureRect:CGRectMake(34,2,32, 32)];
```

```
        [c.mySprite runAction:[CCFadeOut actionWithDuration:0.5]];
    }
        // not relevant code...
}
```

When we wish to draw your attention to a particular part of a code block, the relevant lines or items are set in bold:

```
-(void)step:(ccTime *)dt
{
   [hero update];

   for(Bullet * b in bullets)
   {
     if(b.fired)
     {
        [b update];
     }
     else
     {
        if(self.playerFiring && hero.lastTimeFired > hero.fireInterval)
        {
          [b fire:1 position:hero.mySprite.position
             fspeed:hero.firingSpeed];
          hero.lastTimeFired=0;
        }
     }
   }

   ...
   //enemy updating code
}
```

Any command-line input or output is written as follows:

```
# cp /usr/src/asterisk-addons/configs/cdr_mysql.conf.sample
     /etc/asterisk/cdr_mysql.conf
```

New terms and **important words** are shown in bold. Words that you see on the screen, in menus or dialog boxes for example, appear in the text like this: "Each time you change anything, remember to press the **Reset Cache** button to see the changes".

> Warnings or important notes appear in a box like this.

> Tips and tricks appear like this.

Reader feedback

Feedback from our readers is always welcome. Let us know what you think about this book—what you liked or may have disliked. Reader feedback is important for us to develop titles that you really get the most out of.

To send us general feedback, simply send an e-mail to feedback@packtpub.com, and mention the book title via the subject of your message.

If there is a book that you need and would like to see us publish, please send us a note in the **SUGGEST A TITLE** form on www.packtpub.com or e-mail suggest@packtpub.com.

If there is a topic that you have expertise in and you are interested in either writing or contributing to a book, see our author guide on www.packtpub.com/authors.

Customer support

Now that you are the proud owner of a Packt book, we have a number of things to help you to get the most from your purchase.

> **Downloading the example code for this book**
>
> You can download the example code files for all Packt books you have purchased from your account at http://www.PacktPub.com. If you purchased this book elsewhere, you can visit http://www.PacktPub.com/support and register to have the files e-mailed directly to you.

Errata

Although we have taken every care to ensure the accuracy of our content, mistakes do happen. If you find a mistake in one of our books—maybe a mistake in the text or the code—we would be grateful if you would report this to us. By doing so, you can save other readers from frustration and help us improve subsequent versions of this book. If you find any errata, please report them by visiting `http://www.packtpub.com/support`, selecting your book, clicking on the **errata submission form** link, and entering the details of your errata. Once your errata are verified, your submission will be accepted and the errata will be uploaded on our website, or added to any list of existing errata, under the Errata section of that title. Any existing errata can be viewed by selecting your title from `http://www.packtpub.com/support`.

Piracy

Piracy of copyright material on the Internet is an ongoing problem across all media. At Packt, we take the protection of our copyright and licenses very seriously. If you come across any illegal copies of our works, in any form, on the Internet, please provide us with the location address or website name immediately so that we can pursue a remedy.

Please contact us at `copyright@packtpub.com` with a link to the suspected pirated material.

We appreciate your help in protecting our authors, and our ability to bring you valuable content.

Questions

You can contact us at `questions@packtpub.com` if you are having a problem with any aspect of the book, and we will do our best to address it.

Getting Started with Cocos2d

Before getting started with Cocos2d you need to learn how to set up a project. This will make things easier than starting from scratch. By the end of this chapter, you will know how to install the templates that come with the source code and we'll take a look at the samples included.

In this chapter, we shall:

- ◆ Learn how to get the example projects (called templates) working
- ◆ Play with those templates
- ◆ Take a look at the basic structure of a Cocos2d game

So let's get on with it.

In this book we will always mention the term **iOS programming,** which refers to iPhone, iPod Touch, and iPad programming, as they all share the same iOS and are similar in programming terms.

There are many topics which this book does not cover because they are advanced topics; some of them are not so simple for beginners, but when you feel ready, give them a try.

Downloading Cocos2d for iPhone

Visit `http://www.cocos2d-iphone.org` for downloading the latest files. Search the downloads page, and there you will find the different versions available. As of this writing, Version 0.99.5 is the latest stable version.

Once you have downloaded the file to your computer, uncompress the folder to your desktop, and rename it to `Cocos2d`. Open the uncompressed folder and take a look at its contents. Inside that folder, you will find everything you will need to make a game with Cocos2d. The following is a list of the important folders and files:

- Cocos2d: The bread and butter of Cocos2d.
- CocosDenshion: The sound engine that comes along. We'll explore it in *Chapter 9*.
- Cocoslive: Cocos2d comes packed with its own highscore server. You can easily set it up to create a scoreboard and ranking for your game.
- External: Here are the sources for Box2d and Chipmunk physics engines among other things.
- Extras: Useful classes created by the community.
- Resources: Images, sounds, tilemaps, and so on, used in the tests.
- Templates: The contents of the templates we'll soon install.
- Test: The samples used to demonstrate all the things Cocos2d can do.
- Tools: Some tools you may find useful, such as a ParticleView project that lets you preview how particles will look.
- License files: They are here in case you need to look at them.

We'll start by taking a look at the samples.

Time for action – opening the samples project

Inside the `cocos2d-iphone` folder, you will find a file named `cocos2d-iphone.xcodeproj`. This project contains all the samples and named tests that come with the source code. Let's run one of them.

1. Open the `.xcodeproj` file: In the groups and files panel you will find the source code of all the samples. There are more than 35 samples that cover all of the capabilities of Cocos2d, as shown in the following screenshot:

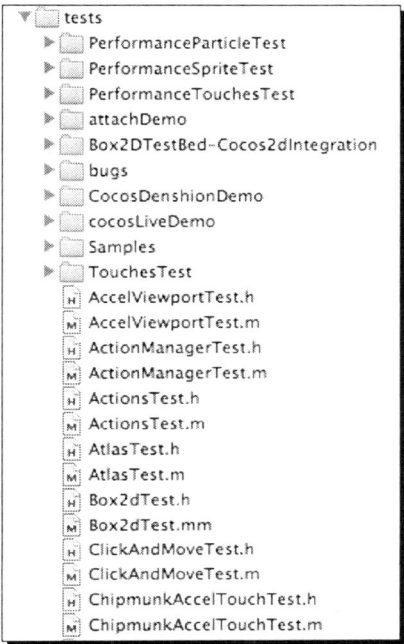

2. Compile and run the SpriteTest: This project comes with a *target* for each of the available tests, so in order to try any of them you have to select them from the overview dropdown.

   Go ahead and select the SpriteTest target and click on **Build and Run**. If everything goes well the test should start running. Play a little with it, feel how it behaves, and be amazed by the endless possibilities.

What just happened?

You have just run your first Cocos2d application. If you want to run another sample, just select it by changing the "Active target". When you do so, the "active executable" should match to the same; if it doesn't select it manually by selecting it from the overview dropdown box. You can see which "active target" and "active executable" is selected from that overview dropdown box, they should be selected.

Have a go hero – trying out the rest of the samples

Try taking a look at all of the samples included with Cocos2d; some are just performance tests, but they are still useful for knowing what to expect from the framework and what it can do.

Although these tests don't make anything that looks like a game, they are useful for learning the basics, and they are very good consulting material. So, when you are in doubt and reading the source code does not help, check these examples, and you will surely find your answer.

Installing the templates

Cocos2d comes with three templates. These templates are the starting point for any Cocos2d game. They let you:

- Create a simple Cocos2d project
- Create a Cocos2d project with Chipmunk as physics engine
- Create a Cocos2d project with Box2d as physics engine

Which one you decide to use for your project depends on your needs. Right now we'll create a simple project from the first template.

Time for action – installing the templates

Carry out the following steps for installing the templates:

1. Open the terminal. It is located in **Applications | Utilities | Terminal**.
2. Assuming that you have uncompressed the folder on your desktop and renamed it as Cocos2d, type the following:

   ```
   cd desktop/Cocos2d
   ./install_template.sh
   ```

You will see a lot of output in the terminal (as shown in the following screenshot); read it to check if the templates were installed successfully.

```
Template dir: /Developer/Platforms/iPhoneOS.platform/Developer/Library/Xcode/Pro
ject Templates/Application/

...creating destination directory: /Developer/Platforms/iPhoneOS.platform/Develo
per/Library/Xcode/Project Templates/Application/cocos2d-0.99.1 Application/
...copying template files
...copying cocos2d files
...copying cocos2d dependency files
...copying CocosDenshion files
...copying cocoslive files
...copying cocoslive dependency files
done!
```

> If you are getting errors, check if you have downloaded the files correctly and uncompressed them into the desktop. If it is in another place you may get errors.

We just installed the Xcode templates for Cocos2d. Now, each time you create a new project in Xcode, you will be given the choice of doing it by using a Cocos2d application. We'll see how to do that in a moment.

> Each time a new version of Cocos2d is released, there is a template file for that version. So, you should remember to install them each time. If you have a lot of older templates and you want to remove them, you can do so by going to `Developer/Platforms/iPhoneOS.platform/Developer/Library/Xcode/Project Templates/Application` and deleting the respective folder.

What just happened?

Templates are very useful and they are a great starting point for any new project. Having these templates available makes starting a new project an easy task. You will have all the Cocos2d sources arranged in groups, your **AppDelegate** already configured to make use of the framework and even a simple starting **Layer**.

Getting Started with Cocos2d

Creating a new project from the templates

Now that you have the templates ready to use, it is time to make your first project.

Time for action – creating a HelloCocos2d project

We are going to create a new project named HelloCocos2d from the templates you have just installed. This won't be anything like a game, but just an introduction on how to get started. The steps are as follows:

1. Open Xcode and select **File | New project** (*Shift + cmd + N*).

2. Cocos2d templates will appear right there along with the other Xcode project templates, as shown in the following screenshot:

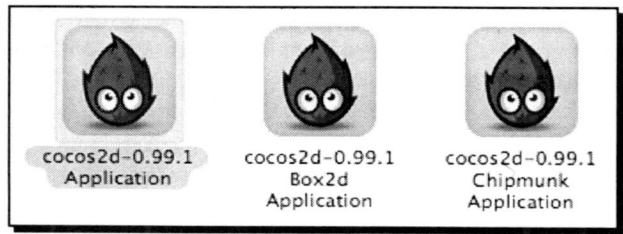

3. Select **Cocos2d-0.99.1 Application.**

4. Name the project `HelloCocos2d` and save it to your `Documents` folder.

Once you perform the preceding steps, the project you just created should open up. Let's take a look at the important folders that were generated:

- `Cocos2d Sources`: This is where the Cocos2d source code resides. Generally, you won't touch anything from here unless you want to make modifications to the framework or want to know how it works.

- `Classes`: This is where the classes you create will reside. As you may see, two classes were automatically created, thanks to the template. We'll explore them in a moment.

- `Resources`: This is where you will include all the **assets** needed for your game.

Go ahead and run the application. Click on **Build and go** and congratulate yourself, as you have created your first Cocos2d project.

Pretty boring, isn't it? As you advance in the book, you will build many more interesting things, but let's stop for a moment and take a look at what was created here.

When you run the application you'll notice a couple of things, as follows:

- The Cocos2d for iPhone logo shows up as soon as the application starts.
- Then a **CCLabel** is created with the text Hello World.
- You can see some numbers in the lower-left corner of the screen. That is the current **FPS** the game is running at.

In a moment, we'll see how this is achieved by taking a look at the generated classes.

What just happened?

We have just created our first project from one of the templates that we installed before. As you can see, using those templates makes starting a Cocos2d project quite easy and lets you get your hands on the actual game's code sooner.

Managing the game with the CCDirector

The CCDirector is the class whose main purpose is *scene* management. It is responsible for switching scenes, setting the desired FPS, the device orientation, and a lot of other things.

The CCDirector is the class responsible for initializing OpenGL ES.

If you grab an older Cocos2d project you might notice that all Cocos2d classes have the "CC" prefix missing. Those were added recently to avoid naming problems. Objective-c doesn't have the concept of namespaces, so if Apple at some point decided to create a Director class, those would collide.

Types of CCDirectors

There are currently four types of directors; for most applications, you will want to use the default one:

- NSTimer Director: It triggers the main loop from an NSTimer object. It is the slowest of the Directors, but it integrates well with UIKit objects. You can also customize the update interval from 1 to 60.
- Mainloop Director: It triggers the main loop from a custom main loop. It is faster than the NSTimer Director, but it does not integrate well with UIKit objects, and its interval update can't be customized.
- ThreadMainLoop Director: It has the same advantages and limitations as the Mainloop Director. When using this type of Director, the main loop is triggered from a thread, but it will be executed on the main thread.
- DisplayLink Director: This type of Director is only available in OS 3.1+. This is the one used by default. It is faster than the NSTimer Director and integrates well with UIKit objects. The interval update can be set to 1/60, 1/30, or 1/15.

Those are the available Directors, most of the times you will not need to make any changes here.

Time for action – taking a first look at the HelloCocos2dAppDelegate

The AppDelegate is the main entry point of your application. Here is where Cocos2d is initialized. There are a lot of useful things you can tweak from the Director in here to change the behavior of your application. Let's take a look.

```
@implementation HelloCocos2dAppDelegate
@synthesize window;
- (void) applicationDidFinishLaunching:(UIApplication*)application
{
    // Init the window
    window = [[UIWindow alloc] initWithFrame:[[UIScreen mainScreen]
       bounds]];
```

```
    // cocos2d will inherit these values
    [window setUserInteractionEnabled:YES];
    [window setMultipleTouchEnabled:YES];

    // Try to use CADisplayLink director
    // if it fails (SDK < 3.1) use the default director
    if( ! [CCDirector setDirectorType:CCDirectorTypeDisplayLink] )
        [CCDirector setDirectorType:CCDirectorTypeDefault];

    // Use RGBA_8888 buffers
    // Default is: RGB_565 buffers
    [[CCDirector sharedDirector] setPixelFormat:kPixelFormatRGBA8888];

    // Create a depth buffer of 16 bits
    // Enable it if you are going to use 3D transitions or 3d objects
    //[[CCDirector sharedDirector] setDepthBufferFormat:
      kDepthBuffer16];

    // Default texture format for PNG/BMP/TIFF/JPEG/GIF images
    // It can be RGBA8888, RGBA4444, RGB5_A1, RGB565
    // You can change anytime.
    [CCTexture2D setDefaultAlphaPixelFormat:kTexture2DPixelFormat_
    RGBA8888];

    // before creating any layer, set the landscape mode
    [[CCDirector sharedDirector] setDeviceOrientation:
    CCDeviceOrientationLandscapeLeft];
    [[CCDirector sharedDirector] setAnimationInterval:1.0/60];
    [[CCDirector sharedDirector] setDisplayFPS:YES];

    // create an openGL view inside a window
    [[CCDirector sharedDirector] attachInView:window];
    [window makeKeyAndVisible];


    [[CCDirector sharedDirector] runWithScene: [HelloWorld scene]];
}

- (void)applicationWillResignActive:(UIApplication *)application {
    [[CCDirector sharedDirector] pause];
}
- (void)applicationDidBecomeActive:(UIApplication *)application {
    [[CCDirector sharedDirector] resume];
}
```

```
- (void)applicationDidReceiveMemoryWarning:
    (UIApplication *)application {
    [[CCTextureCache sharedTextureCache] removeUnusedTextures];
}
- (void)applicationWillTerminate:(UIApplication *)application {
    [[CCDirector sharedDirector] end];
}

- (void)applicationSignificantTimeChange:(UIApplication *)application
{
    [[CCDirector sharedDirector] setNextDeltaTimeZero:YES];
}
- (void)dealloc {
    [[CCDirector sharedDirector] release];
    [window release];
    [super dealloc];
}

@end
```

What just happened?

A lot is happening in here. Don't worry if you don't understand it yet, as you won't have to deal with most of this stuff until you have advanced more into your game.

Let's analyze each line in here, as follows:

```
// Try to use CADisplayLink director
    // if it fails (SDK < 3.1) use the default director
    if( ! [CCDirector setDirectorType:CCDirectorTypeDisplayLink] )
        [CCDirector setDirectorType:CCDirectorTypeDefault];
```

These lines of code set the type of director that will be used. If you are targeting your game for OS 3.1 + it will use the `DisplayLink` Director. Let's take a look at each of them.

Let's continue looking at the code generated in the AppDelegate.

```
// Use RGBA_8888 buffers
    // Default is: RGB_565 buffers
    [[CCDirector sharedDirector] setPixelFormat:kPixelFormatRGBA8888];

    // Create a depth buffer of 16 bits
    // Enable it if you are going to use 3D transitions or 3d objects
//  [[CCDirector sharedDirector] setDepthBufferFormat:kDepthBuffer16];
```

```
    // Default texture format for PNG/BMP/TIFF/JPEG/GIF images
    // It can be RGBA8888, RGBA4444, RGB5_A1, RGB565
    // You can change anytime.
    [CCTexture2D setDefaultAlphaPixelFormat:kTexture2DPixelFormat_
RGBA8888];
```

The preceding lines set the Texture's format and definition. We'll talk about this in the next chapter.

```
    [[CCDirector sharedDirector] setDeviceOrientation:
    CCDeviceOrientationLandscapeLeft];
```

The preceding line of code sets the orientation of the device. You can choose from any four types of orientations.

```
    [[CCDirector sharedDirector] setAnimationInterval:1.0/60];
```

This sets the frames per second that the application will run at. By default, it runs at 60 fps but sometimes you may need to set it at 30 fps for performance reasons. 60 fps is also the highest framerate that the iOS devices can support.

```
    [[CCDirector sharedDirector] setDisplayFPS:YES];
```

Remember the numbers that appear at the lower-left corner? They show the current FPS. These can be removed by commenting this line or setting it to NO.

Finally:

```
    [[CCDirector sharedDirector] runWithScene: [HelloWorld scene]];
```

This `runWithScene` method tells Cocos2d to start running with a given CCScene. In this case, we are starting it with the scene created by HelloWorld.

Scene management

The CCDirector handles the scene management. It can tell the game which scene to run, suspend scenes, and push them into a stack. In *Chapter 5*, you'll learn how to do this, for now should know that in the AppDelegate you need to tell the Director which is the scene you wish run when starting the application.

Take a look at the following method that is implemented. Those are methods found in any iPhone application, but the template has done the work of adding some useful and necessary calls.

```
-   (void)applicationWillResignActive:(UIApplication *)application {
    [[CCDirector sharedDirector] pause];
}
```

When your game is about to stop being active (for example, when you lock the screen), the `applicationWillResignActive:` method is called. The template added the `pause` method from the `CCDirector` class. This method will pause all the timers and set the FPS to a low value, so the application does not consume much CPU.

```
- (void)applicationDidBecomeActive:(UIApplication *)application {
    [[CCDirector sharedDirector] resume];
}
```

On the other side, when the application becomes active again (for example, you unlocked the screen) `applicationDidBecomeActive:` method will be called. The template will add the `resume` method from the `CCDirector` class. This method resumes the timers.

In the following chapters, you'll learn how to display a UIAlert, so that the action does not resume instantly. Later on, you'll learn how to do a nice pause screen with options to resume and quit the game.

```
- (void)applicationWillTerminate:(UIApplication *)application {
    [[CCDirector sharedDirector] end];
}
```

When you quit your game (be it by pressing the home button or answering a call) the `applicationWillTerminate:` method will be called. This is a good time to save your game's state, if you need to.

Doing everything with CCNodes

CCNodes are the main elements in the Cocos2d structure. Everything that is drawn or contains things that are drawn is a CCNode. For example, CCScene, CCLayers, and CCSprites are the subclasses of CCNode.

Time for action – peeking at the HelloWorldScene class

1. Start by opening the `HelloWorldScene.h` file. Let's analyze it line by line:

    ```
    #import "cocos2d.h"
    ```

    Each class you create that makes use of Cocos2d should import its libraries. You do so by writing the preceding line.

    ```
    // HelloWorld Layer
    @interface HelloWorld : CCLayer
    {
    }

    // returns a Scene that contains the HelloWorld as the only child
    ```

```
+(id) scene;
```

```
@end
```

These lines define the Interface of the HelloWorld **CCLayer**.

A CCLayer is where all the content of your game goes. We'll explain it better soon, but for now, think of them as in any graphic design software, where you can have as many layers as you want and each of them contains different elements. Layers are also responsible for handling touches and accelerometer events. That is all there is for that file.

2. Take a look at the `HelloWorldScene.m` file, where the action happens:

```
// on "init" you need to initialize your instance
-(id) init
{
    // always call "super" init
    // Apple recommends to re-assign "self" with the "super"
      return value
    if( (self=[super init] )) {

        // create and initialize a Label
        CCLabel* label = [CCLabel labelWithString:@"Hello
          World" fontName:@"Marker Felt" fontSize:64];

        // ask director the the window size
        CGSize size = [[CCDirector sharedDirector] winSize];

        // position the label on the center of the screen
        label.position =  ccp( size.width /2 ,
          size.height/2 );

        // add the label as a child to this Layer
        [self addChild: label];
    }
    return self;
}
```

The preceding code is the one that will be called when the layer is initialized. What it does is create a **CCLabel** to display the **Hello World** text.

```
CCLabel* label = [CCLabel labelWithString:@"Hello World"
fontName:@"Marker Felt" fontSize:64];
```

`CCLabel` is one of the three existent classes that allow you to show text in your game. We'll do a lot of things with labels throughout this book.

What we are doing here is creating a CCLabel object named label. We are initializing it with the String `"Hello World"` using the `"Marker Felt"` font, with a 64 font size.

As you may notice, the CCLabel is instantiated using a convenience method, so you won't have to worry about releasing it later.

> Most Cocos2d classes can be instantiated using convenience methods, thus making memory management easier. To learn more about memory management check the Apple documents at the following URL:
> `http://developer.apple.com/library/mac/#documentation/Cocoa/Conceptual/MemoryMgmt/MemoryMgmt.html`

```
CGSize size = [[CCDirector sharedDirector] winSize];
```

The preceding line gets the size of the current window. Right now the application is running in landscape mode so it will be 480 * 320 px.

> Remember that the screen sizes might vary from device to device and the orientation you choose for your game. For example, in an iPad application in portrait mode, this method would return 768 * 1024.

```
label.position =  ccp( size.width /2 , size.height/2 );
```

This line sets the label's position in the middle of the screen.

> Cocos2d includes many helper macros for working with vectors. **Ccp** is one of those helper macros. What it does is simply create a CGPoint structure by writing less code.

3. Now, all that is left is to actually place the label in the layer.

   ```
   [self addChild: label];
   ```

   You must always add any new object as a child of a layer (or another CCNode) by calling `addChild`. This allows the framework to actually render the object. There are a few more things you can do, such as setting the **Z-order** and assigning a **tag** to that object. We'll see how to do that soon.

> You can find further information about parent-child relationships in the Cocos2d documentation at:
> `http://www.cocos2d-iphone.org/wiki/doku.php/prog_guide:basic_concepts`

What just happened

We took a look at the code generated by the template. This particular template just creates a scene, which contains a layer that displays some text. Texts are displayed using one of the three different types of labels which are subclasses of CCNode.

Everything that is a subclass of CCNode has the following features:

- They can contain other CCNodes: In the preceding example, a CCLabel is being added to a CCLayer, but with both of them being CCNodes you could also create a deeper hierarchy and add some other element, such as a Sprite, as a child of the label.
- They can schedule periodic callbacks: This means you can have them execute certain methods in a period of time you set. We'll see a lot of examples of this throughout the book as it is a very useful feature.
- They can execute actions: For example, you could tell the CCLabel we had in the previous example to move to the position (0,0) in 1 second. Cocos2d allows for this kind of action in a very easy fashion.

CCNodes properties

In the preceding example we changed one of the label's properties.

```
label.position =  ccp( size.width /2 , size.height/2 );
```

This is only one of the several properties CCNodes have that can be modified to suit your needs.

Let's have a quick look at some of them:

- `Anchor point`: Sets the anchor point of the node. By default, it is placed at (0,0) of the node; that being the center. An exception to these are CCScene and CCSprite whose anchor point is set to (0.5,0.5). The anchor point also affects how the objects are rotated and scaled.
- `Position`: Sets the position of the node relative to its parent node.
- `Scale`: Changes the scaling of the node.

- **Rotation:** Changes the rotation of the object.
- **Visible:** Whether it is visible or not.
- **Z-order:** Objects with a higher z-order will appear on top of others with a lower z-order.

Handling CCNodes

As you learned before, nodes can contain other nodes. Cocos2d provides several methods for adding nodes inside other nodes, retrieving them, and even removing them. These are as follows:

Method	Description
`-(id) addChild(CCNode *)node`	This method adds the CCNode node as a child of the CCNode you called this method from. It's z-order will be 0.
`-(id) addChild(CCNode *)node z:(int)z`	The same as above but lets you specify a z-order for the child.
`-(id) addChild(CCNode *)node z:(int)z tag:(int)tag`	The same as above but also lets you specify a tag for the child. This will allow you to retrieve the child later.
`-(id) removeChild: (CCNode *)node cleanup:(BOOL)cleanup`	Removes the node from its parent and if specified cleans up all its actions and schedulers.
`-(id) removeChildByTag: (int)tag cleanup:(BOOL)cleanup`	The same as above but instead of passing the node, you pass the tag value for that node.
`-(id) removeAllChildernWithCleanup: (BOOL)cleanup`	It removes all children from the parent.
`-(CCNode*) getChildByTag:(int) tag`	Gets a child from the object with the desired tag.
`-(NSArray *)children`	Returns an array with all the children of the node.

When a CCNode is added to or removed from the stage, a couple of useful callback methods that are called, which are as follows:

- **onEnter:** This is called when you add the CCNode as a child of a CCLayer. Adding a CCNode as the child of another node will not fire this method unless the parent node is already on the stage. If it enters the stage with a transition, this method will be called when the transition starts.

> A transition is a nice way to go from one scene to another. Instead of instantly removing one scene and showing the next one, Cocos2d can, for example, fade them, have them move out of the screen, and perform many other nice effects. We'll see how to do this later in the book.

- `onEnterTransitionDidFinish`: The same as preceding method, but if it enters with a transition, this method will be called when the transition ends.
- `onExit`: This will be called when the CCNode is removed. If it is removed with a transition, it will be called after the transition ends.

Have a go hero – doing more with the HelloWorldScene Class

You have just learned how to include simple text into your layer, why don't you try the following?

- Create another CCLabel
- Change its text, font, and size to something you like
- Add this new label as a child of the other label
- Try changing the positions of both labels one by one

You may notice that moving the label that is the parent of the other one causes both of them to move. This is because of the parent-children relationship between them. This is very useful in most cases.

Checking your timing

Sometimes you will need to call a method many times every two seconds. Normally, you would have to check every tick in your game loop to see how many milliseconds have passed and add them up. Imagine doing this for every object that needs to know how much time has passed since it did something. Fortunately, Cocos2d has a way of doing this quite easily. Let me introduce you to Cocos2d Schedulers.

Time for action – using timers to make units shoot each second

Imagine you are making the next blockbuster game like Castle Defense. You need your deployed units to fire at the enemy troops every second, once they have been created. Let's do a simple text example of this.

For this small example, you can use the HelloCocos2d project we started before or create a new one using the simple template just as we did back then.

Let's begin by creating the Unit class.

1. In Xcode go to **File | New File** (*cmd + N*).

2. Use Objective-C class as template for this class. We'll change its content in a moment.

3. Click on **Next** and name the new class as `Unit`.

4. Xcode should have created two files in your `Classes` folder as shown in the following screenshot:

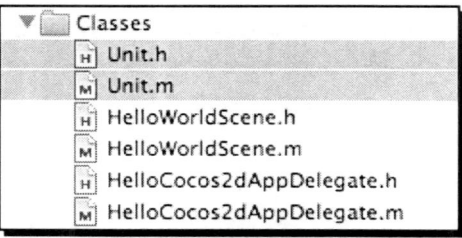

5. Open `Unit.h`. It should look like the following:

   ```
   #import <Foundation/Foundation.h>

   @interface Unit : NSObject {
   }

   @end
   ```

6. Modify the Interface of this class to make use of Cocos2d.

   Begin by importing the Cocos2d.h file. Every class that makes use of Cocos2d should include this file.

   ```
   #import "cocos2d.h"
   ```

   Unit should inherit from CCNode to be able to schedule methods, so let's make the corresponding changes.

   ```
   @interface Unit
     : CCNode {
   }
   ```

Chapter 1

7. Import the `HelloWorldScene.h`. We'll need this class soon.

```
#import "HelloWorldScene.h";
```

That is all you must change for now in the Unit.h file. Now, open the Unit.m file. You should see something like this:

```
#import "Unit.h"
@implementation Unit
@end
```

What we have to do now is fill it up.

8. Create the `init` method for the `Unit` class. This one is a simple example so we won't be doing a lot here:

```
-(id) initWithLayer:(HelloWorld*) game
{
    if ((self = [super init]))
    {
      [game addChild:self];
      [self schedule:@selector(fire) interval:1];
    }
    
    return (self);
}
```

This init method takes the HelloWorld layer as a parameter. We are doing that because when the object is instantiated it will need to be added as a child of the layer node.

9. `[game addChild:self];`

When adding the unit object as a child of the layer node it allows it to schedule methods.

> If you are scheduling a method inside a custom class and it is not running, check whether you have added the said object as a child of a layer. Not doing so won't yield any errors but the method won't run!

`[self schedule:@selector(fire) interval:1];`

This line is the one that does the magic! You pass the desired selector you want to run in the schedule parameter and a positive float number as the interval in seconds.

[29]

Getting Started with Cocos2d

10. Now, add the `fire` method.

```
-(void)fire
{
  NSLog(@"FIRED!!!");
}
```

You did expect a bullet being fired with flashy explosions, didn't you? We'll do that later! For now content yourself with this. Each second after the Unit instance is created a "FIRED!!!" message will be output in the Console.

We just need to make a couple of changes to the HelloWorldScene class to make this work.

11. In the `HelloWorldScene.h` file, add the following line:

```
#import "Unit.h"
```

12. Then in the HelloWorldScene.m file let's create an instance of the `Unit` class.

```
Unit * tower = [[Unit alloc]initWithLayer:self];
```

As you can see we are passing the HelloWorld layer to the Unit class to make use of it.

That is all, now Build and Run the project. You should see the following output:

```
2010-04-13 14:47:10.114 HelloCocos2d[1240:207] FIRED!!!
2010-04-13 14:47:11.132 HelloCocos2d[1240:207] FIRED!!!
2010-04-13 14:47:12.147 HelloCocos2d[1240:207] FIRED!!!
2010-04-13 14:47:13.164 HelloCocos2d[1240:207] FIRED!!!
2010-04-13 14:47:14.164 HelloCocos2d[1240:207] FIRED!!!
2010-04-13 14:47:15.180 HelloCocos2d[1240:207] FIRED!!!
2010-04-13 14:47:16.180 HelloCocos2d[1240:207] FIRED!!!
```

As you can see, the unit created is firing a bullet each second, defeating every enemy troop on its way.

Be careful when scheduling a method which outputs to the console using `NSLog()`. Doing this will reduce the FPS drastically.

What just happened?

CCNodes can schedule selectors to run at an interval of seconds. This gives them a lot of versatility. You can use timers in the following two ways:

- To call a method at an interval of every X seconds
- To delay a method call

In the previous example, we used timers to have a Unit object fire a bullet each second after its creation.

Delaying a method call

You can use timers to just call a method once, but instead of at that precise moment you could have it scheduled and called some seconds after that.

Time for action – destroying your units

Usually, you will want to delay the execution of some methods. For example, when one of your units is hit, you will want to give a visual feedback like an explosion, some movement, or something nice, and then remove it from the screen (and from its parent node).

Continuing from the previous example, modify Unit.m to look like the following:

```
#import "Unit.h"

@implementation Unit
-(id) initWithLayer:(HelloWorld*) game
{
    if ((self = [super init]))
    {
      [game addChild:self];
      [self fireAndDestroy];
    }

    return (self);
}

-(void)fireAndDestroy
{
    NSLog(@"FIRED!!!");
    NSLog(@"Destroying...");
    [self schedule:@selector(destroy) interval:3];
}
```

```
-(void)destroy
{
    [self unschedule:@selector(destroy)];
    NSLog(@"Unit Destroyed.");
    [self.parent removeChild:self cleanup:YES];
}

-(void)dealloc
{
    [super dealloc];
}
@end
```

You should see the following output now:

```
2010-04-13 16:04:34.734 HelloCocos2d[1413:207] FIRED!!!
2010-04-13 16:04:34.738 HelloCocos2d[1413:207] Destroying...
2010-04-13 16:04:37.777 HelloCocos2d[1413:207] Unit Destroyed.
```

Notice how the `Unit Destroyed` message is output three seconds after the previous ones.

What just happened?

For starters, we have made the worst units of any game. These units will fire a bullet and then start destroying themselves. After a couple of seconds of explosions (don't you see them?), they will be gone. So, let's go through the new code step by step, as follows:

```
[self fireAndDestroy];
```

As soon as the object is initialized, the `fireAndDestroy` method is called.

```
-(void)fireAndDestroy
{
    NSLog(@"FIRED!!!");
    NSLog(@"Destroying...");
    [self schedule:@selector(destroy) interval:3];
}
```

This method just prints some text to the Console and then schedules the `destroy` method to run every three seconds.

```
-(void)destroy
{
    [self unschedule:@selector(destroy)];
    NSLog(@"Unit Destroyed.");
    [self release];
}
```

We just want this method to be called once. So, we use the `unschedule` CCNode method to stop the selector that is passed from being called over and over. Then it prints a message and we release the object.

So, what we are doing here is having a method run after three seconds and then stopping it, thus calling it just once.

That is all there is for CCNodes right now. Remember that you will use them a lot when making your games, as they are the base class for almost everything that you wish to show onscreen. In the next chapter, you will learn how to use CCSprites, another subclass of CCNode.

Debugging cocos2d applications

Sometimes things go wrong. As a matter of fact, a lot of things will go wrong while you program your game. Your game will crash, things will not appear onscreen, and a lot of other problems may arise.

Fortunately, Cocos2d includes some simple messages that will help you with your debugging.

Time for action – checking Cocos2d debug messages

Let's take a look at the HelloCocos2d project and the debug message that it generates. They will be few, but as you add more elements to your game, you will be able to get a lot of useful information from this data, as shown here:

- Run the HelloCocos2d application.
- Once it is running, open the Console. To do this go to **Run | Console** (*Shift + cmd + R*)
- You will see the following output:

```
2010-04-09 15:05:13.189 HelloCocos2d[3197:207] cocos2d: cocos2d v0.99.1
2010-04-09 15:05:13.207 HelloCocos2d[3197:207] cocos2d: Using Director Type:CCDisplayLinkDirector
2010-04-09 15:05:13.388 HelloCocos2d[3197:207] cocos2d: GL_VENDOR: Apple Computer, Inc.
2010-04-09 15:05:13.389 HelloCocos2d[3197:207] cocos2d: GL_RENDERER: Apple Software Renderer
2010-04-09 15:05:13.389 HelloCocos2d[3197:207] cocos2d: GL_VERSION: OpenGL ES-CM 1.1 APPLE
2010-04-09 15:05:13.390 HelloCocos2d[3197:207] cocos2d: GL_MAX_TEXTURE_SIZE: 2048
```

Getting Started with Cocos2d

```
2010-04-09 15:05:13.391 HelloCocos2d[3197:207] cocos2d: Supports PVRTC: YES
2010-04-09 15:05:13.391 HelloCocos2d[3197:207] cocos2d: GL_MAX_MODELVIEW_STACK_DEPTH: 16
2010-04-09 15:05:13.425 HelloCocos2d[3197:207] cocos2d: Frame interval: 1
```

There you can see the current version of Cocos2d, the type of CCDirector it is using (we talked about them a while back), the version of OpenGL it is using, and so on.

What just happened?

We have just seen how to open the Xcode's Console. Now, you can get a lot more information from Cocos2d debug messages, such as when a particular object is dealloced.

Time for action – checking deallocing messages

Cocos2d debug mode can inform you about a lot of things, such as when there is some error retrieving a file or having you know when an object is removed from memory (you will see a "cocos2d:deallocing <object>" message). Let's have a look:

- While the application is running, press the **Home** button. This will cause the application to gracefully end and the Cocos2d objects that were living will be dealloced.
- Open the console again.
- You will see the following output:

  ```
  2010-04-09 15:14:35.284 HelloCocos2d[3197:207] cocos2d: deallocing <CCScheduler: 0x3a2b2f0>
  2010-04-09 15:14:35.287 HelloCocos2d[3197:207] cocos2d: deallocing <CCTextureCache = 03A0E9A0 | num of textures = 1>
  ```

  These two messages show what was dealloced in this particular case. What these classes do does not matter right now. However, **CCScheduler** is responsible of triggering scheduled callbacks and **CCTextureCache** is responsible of handling the loading of textures.

What just happened?

The preceding messages are the types of messages you can get from the framework. These ones in particular are deallocing messages that allow us to know when Cocos2d has, for example, released memory for a given texture which it is not using anymore.

Time for action – knowing your errors

Let's take a look at one more example. When you make a mistake and you want to use an image file from the resources folder, if you mistype its name, you will get an exception. Normally, you would have to take a look at Xcode's debugger and check where the error happens. Fortunately, Cocos2d debug comes to your rescue!

- Add the following lines of code right after adding the label:

  ```
  CCSprite * image = [CCSprite spriteWithFile:@"Icoun.png"];
  [self addChild:image];
  ```

  That line of code creates a Sprite from an image file in your resource folder. As you may notice, `"Icoun.png"` is not present in the project's resource folder, so when the application is run and execution gets to that line of code, it will crash.

- Run the application and see it crash.
- Open the Console, and you will see the following output:

  ```
  2010-04-09 16:07:46.875 HelloCocos2d[4394:207] cocos2d: CCTexture2D. Can't create Texture. UIImage is nil
  2010-04-09 16:07:46.875 HelloCocos2d[4394:207] cocos2d: Couldn't add image:Icoun.png in CCTextureCache
  2010-04-09 16:07:46.876 HelloCocos2d[4394:207] *** Assertion failure in -[HelloWorld addChild:], /Users/pabloruiz/Documents/HelloCocos2d/libs/cocos2d/CCNode.m:300
  ```

  The debug messages tell you exactly what is failing. In this case, it couldn't use the image `icoun.png`. Why? This is because it is not there!

- Change the string to match the file's name to see the error go away.

What just happened?

Cocos2d debug messages can really help you save time when searching for these kinds of bugs. Thanks to the built-in debug messages, you can get an idea of what is happening while the application is running.

Time for action – removing debug messages

Sometimes you will need to get a better look at your own debug messages or you will notice your application is running very slowly for no apparent reason. This could be caused by all the debug messages being written to the console. So, let's take a look at how to disable them:

1. Go to **Project | Edit active target**.

2. Search for **gcc_preprocessor_defination**, and you will find the flag **COCOS2D_DEBUG** set to **1**.

3. Change it to 0 to disable it.

4. Rebuild your project.

5. Cocos2d debug messages will now disappear.

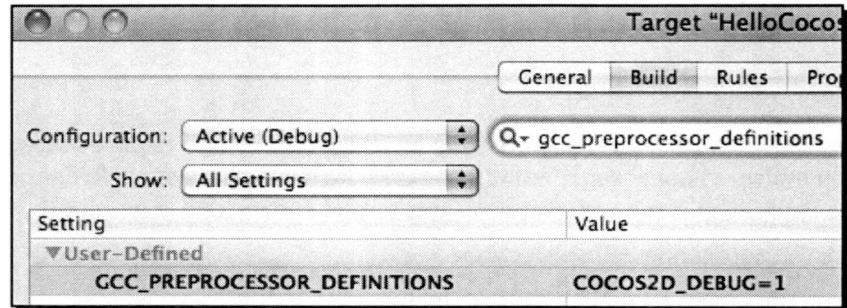

 Alternatively, you can have your project run in release configuration. To do that, select it from the overview dropdown under **Active Configuration**.

What just happened?

As debug messages are written to the console, many times when you have a lot of things going around in your game it will start running slowly. In such cases, you may want to prevent Cocos2d from logging all that useful data. If you follow the preceding steps you will be able to switch the debug logging on and off at will.

Summary

In this chapter, we've explored the basics of creating your first project.

- We began by exploring the samples that are included with Cocos2d. Then we went a step further and created a brand new project from the templates. We also took a look at the code created by these templates.

- Then we learned about the basics of Cocos2d - how to configure the CCDirector, how to use CCNodes, and we went over the basic structure of a Cocos2d application.

- Finally, we learned how to interpret the debug messages given by Cocos2d.

In the next chapter, we will learn everything there is to know about CCSprites by building the first game of the book, "Colored Stones".

2
Playing with Sprites

A **sprite** is a two dimensional image that represents an element of your game; it can be the main character, an enemy, projectiles, or backgrounds. These sprites can also be transformed; that means you can change their position, rotation, and scaling, among other things. Cocos2d allows the usage of sprites through the `CCSprite` class.

CCSprites are subclasses of CCNode, that means you can have them do what CCNodes do, like adding them as children of other CCNodes, scheduling methods for them and so on.

In this chapter, you will learn how to use sprites, and to that end we will start building the first of the games of the book, "Colored Stones".

In this chapter, we shall:

- Make use of sprites
- Learn how to change properties of sprites
- Create sprites using Spritesheets with the `CCSpriteBatchNode` class
- Implement touches on sprites
- Use OpenGL calls

So, let's get started.

Playing with Sprites

Making a puzzle game

In this chapter, we will start building the first of the three games we will make through this book.

We'll call it "Colored Stones". Since this is your first project with Cocos2d, we will begin with a basic puzzle game. This game will feature an 8 X 7 grid where different types of stones will fit. The objective of the game is making a lot of points by destroying these stones. Doing so requires the player to align three or more stones vertically or horizontally by swapping their positions. To do that he will touch a stone and do a swiping motion.

The more stones the player destroys in one go the more points he/she will be awarded. Once these stones are destroyed new ones will fall from the sky.

In the following chapters, we will enhance this game to be more visually appealing and we will also add some features to it.

Beginning a new project

We'll use the basic Cocos2d template as a starting point for the Coloured Stones game, so the first thing to do is to start a new project in Xcode.

Time for action – creating a new project

1. Create a new project from the templates like we did in the previous chapter. Go to **File | New project** and then select the **Cocos2d template** and let's name the project **Coloured Stones**. You may place it anywhere you like.

   You should now have your new project created and opened. Let's clean it up first to start working on it, as follows:

   - Rename the `HelloWorldScene` files to something more descriptive for this project. I will rename them as `GameScene` since that will be the class that will handle the scene where the action happens.
   - Inside the GameScene files, change the name of the CCLayer it contains to GameLayer. This is the only layer we will work with for now.
   - Remove the unnecessary code the template created. That would be the CCLabel that is created and placed in the init method.
   - As you have changed some files and class names, you should look everywhere they are used and make the changes for the project to work.

Your `GameScene` files should look like the following; I have removed some comments for brevity:

```
#import "cocos2d.h"
@interface GameLayer : CCLayer
{
}
// returns a Scene that contains the HelloWorld as the only child
+(id) scene;
@end
// Import the interfaces
#import "GameScene.h"
@implementation GameLayer
+(id) scene
{
   // 'scene' is an autorelease object.
   CCScene *scene = [CCScene node];

   // 'layer' is an autorelease object.
   GameLayer *layer = [GameLayer node];

   // add layer as a child to scene
   [scene addChild: layer];

   // return the scene
   return scene;
}
// on "init" you need to initialize your instance
-(id) init
{
   // always call "super" init
   // Apple recommends to re-assign "self" with the "super" return
      value
   if( (self=[super init] )) {

   }
   return self;
}
- (void) dealloc
{
   [super dealloc];
}
@end
```

2. In the `ColouredStonesAppDelegate.m` file, you must now import the `GameScene.h` file instead. Also, you must now start the application by running the scene that contains the GameLayer layer. `ColouredStonesAppDelegate.m` should look like the following:

```
#import "ColouredStonesAppDelegate.h"
#import "cocos2d.h"
#import "GameScene.h"

@implementation ColouredStonesAppDelegate

@synthesize window;

- (void) applicationDidFinishLaunching:(UIApplication*)application
{
    //The CCDirector setup code
    ...

[[CCDirector sharedDirector] runWithScene: [GameLayer scene]];
}
//The rest of the ColouredStonesAppDelegate methods
@end
```

Ok, now we really have a blank slate to start working with. Before doing anything else, save your project and try running it. If there are no problems, you should just see a black screen with the FPS label in the lower-left corner, as shown in the following screenshot:

What just happened?

When using a template, Cocos2d automatically places some placeholder code for you. That code is not always suitable for your project. So, what we did here was change the generated classes' names and eliminate the content that was not useful. All those changes left us with a blank slate for us to work on.

Displaying images with CCSprites

Let's start simple. Almost every game you make will have a background image. It could be static (like the one we will make in a moment) or be constantly moving. It could also be animated or just a still image. It could be made from just one image or several ones. The fact is that every game will handle the backgrounds differently and what we will do next is no definitive guide on how to handle your backgrounds.

> A word of caution: As tempting as it would be to make large, animated, flashy moving backgrounds, have in mind that the iPhone has its limitations. Using a couple of huge images will reduce the FPS drastically soon enough. If you find yourself placing lot of those, try splitting them into smaller images. In Chapter 8, you will learn how to use tilemaps, which help you build large backgrounds using lots of small images.
>
> A word of caution: In most games, placing many CCSprites on the screen will reduce the performance. In order to get better results Spritesheets are used (handled by the CCSpriteBatchNode). This technique consists of putting as many image elements in a single huge image and picking the needed sprite from there. We'll see how to do this later in this chapter.

A background image, just like any other element that is supposed to be rendered from an image, will be a CCSprite. Thus you will be able to translate it, rotate it, scale it, and do a lot more things. Let's begin.

Time for action – adding a background image to the game

For this simple game, we'll start by using a static background, just a still image to define the game board and where the other elements should go. For this game, we won't be creating any menus or other screens, but I will leave the necessary space in the design for you to add those, once you learn more stuff through the book.

1. In the companion files, inside Chapter 2, in the `assets` folder there is a `background.png` file. Include it in the project by dragging it to the `Resources` folder as shown in the following screenshot:

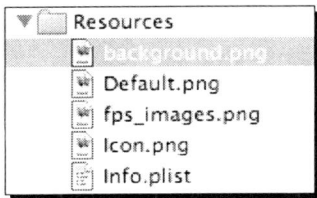

Playing with Sprites

Now that you have the image, we'll be using it as background added to the project. Let's create a CCSprite to display it.

2. In your `GameScene.m` file, add the following lines to the GameLayer's `init` method:

```
CCSprite * background = [CCSprite spriteWithFile:@"background.png"];
[self addChild:background z:0];
[background setPosition:ccp(240,160)];
```

3. Click on **Build and Run**, and you should see your background image nicely centred on the screen, as shown in the following screenshot:

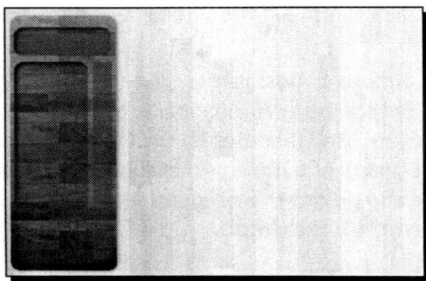

What just happened?

With just those three lines of code you were able to place an image in your game. Let's go through them, line by line.

```
CGSize wins = [[CCDirector sharedDirector] winSize];
CCSprite * background = [CCSprite spriteWithFile:@"background.png"];
```

This line of code creates an instance of the `CCSprite` class. We are naming it *background*. Using a convenience method we initialize it with the image passed as the parameter to the `spriteWithFile` Class method.

 Notice how you didn't have to pass any folder location to the method. Cocos2d handles it nicely.

```
[self addChild:background z:0];

[background setPosition:ccp(wins.width/2,wins.height/2)];
```

Those two lines do the same thing that we did before with the CCLabel. Since `CCSprite` is a subclass of `CCNode` we are able to add it as a child of another CCNode and modify its position.

Creating CCSprites

Cocos2d supports several image file types for your sprites:

- `.Png`
- `.Bmp`
- `.Tiff`
- `.Jpeg`
- `.Pvr`
- `.Gif`

Mostly you will be using either `.png` or `.pvr` images. Pvr stands for PowerVR and it is optimized for the GPU inside the iPhone. They are compressed and this means they take a lot less memory than `.png` files. You should use them whenever possible. The disadvantage they have is that they are not suited for detailed images as they are 2 to 4 bit textures.

Pixel formats

Pixel format is the way a texture is stored in GPU memory. The more bits per channel an image uses, the higher its quality, but also the memory it consumes and its loading time.

When creating sprites, you can choose which pixel format to use for them. Which one you choose will depend on the images in question. Some of them will still look fine with low bit pixel formats.

- `RGBA8888` (`kTexture2DPixelFormat_RGBA8888`): This is the pixel format that offers the maximum possible quality of the images. The trade off is that it consumes a lot of memory (twice as much as the 16 bit textures, and is also slower to render). An image using this pixel format will consume 4 MB of memory if it is 1024 * 1024 or 16 MB if it is 2048 * 2048; while using RGBA4444 would take half of those values.
- `RGBA4444`(`kTexture2DPixelFormat_RGBA4444`): This is a 16 bit pixel format that offers good quality, speed, and memory consumption.
- `RGB5_A1`(`kTexture2DPixelFormat_RGB5A1`): This 16 bit channel offers good quality in the RGB channels but is very poor in the A channel, as it uses just 1 bit for it. It gives good speed and memory consumption.
- `RGB565`(`kTexture2DPixelFormat_RGB565`): It has no alpha support but gives the best possible quality for 16 bit textures.

You can change the pixel format that you want to use for the next textures by calling the following method at any time:

```
[CCTexture2D setDefaultAlphaPixelFormat:kTexture2DPixelFormat_
RGBA8888];
//Use the pixel format you want.
```

More ways of creating CCSprites

The way we created a CCSprite in the preceding example is just one way of doing it. Cocos2d allows you to create your sprites from a variety of forms, which are as follows:

- Textures: You can create a sprite from a `CCTexture2D`. This class allows the creation of OpenGl 2D textures from images, text or, raw data
- Sprite frames: `CCSpriteFrameCache` holds all the frames you create for animations
- Files: As we did before, you can create sprites from image files
- CGImages: This let's you create your sprites from `CGImageRef`
- Spritesheets: A spritesheet is an image that can hold a lot of other images for you to use as sprites

Time for action – creating the Stone class

With everything you have learned so far about sprites, let's begin building the game as follows:

1. The first thing we'll be doing is creating the `Stone` class. This class will handle the visual representation of the stones and also handle the touching of them.

    Next is the content of the `Stone` class interface:

    ```
    Stone.h
    #import <Foundation/Foundation.h>
    #import "cocos2d.h"
    #import "GameScene.h"

    @class GameLayer;

    typedef enum tagState {
        kStateGrabbed,
        kStateUngrabbed
    } touchState;

    @interface Stone : CCNode <CCTargetedTouchDelegate> {
        CCSprite * mySprite;
        GameLayer * theGame;
    ```

```objc
    int stoneType;
    int curVGroup;
    int curHGroup;
    touchState state;
    BOOL disappearing;
    CGPoint initDir;
}
@property(readwrite,nonatomic) touchState state;
@property(readwrite,nonatomic,retain) CCSprite * mySprite;
@property(readwrite,nonatomic,retain) GameLayer * theGame;
@property(readwrite, assign)int stoneType;
@property(readwrite, assign)int curVGroup;
@property(readwrite, assign)int curHGroup;
@property(readwrite, assign)BOOL disappearing;
@property(readwrite, assign)CGPoint initDir;
-(id) initWithGame:(GameLayer*) game;
-(void)placeInGrid:(CGPoint)place pt:(int)pt pl:(int)pl ;
-(NSString *)setStoneColor:(int)stoneT;
@end
```

Stone also adopts the `CCTargetedTouchDelegate` protocol. We will inspect this later but this protocol tells you, the programmer, that objects of this class respond to touches.

I have extended CCNode by adding some properties for handling a variety of things:

- `mySprite`: This contains the CCSprite that will show the stone image; we'll be using this a lot.
- `theGame`: This is just a reference to the actual GameLayer.
- `stoneType`: An integer value for the current type of the stone. If there are three or more adjacent stones with the same type, they will be removed.
- `state`: This is used in the code that handles the touch.
- The rest of the ivars are used for other calculations.

`Stone` class inherits from `CCNode` class, thus it can contain other CCNodes like the sprite image.

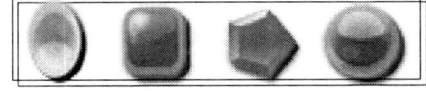

Playing with Sprites

2. Next is the implementation of the Stone class:

Stone.m

```
#import "Stone.h"

@implementation Stone

@synthesize
state,mySprite,theGame,stoneType,curVGroup,curHGroup,disappearing,
initDir;

-(id) initWithGame:(GameLayer*) game
{
  if ((self = [super init]))
  {
    self.theGame = game;

    [game addChild:self];

    self.state = kStateUngrabbed;


  }

    return (self);
}
-(void)placeInGrid:(CGPoint)place pt:(int)pt pl:(int)pl
{

  int sType = arc4random() % 4;
  if(sType == pt || sType == pl)
  {   [self placeInGrid:place pt:pt pl:pl];
      return;
  }
  else
  {
    NSString * color =[self setStoneColor:sType];
    mySprite = [CCSprite spriteWithFile:[NSString
             stringWithFormat:@"s%@.png",color]];
    [self addChild:mySprite z:1];

    self.stoneType =sType;
    [self.mySprite setPosition:place];
```

```
      }
   }

   -(NSString *)setStoneColor:(int)stoneT
   {
     self.stoneType = stoneT;
     NSString * color;
     switch (self.stoneType)
     {
       case 0:
       color = @"Red";
         break;
       case 1:
       color = @"Blue";
         break;
       case 2:
       color = @"Yellow";
         break;
       case 3:
       color = @"Green";
         break;
     }

       return color;
   }
```

If you run the game now, you won't see any change, because we still have to place those stones in the grid.

What just happened?

First we have the `Stone` class init method. It takes the `GameLayer` as a parameter and assigns it to its own `theGame` ivar. This will let us access the GameLayer directly from any stone object. The stone object is then added as a child of the GameLayer with a z-order of two, so it appears on top of the background and some other elements we may add later.

The `Stone` object contains a state property which is set to `kStateUngrabbed`. This means it is not currently being touched.

The `placeInGrid` method will be called when the game starts for each stone. This method places each one in a space of the 8 * 7 grid, so that initially none of them match:

```
int sType = arc4random() % STONE_TYPES;
   if(sType == pt || sType == pl)
   {
```

Playing with Sprites

```
        [self placeInGrid:place pt:pt pl:pl];
        return;
}
```

`placeInGrid` method takes a CGPoint and two ints as parameters.

The `place` variable tells the stone where to place the sprite in the screen. The other two ints inform which two types the stone can't be.

 For example, if you had a red stone and another red stone next to it, the following one could not be a red one when the game starts; if it was, there would be a match as soon as the game starts. So, to avoid that, each stone when placed, knows which type the previous left and down ones were.

This method first selects one number at random from zero to three. This will be the stone's type.

Then if the selected type matches one of the two types that are adjacent to this one, it calls this method again. This will happen until the stone is of a different type. When it does, we create a string using the `setStoneColor` method, which assigns the selected type to the stone and returns a string with the color's name, so we can load the right image file for that stone.

```
        mySprite = [CCSprite spriteWithFile:[NSString
                    stringWithFormat:@"s%@.png",color]];
        [self addChild:mySprite z:1];
```

Once the type is selected, we create an `NSString` object from that. Then we create a sprite from an image file that corresponds to the selected type. This is a simple way for starting, but most times you don't want to load images directly, each from a single file, for performance issues. Later in this chapter, we will take a look at other methods.

So then, the sprite object is added as a child of the stone object with a z-order of two. That way it appears on top of the background and some other elements we may add later.

Let's create the grid now, so you can see all the stones in place.

Creating the game board

Now that we have the stones ready, let's arrange them on the screen. For that, we are going to create a C array that contains all of the stones.

Time for action – placing stones in the grid

1. First, replace the GameScene.h contents with the following:

   ```
   #import "cocos2d.h"
   #import "Stone.h"

   @class Stone;

   // HelloWorld Layer
   @interface GameLayer : CCLayer
   {
     Stone *grid[8][7];
     BOOL allowTouch;
     int score;
   }

   @property(readwrite, assign)BOOL allowTouch;
   @property(readwrite, assign)int score;

   +(CCScene) scene;
   -(id) init;
   -(void)placeStones;
   -(void)checkGroups:(bool)firstTime;
   -(void)moveStonesDown;
   -(void)swapStones:(Stone *)stone dir:(int)dir;
   -(void)checkGroupsAgain;
   @end
   ```

2. In the init method of the GameLayer class, add the following code after where you created the background:

   ```
   CCSprite * gridBackground = [CCSprite spriteWithFile:@"grid.png"];
      [self addChild:gridBackground z:0];
      [gridBackground setPosition:ccp(305,154)];

      // Creating the stones
      for(int i =0; i< GRID_WIDTH ; i++)
      {
        for(int j =0; j< GRID_HEIGHT ; j++)
         {
           Stone * s = [[Stone alloc]initWithGame:self];
           grid[i][j] = s;
           [s release];
         }
      }
      [self placeStones];
   ```

Playing with Sprites

3. Also define the following constants on top of the file:

```
#define GRID_WIDTH 8
#define GRID_HEIGHT 7
#define GRID_OFFSET ccp(158,35)
#define MAX_TIME 230
```

`GRID_HEIGHT` and `GRID_WIDTH` will be used a lot for calculations and `GRID_OFFSET` represents the position of the first element of the array. So if you want to reposition the whole grid you should change this constant.

4. Write the `placeStones` method, which handles the initial layout of the stones inside the board, as follows:

```
-(void)placeStones
{
  for(int i =0; i< GRID_WIDTH ; i++)
  {
    for(int j =0; j< GRID_HEIGHT ; j++)
    {
      Stone * leftS = nil;
      Stone *leftmostS= nil;
      Stone * topS= nil;
      Stone *topmostS= nil;
      int prohibitedLeft = -1, prohibitedTop = -1;
      if(i>=2)
      {
        leftS = (Stone *)grid[i-1][j];
        leftmostS = (Stone *)grid[i-2][j];
      }
      if(j>=2)
      {
        topS = (Stone *)grid[i][j-1];
        topmostS = (Stone *)grid[i][j-2];
      }
      if(leftS && leftmostS && leftS.stoneType == leftmostS.stoneType)
      {
        prohibitedLeft = leftS.stoneType;
      }
      if(topS && topmostS && topS.stoneType == topmostS.stoneType)
      {
        prohibitedTop = topS.stoneType;
      }
```

```
            [grid[i][j] placeInGrid:ccp(42*i + GRID_OFFSET.x,42*j +
                GRID_OFFSET.y) pt:prohibitedTop pl:prohibitedLeft];
        }
      }
    }
```

5. Run the game now, and you should see a board filled up with lots of beautiful stones, as shown in the following screenshot:

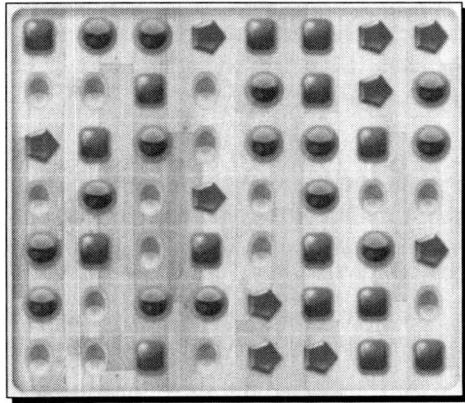

What just happened?

Let's see what is happening in the init method of the GameLayer class:

```
CCSprite * gridBackground = [CCSprite spriteWithFile:@"grid.png"];
  [self addChild:gridBackground z:0];
  [gridBackground setPosition:ccp(305,160)];
```

Here we are adding another image that represents the grid background.

Let's move further in the code:

```
for(int i =0; i< GRID_WIDTH ; i++)
{
  for(int j =0; j< GRID_HEIGHT ; j++)
  {
    Stone * s = [[Stone alloc]initWithGame:self];
    grid[i][j] = s;
    [s release];
  }
}
```

Playing with Sprites

Here we loop through the grid array, instantiating stone objects and storing them inside each grid slot. We then end up with 56 stone objects.

As `Stone *s` is being retained by the GameLayer, we have to release it in there.

As an iPhone developer, you will find yourself optimizing a lot to make your game work as expected. To that end, it is very important that you are not continually creating and destroying objects mid-game. So even in this simple game we will be using the concept of reusing your objects. This method consists, in our case, of moving the stones away, outside of the screen, when they are matched, and then when new stones fall, using the same ones that were *removed* before. So, the 56 stone objects we created are all we are going to use.

This method helps a lot to improve the performance of the game, although it adds a layer of complexity to the code. Anyway, it is worth trying and we will be doing this a lot, for most elements that appear throughout the book.

Finally in the `init` method, we are calling the `placeStones` method, which is responsible for handling the initial placement of the stones. Let's analyze what the `placeStones` method does. If you think about it for a while, you will come to the following conclusions:

- The first stone can be any color
- As they match when there are three or more in the same line, we also don't care about the second stone's color
- Now, the second one must be of a different color from the previous two if those were of the same one
- The above applies to vertical and horizontal match

So, with that in mind, let's see what we did before:

- First, we loop through all the stones in the grid. For each of them, we retrieve the previous ones, vertically and horizontally, (except for the first two columns and rows which don't have previous stones).
- Once we have those, we compare their `stoneType` fields. If they match, we need to avoid placing another stone of the same one, so we assign that value to two auxiliary variables. `prohibitedLeft` and `prohibitedTop` hold the stoneType that can not be used for the next stone. Those are the values we then pass to the stone's `placeInGrid` method like we saw before.

The result is that there will never be three stones of the same type aligned at the beginning of any game.

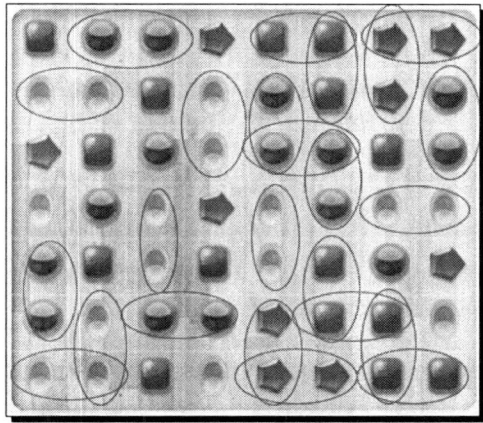

Have a go hero – finding another way to place the stones

While writing this, I came up with other methods for making the initial placement. Although the one I chose is not the best way to do it, it serves its purpose and it is simple enough to understand. Some ideas for you to try:

- You could place all of them regardless of their type, and then find the ones matching and change them.

- You could have each stone hold a reference to the adjacent ones (at least two of them) and them check those when adding a new one instead of looking at the whole grid.

- You could drop the whole random placement thing and create premade levels. This would mean having a plist with different configurations and each stone's type and grid coordinates.

Interacting with sprites

The `CCTouchDispatcher` class is responsible for handling touches in Cocos2d. It can do it in the following two ways:

1. **Standard**: It acts as the CocoaTouch handler, where a set of touches is passed to the delegate and you may loop through them to act accordingly.

2. **Targeted**: It receives just one touch and can *swallow* touches to avoid propagation of the event. You should avoid propagation of touch events to the lower elements. It can be a horrible bug to track down if something is not working as expected.

Playing with Sprites

The `CCTouchHandler` class is responsible for handling the touches for a given CCNode. We will be using target touches for the Stone class. This means the Stone class will handle what happens when touched by itself. If we were using standard touches in the GameLayer, we would have to code a way for us to retrieve the stone we are touching.

In order for the stones to receive touch events, we must do two things:

1. First, we have to register the `stone` class to be able to receive touches.
2. Then we must implement the `touches` methods, so the stone know what to do when a finger is pressed or removed from the screen.

Time for action – registering the stones for receiving touches

As we saw before, the `onEnter` and `onExit` methods are called, respectively, when a CCNode is added as a child of another CCNode or when it is removed. To be able to register a touch, objects must add themselves to the `CCTouchDispatcher` and then remove themselves when they are to be destroyed.

```
- (void)onEnter
{
    [[CCTouchDispatcher sharedDispatcher] addTargetedDelegate:self
     priority:0 swallowsTouches:YES];
    [super onEnter];
}

- (void)onExit
{
    [[CCTouchDispatcher sharedDispatcher] removeDelegate:self];
    [super onExit];
}
```

What just happened?

The `CCTouchDispatcher addTargetedDelegate` method takes the `object`, `priority`, and `swallowsTouches` as its parameters.

A higher priority determines which `object` will receive the touches first, and the `swallowsTouches` report if the object will swallow the touches, thus making the objects below not receive them.

Now we have to implement the methods to actually tell the stones what to do when touched.

Time for action – handling touches for swapping stones

The objective of the game is to match three or more adjacent stones. In order to do this, the player will swap stones by making a swipe gesture. The user will touch a stone and then move his finger to the left, right, up, or down. When the finger is released, the selected stone and the adjacent one (in the direction where the finger was released) will swap positions. This will then trigger a method that checks for matches. Let's take a look at the following code for handling the touches:

```
- (BOOL)ccTouchBegan:(UITouch *)touch withEvent:(UIEvent *)event
{
  if (state != kStateUngrabbed) return NO;
  if ( ![self containsTouchLocation:touch]) return NO;
  if (!theGame.allowTouch) return NO;

  CGPoint location = [touch locationInView: [touch view]];
  location = [[CCDirector sharedDirector] convertToGL: location];

  self.initDir = location;

  state = kStateGrabbed;
  return YES;
}

- (void)ccTouchEnded:(UITouch *)touch withEvent:(UIEvent *)event
{
  NSAssert(state == kStateGrabbed, @"Unexpected state!");

  CGPoint location = [touch locationInView: [touch view]];

  location = [[CCDirector sharedDirector] convertToGL: location];

  CGPoint aux = ccpNormalize(ccp(location.x-initDir.x,location.y-
    initDir.y));
  int dir =0;

  if(fabsl(aux.x) >= fabsl(aux.y))
  {
    if(aux.x>=0)
      dir=1;
    else
      dir=2;
  }
  else
```

Playing with Sprites

```
    {
      if(aux.y>=0)
         dir=3;
      else
         dir=4;
    }

    [theGame swapStones:self dir:dir];


    state = kStateUngrabbed;
}

- (BOOL)containsTouchLocation:(UITouch *)touch
{
   return CGRectContainsPoint(self.rect, [self
      convertTouchToNodeSpaceAR:touch]);
}

- (CGRect)rect
{
   //CGSize s = [self.texture contentSize];
   CGRect c = CGRectMake(mySprite.position.x-
      (self.mySprite.textureRect.size.width/2) * self.mySprite.scaleX
        ,mySprite.position.y-(self.mySprite.textureRect.size.height/2)*
         self.mySprite.scaleY,self.mySprite.textureRect.size.width*
         self.mySprite.scaleX,self.mySprite.textureRect.size.height *
         self.mySprite.scaleY);
   return c;
}
```

Now, before you are able to interact with your stone objects, there is one more thing we must do before you can run the game and have the stones change places.

What just happened?

The following is the code for handling the swipe gesture; even if it is a very simplistic implementation, it does work fine for our needs. Let's break it down:

There are four methods that handle the touches for the targeted touch handler, which are as follows:

- `- (BOOL)ccTouchBegan:(UITouch *)touch withEvent:(UIEvent *)event`
- `- (void)ccTouchMoved:(UITouch *)touch withEvent:(UIEvent *)event`

- (void)ccTouchEnded:(UITouch *)touch withEvent:(UIEvent *) event
- (void)ccTouchCancelled:(UITouch *)touch withEvent:(UIEvent *) event

These methods are called respectively when the player puts his finger on the screen, moves it, removes it, and cancels the touches.

In this case, we are just using two of them. Let's take a look at the ccTouchBegan method first:

```
if (state != kStateUngrabbed) return NO;
if ( ![self containsTouchLocation:touch]) return NO;
if (!theGame.allowTouch) return NO;
```

The preceding three lines check for different things to see if we should compute the received touch.

- The first line checks if the object is already being touched. If it is, it will not handle a second touch until it is let go.
- The containsTouchLocation method checks whether the user is really touching the object or somewhere else. It does so by calling the CGRectContainsPoint method, which checks if a touch is within the boundaries of a CGRect.
- The rect method returns a CGRect object representing the boundaries of the object. In this case, we are making a CGRect of the exact size of the stone's sprite, but you could make it bigger or smaller if you needed to.
- The allowTouch variable prevents the player touch a stone again until they are placed correctly and there are no more matches.

```
CGPoint location = [touch locationInView: [touch view]];
    location = [[CCDirector sharedDirector] convertToGL: location];
```

These lines return a CGPoint object with the actual point if the screen that was touched. The CCDirector's convertToGL method takes the location of the touch and changes it to match the current orientation the device was set to.

```
self.initDir = location;
```

This line sets the initDir variable to the location of the touch, so we can then compute the direction of the swipe.

```
state = kStateGrabbed;
```

Finally, we set the state of the object to kStateGrabbed. This means it is currently being touched.

Playing with Sprites

In the `CCTouchEnded` method, we will compare the location where the finger was lifted off with the `initDir` to find out the direction of the swipe.

```
CGPoint aux = ccpNormalize(ccp(location.x-initDir.x,location.y-
initDir.y));
   int dir =0;

   if(fabsl(aux.x) >= fabsl(aux.y))
   {
     if(aux.x>=0)
        dir=1;
     else
        dir=2;
   }
   else
   {
     if(aux.y>=0)
        dir=3;
     else
        dir=4;
   }
```

First we subtract those two vectors and normalize them. Then we need to find out which component of the resulting vector is greater, to know which direction the user moved his finger towards.

Once we do so, we call the `swapStones` method of the GameLayer object, passing the touched stone and the direction along. This method will actually handle the swapping.

Have a go hero – canceling the swap

The preceding method has one problem. What happens if the user touches a stone and then wants to cancel? He can't! Can you guess a way to solve that? I'll give you a hint: Try checking the positions of the centre of the touch stone and where the finger was lifted off. If the distance between them is a little one, you can avoid calling the `swapStones` method.

To find out the distance between two CGPoints use the `ccpDistance` method, which takes two CGPoints as its parameters.

Time for action – swapping the stones around

Back when we wrote the stone class object, we laid the foundations for swapping the stones' positions. If you remember well, we were handling the touches, and once we found out which direction the finger was moved to we called the `swapStones` method. Without further ado, here it is:

```
-(void)swapStones:(Stone *)stone dir:(int)dir
{
 for(int i =0; i< GRID_WIDTH ; i++)
 {
  for(int j =0; j< GRID_HEIGHT ; j++)
  {
   if(grid[i][j] == stone)
    {
      switch (dir)
      {
       case 1:
       if(i<GRID_WIDTH-1)
        {
          grid[i][j] = grid[i+1][j];
          grid[i+1][j] = stone;
          [grid[i][j].mySprite setPosition:ccp(42*i + GRID_OFFSET.x,42*j
          + GRID_OFFSET.y)];
          [grid[i+1][j].mySprite setPosition:ccp(42*(i+1) +
          GRID_OFFSET.x,42*j + GRID_OFFSET.y)];

          return;
        }
        break;
        case 2:
        if(i>0)
        {
         grid[i][j] = grid[i-1][j];
         grid[i-1][j] = stone;
         [grid[i][j].mySprite setPosition:ccp(42*i + GRID_OFFSET.x,42*j
         + GRID_OFFSET.y)];
         [grid[i-1][j].mySprite setPosition:ccp(42*(i-1) +
         GRID_OFFSET.x,42*j + GRID_OFFSET.y)];

         return;
```

```
            }
            break;
            case 3:
            if(j<GRID_HEIGHT-1)
            {
             grid[i][j] = grid[i][j+1];
             grid[i][j+1] = stone;
             [grid[i][j].mySprite setPosition:ccp(42*i + GRID_OFFSET.x,42*j
                + GRID_OFFSET.y)];
             [grid[i][j+1].mySprite setPosition:ccp(42*i +
                GRID_OFFSET.x,42*(j+1) + GRID_OFFSET.y)];

             return;
            }
            break;
            case 4:
            if(j>0)
            {
             grid[i][j] = grid[i][j-1];
             grid[i][j-1] = stone;
             [grid[i][j].mySprite setPosition:ccp(42*i + GRID_OFFSET.x,42*j
                + GRID_OFFSET.y)];
             [grid[i][j-1].mySprite setPosition:ccp(42*i +
                GRID_OFFSET.x,42*(j-1) GRID_OFFSET.y)];

             return;
            }
            break;
       }
      }
   }
  }

 }
```

Try running the game now. Finally, you should see a nicely arranged grid with stones, and of course you should be able to swap the positions of the tiles.

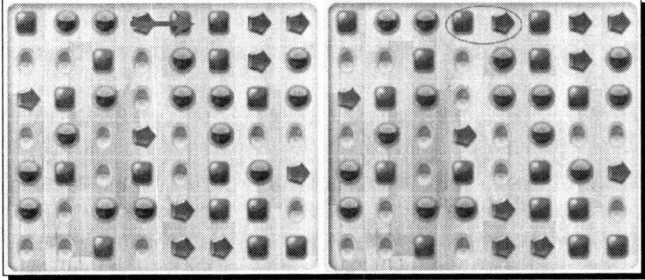

In the next chapter, we will animate the swapping to look better.

What just happened?

The swapStones method receives the actual stone that was initially touched and the direction of the swipe, that is, which stone must the touched one switch with.

First, we need to loop through the entire grid to find the place where the touched stone is. For that we compare the current grid place with the stone object passed along.

Once we find the one, we act accordingly depending on the direction. Let's analyze just one of them:

```
if(i<GRID_WIDTH-1)
{
  grid[i][j] = grid[i+1][j];
  grid[i+1][j] = stone;
  [grid[i][j].mySprite setPosition:ccp(42*i + GRID_OFFSET.x,42*j +
    GRID_OFFSET.y)];
  [grid[i+1][j].mySprite setPosition:ccp(42*(i+1) +
  GRID_OFFSET.x,42*j +
    GRID_OFFSET.y)];
  [self checkGroups:YES];
  return;
}
```

If we wanted to swap the touched stone with the right one, the preceding code is the one that would be run.

First, we check whether the swapping is really possible, if we touched the eight stone of any row and moved the finger to the right that swapping would never occur! (Unless you wanted this game to be cooler and made it possible to also swap the first and last stones)

Once we check that we can do the swapping, we just have to assign the value of the next grid's content to the current one, and then assign the stone object passed along to the next grid's content. We then change the sprite's positions to match this change.

Playing with Sprites

Finally, we call the `checkGroups` method, which will check if after the swapping there are any matches. We pass YES to it, as it is the first time we'll check a match since touching the screen.

 Notice that after we swap, we return from the function. If we didn't do this the game would crash, as once we swap, the next stone is equal to the stone passed. So when the loop reaches the next one it will be the same over again. This will repeat until we swap all the stones of the current column or row!

Have a go hero – doing more with the CCTouchDispatcher

The proposed method for handling the swapping is just one way to do it. Can you think of other ways to select two stones to swap? For example, you could do the following:

- On `CCTouchBegan` store a reference of the touched stone
- On `CCTouchEnded` store a reference to the place where the finger was let go
- Then retrieve which stone is placed where the finger was lifted off and compare to the first stone

Time for action – checking for matches

Now that we have the stones placed and the swapping working, we just need to check and react to stones matching. First we'll do the checking, which basically consists of grouping the stones that match. The following is the code:

```
-(void)checkGroups:(bool)firstTime
{
  int curHGroup = 0;
  int curVGroup = 0;
  int lastGroup =-1;
  NSMutableArray * groupings = [[NSMutableArray alloc]init];

  for(int i =0; i< GRID_WIDTH ; i++)
  {
    for(int j =0; j< GRID_HEIGHT ; j++)
    {
      Stone * d = (Stone *)grid[i][j];
      d.disappearing = NO;
      Stone * l =nil;
      Stone * t =nil;
```

```
if(i>0)
  l = (Stone *)grid[i-1][j];
if(j>0)
    t = (Stone *)grid[i][j-1];

  //IF there is a previous stone in the grid we compare the
   actual one with that one. If they
  //are of the same type we add it to that group.
  //If not, we create a new horizontal group and add the stone
   to that one.

if(l && l.stoneType == d.stoneType)
{
  [[groupings objectAtIndex:l.curHGroup] addObject:grid[i][j]];
  grid[i][j].curHGroup = l.curHGroup;

}
else
{
  curHGroup = lastGroup +1;
  NSMutableSet * group = [[NSMutableSet alloc]init];
  [groupings addObject:group];
  [group release];
  [[groupings objectAtIndex:curHGroup] addObject:grid[i][j]];
  grid[i][j].curHGroup = curHGroup;
  lastGroup = curHGroup;
}

    //The same for grouping vertically

if(t &&  t.stoneType == d.stoneType)
{
  [[groupings objectAtIndex:t.curVGroup] addObject:grid[i][j]];
  grid[i][j].curVGroup = t.curVGroup;
}
else
{
  curVGroup = lastGroup+1;

  NSMutableSet * group2 = [[NSMutableSet alloc]init];
  [groupings addObject:group2];
  [group2 release];
  [[groupings objectAtIndex:curVGroup] addObject:grid[i][j]];
```

Playing with Sprites

```
          grid[i][j].curVGroup = curVGroup;
          lastGroup = curVGroup;
        }
      }
    }

    BOOL moveStones = NO;
    for (NSMutableSet * n in groupings)
    {
      if([n count]>=3)
      {
        for(Stone * c in n)
        {
            c.disappearing = YES;
            moveStones = YES;
            [c.mySprite setOpacity:0];
        }

      }
    }

    //We are done with the groupings array, release it.
    [groupings release];

    if(moveStones)
    {
      [self moveStonesDown];
    }
    else
    {
      self.allowTouch = YES;
    }
}
```

We also have to add the call to this new method. We'll do it in the `swapStones` method we wrote before. The code inside those loops should look as follows:

```
    if(grid[i][j] == stone)
    {
      switch (dir) {
      case 1:
      if(i<GRID_WIDTH-1)
      {
        grid[i][j] = grid[i+1][j];
        grid[i+1][j] = stone;
```

```
    [grid[i][j].mySprite setPosition:ccp(42*i + GRID_OFFSET.x,42*j +
       GRID_OFFSET.y)];
    [grid[i+1][j].mySprite setPosition:ccp(42*(i+1) +
     GRID_OFFSET.x,42*j +
       GRID_OFFSET.y)];
    [self checkGroups:YES];
    return;
}
  break;
  case 2:
if(i>0)
{
  grid[i][j] = grid[i-1][j];
  grid[i-1][j] = stone;
  [grid[i][j].mySprite setPosition:ccp(42*i + GRID_OFFSET.x,42*j +
       GRID_OFFSET.y)];
  [grid[i-1][j].mySprite setPosition:ccp(42*(i-1) +
   GRID_OFFSET.x,42*j +
       GRID_OFFSET.y)];
  [self checkGroups:YES];
  return;
}
  break;
  case 3:
if(j<GRID_HEIGHT-1)
{
  grid[i][j] = grid[i][j+1];
  grid[i][j+1] = stone;
  [grid[i][j].mySprite setPosition:ccp(42*i + GRID_OFFSET.x,42*j +
       GRID_OFFSET.y)];
  [grid[i][j+1].mySprite setPosition:ccp(42*i +
   GRID_OFFSET.x,42*(j+1) + GRID_OFFSET.y)];
  [self checkGroups:YES];
  return;
}
  break;
  case 4:
if(j>0)
{
  grid[i][j] = grid[i][j-1];
  grid[i][j-1] = stone;
  [grid[i][j].mySprite setPosition:ccp(42*i + GRID_OFFSET.x,42*j +
       GRID_OFFSET.y)];
```

Playing with Sprites

```
    [grid[i][j-1].mySprite setPosition:ccp(42*i +
     GRID_OFFSET.x,42*(j-1) +
       GRID_OFFSET.y)];
    [self checkGroups:YES];
    return;
  }
    break;
}
```

What just happened?

The checkgroups takes a `Bool` parameter we call first time. We won't need this yet, but it will allow us to know later if we are checking groups as a result of player input or if we are checking after new stones fall.

First we must create an `NSMutableArray`. This will hold all the different groups of matching stones. Next, we loop through the grid to retrieve each stone and the adjacent ones. We then compare their types to see if they match.

If the current stone does not match with the previous one, we can assume it could be the first stone of a future group, so we create a new `NSMutableSet` and store it there. If it does match, we add the stone to the previous group.

This way we will end up with an array of **NSSets** that contain sets of stones (they could be holding from one to more than five).

Once every stone has been checked, we can do whatever we want with the resultant groups. Right now let's just make the stones instantly disappear:

```
BOOL moveStones = NO;
for (NSMutableSet * n in groupings)
{
  if([n count]>=3)
  {
    for(Stone * c in n)
    {
      c.disappearing = YES;
      moveStones = YES;
      [c.mySprite setOpacity:0];
      score += 100 * [n count];
      NSLog(Score: %d,score);
    }
  }
}
```

In the preceding code, we travel the array that contains all the sets, and if they have three or more stones inside we set their opacity to 0, thus making them invisible.

Also, we are computing the actual score by logging it into the console.

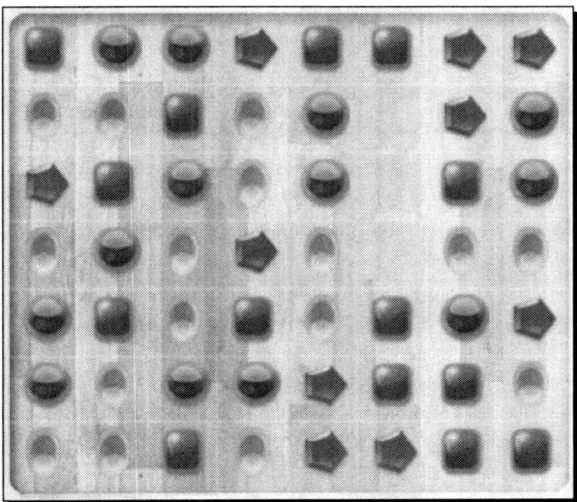

We also are marking these stones as disappearing. This will be of use later when switching stones from their place. Remember that if any stone is removed, all the ones that are above it should fall from their place, and later more of them will fall from the sky to replace the removed ones.

Finally, we are setting moveStones to YES if we find at least one group that matches:

```
if(moveStones)
{
    [self moveStonesDown];
}
else
{
    self.allowTouch = YES;
}
```

If there was a match we would need to make the other stones fall; if not we just let the player continue with his stone swapping frenzy.

Playing with Sprites

Making them fall!

All that is left now is to have the stones fall from their comfortable places and have *new* ones fall from the sky to occupy the newly free slots. We won't be using any animations or actions for the time being, so they will just appear in the corresponding slot. In the next chapter we'll modify this to do just that.

Time for action – refilling the grid

So, we need to do something with the stones we marked as disappearing a while before. We must have them free the space they are occupying and let the ones from above fall. Then once they are not in the grid anymore we will reuse them to make new ones appear.

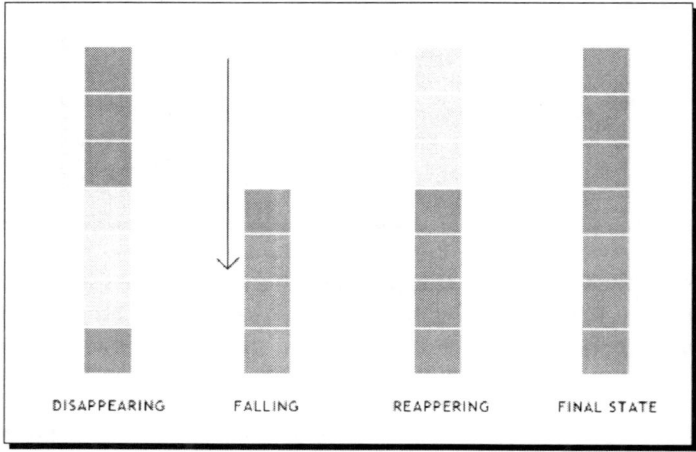

The following is the code that gets the job done:

```
-(void)moveStonesDown
{
    self.allowTouch = NO;
    NSMutableArray * removeds = [[NSMutableArray alloc]init];
    
    for(int i =0; i< GRID_WIDTH ; i++)
    {
        int nilCount =0;
        for(int j =0; j< GRID_HEIGHT ; j++)
        {
            Stone * d = grid[i][j];
            if(nilCount >0)
            {
```

```
                grid[i][j] = nil;
                grid[i][j -nilCount] = d;
            }

            if(d.disappearing)
            {
                nilCount ++;
                [removeds addObject:d];
            }

            if(nilCount >0 && !d.disappearing)
            {
                [d.mySprite setPosition:ccp(42*i + GRID_OFFSET.x,42*
                (j-nilCount) + GRID_OFFSET.y)];
            }
        }

        int q =0;

        for(Stone * stone in removeds)
        {
            [stone.mySprite setOpacity:255];
            int stoneT = arc4random() % STONE_TYPES;
            CGRect color =[stone setStoneColor:stoneT];
            [stone.mySprite setTextureRect:color];

            [stone.mySprite setPosition:ccp(42*i +
             GRID_OFFSET.x,42*(GRID_HEIGHT -nilCount +q) +
             GRID_OFFSET.y)];

            grid[i][GRID_HEIGHT -nilCount +q] = stone;
            q++;
        }
        [removeds removeAllObjects];
    }
    [self schedule:@selector(checkGroupsAgain) interval:2.5];
}
```

What just happened?

First we are disallowing the player from touching any other stone while a stone is moving. That is because we can't have him make new matches while we are still computing older ones.

Then we initialize an `NSMutableArray` that will be holding the stones that are supposed to be eliminated from the grid.

Playing with Sprites

Before I explain the code, let me tell you there are two ways of handling the creation and elimination of game elements, which are as follows:

- You can create them and destroy them as needed. In our game this would mean each time that the stones are matched and removed they are destroyed, and when you need to make new ones fall, you initialize more objects from the Stone class.

- You can create all the objects you need on `init`, and then reuse them. That would mean that each time a stone is eliminated, it is not really being destroyed, but its opacity is set to 0 (you could also position it outside of the screen) and it is added to an array that will hold all of these "destroyed" elements for later use.

As you may already have noticed, I will be doing this with the second method. It does require more coding and thinking but the performance boost it gives makes it worth it. Imagine a case where you have a lot more elements going around, like in the second game we will create with lots of bullets and planes, and so on. If you were to create and destroy that many elements all the time, during the game's lifetime performance would drop considerably.

What we are trying to achieve here is to have the stones that are on top of the removed ones occupy their places and then use those removed pieces to occupy the places above, that are now free.

Take a look at just the first column; it contains seven stones, one on top of the other. For example, let's say we matched the third, fourth, and fifth stones from bottom to top. The final result would be as follows:

- The first and second stones are below the ones removed and they won't fall, so they should remain untouched.

- The third, fourth, and fifth ones matched, so we must remove them from the grid, make them invisible, and add them to the array that holds the removed stones.

- The sixth and seventh stones must fall to occupy the third and fourth slot.

- The third removed stones must be placed in the, now, empty fifth, sixth, and seventh.

- Check again if after the movements there are new groups of matching stones. If there are, we repeat the whole process again.

Analyzing the logic

Now that we know what is to be done, let's analyze the code that makes this happen for the preceding example.

While we are travelling the grid array, we must check a couple of the following things:

- We leave the first and second stones untouched:

```
if(nilCount >0)
  {
    grid[i][j] = nil;
    grid[i][j -nilCount] = d;
  }
```

The `nilCount` variable will be incremented each time we encounter a stone marked as disappearing, so the ones below will skip that code.

Once we reach at least one stone supposed to disappear, what we do is set the grid slot that holds that stone to `nil` (thus eliminating the reference the grid has to the stone) and then assign a stone below the to `d` (which is a reference to the current stone).

- Next, we have to remove the stones that match:

```
if(d.disappearing)
  {
    nilCount ++;
    [removeds addObject:d];
  }
```

If the stone we are looking at is marked as disappearing, we increment `nilCount`, so the next stone we travel will execute the code I explained in step 1. Also, we add that stone to the array that holds the removed ones.

- Now we have to handle the actual movement of the sprites of the stones that must fall from their places (the sixth and seventh ones)

```
if(nilCount >0 && !d.disappearing)
  {
    [d->mySprite setPosition:ccp(42*i + GRID_OFFSET.x,42*
      (j-nilCount) + GRID_OFFSET.y)];
  }
```

In the next chapter, we will animate this behavior with *Actions*, but for now we just set the position, so they move instantly there.

- Now we have three empty slots and we should fill them with three *new* stones:

```
for(Stone * stone in removeds)
  {
    [stone.mySprite setOpacity:255];
    int stoneT = arc4random() % STONE_TYPES;
    CGRect color =[stone setStoneColor:stoneT];
    [stone.mySprite setTextureRect:color];
```

Playing with Sprites

```
        [stone.mySprite setPosition:ccp(42*i + GRID_OFFSET.x,42*
        (GRID_HEIGHT - nilCount +q) + GRID_OFFSET.y)];

        grid[i][GRID_HEIGHT -nilCount +q] = stone;
        q++;
    }        [removeds removeAllObjects];
```

As discussed before, we take the stones that are contained in the `removeds` array and place them again in the grid but in the fifth, sixth, and seventh positions. We also call the `setStoneColor` method from the `Stone` class. That method will change the stone type of the stone, so they are not three matching stones again (although as we are doing it at random, it can happen, but that is ok.).

- Finally, we have to check if there is, now, another matching set:

```
[self schedule:@selector(checkGroupsAgain) interval:2.5];
```

This line calls the `checkGroupsAgain` method after `2.5` seconds. We are delaying the call to give the player time to see the stones matching. If it happened instantly it would be very confusing.

The following are the contents of the `checkGroupsAgain` method:

```
-(void)checkGroupsAgain
{
    [self unschedule:@selector(checkGroupsAgain)];
    [self checkGroups:NO];
}
```

All it does is unschedule the same method (so it is not called continually every 2.5 seconds) and then call the `checkGroups` method again. This is not the first time we called this method since we touched the screen, so we pass `NO` to it.

If the `checkGroups` method finds a matching set, all the process will repeat again, and if it doesn't, the user will be able to swap stones again.

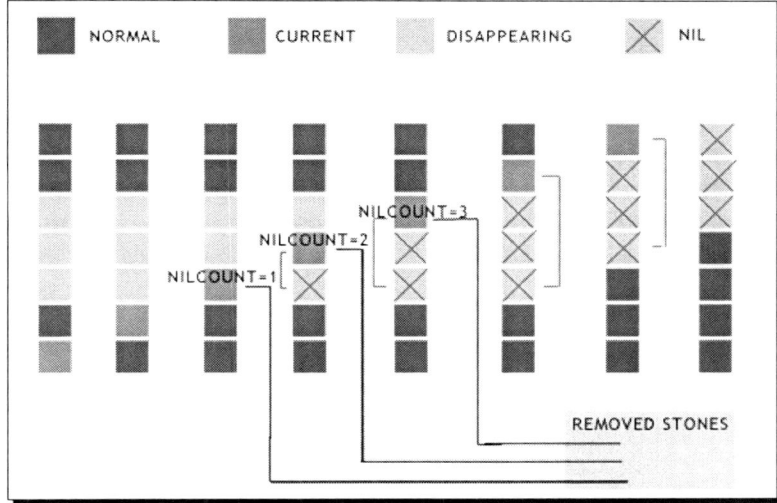

Build and run the project now, you should be able to see all of this working! Relax for a moment and enjoy, as the most complicated part is done.

Playing with CCSprite's properties

Sprites have a lot of properties you can play with, for example you can change their rotation, position, scaling, opacity, and tinting. We have already been using some of them in our examples.

Of course, you can apply many transformations at the same time, and these transformations can be applied to the sprite's children at the same time.

Playing with Sprites

Time for action – making a time bar

Our game is missing a lose condition; we must make the player feel the pressure of time when choosing which stones to swap. So, let's make the game last one minute. After that time is over, points are reset and the player has to start over. We will represent the remaining time with a **bar**. This bar will start fill up and drain over time. If the player swaps stones and he doesn't match any stones, the bar will drain even more, if he matches four or more stones, it will fill up a little, thus giving him more time. The following screenshot shows how it will look:

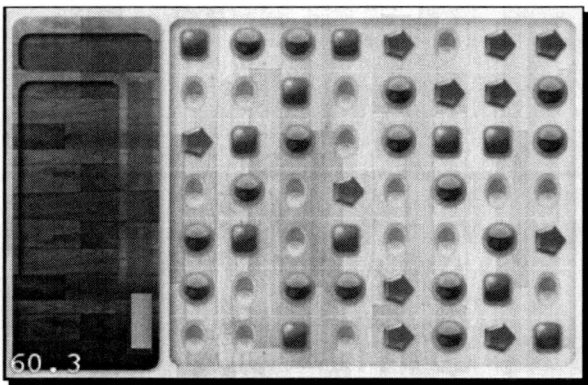

Carry out the following steps:

1. First, add the following code in your GameLayer's `init` method:

   ```
   remainingTime = MAX_TIME;
   
   bar = [CCSprite spriteWithFile:@"bar.png"];
   [self addChild:bar];
   [bar setPosition:ccp(113,25)];
   [bar setScaleY:remainingTime];
   [bar setAnchorPoint:ccp(0.5,0)];
   
   [self schedule:@selector(drainTime) interval:0.20];
   ```

2. Then add the `drainTime` method:

   ```
   -(void)drainTime
   {
       if(remainingTime>0)
           remainingTime--;
       [bar setScaleY:remainingTime];
   ```

```
    if(remainingTime <=0)
    {
       score= 0;
       NSLog(@"You lost!");
       remainingTime = MAX_TIME;
    }
}
```

Now, we have to make the time remaining change depending on whether the player matched none or more than three stones.

3. In the `checkGroups` method make the following changes:

```
for (NSMutableSet * n in groupings)
   {
       if([n count]>=3)
       {
          //... other code...
       }
       if([n count]>=4)
       {
          [self changeTime:50];
       }
   }
[groupings release];

   if(moveStones)
   {
      //... other code...    }
   else
   {
      if(firstTime)
         [self changeTime:-50];
      //... other code...
   }
```

4. The `changeTime` method does the following:

```
-(void)changeTime:(int)time
{
   remainingTime += time;
   if(remainingTime>=MAX_TIME)
      remainingTime = MAX_TIME;
   else if(remainingTime<=0)
      remainingTime =0;
}
```

That is all; let's see how it works.

Playing with Sprites

What just happened?

We made a time bar in quite a simple fashion, that is, by using a 1 pixel height image, we scale it up to look a lot higher. Then as the remaining time changes, we scale it down (or up again if we acquired more time).

Take a look at the following lines:

```
bar = [CCSprite spriteWithFile:@"bar.png"];
[self addChild:bar];
[bar setPosition:ccp(113,7)];
[bar setScaleY:remainingTime];
[bar setAnchorPoint:ccp(0.5,0)];
```

As you can see, we are applying three transformations to the sprite's properties. We are modifying its position, its scaling (only its height), and its anchorPoint.

The anchorPoint is measured in percentage and not in pixels as you might expect. This has its pros and cons, but what is important is that you remember that.

The anchorPoint is another property that CCNodes have. By default, it is placed at the bottom left part of the node and it is the point where all the transformations and positioning will occur. It is expressed as a percentage where 0 is the leftmost part of the node and 1 is the rightmost. So, when you move a CCNode to, let's say, position (100,100) the centre of the sprite will be placed at that position. Also, if you were to rotate it, it would rotate around its centre. The anchorPoint does not necessarily need to be inside the node. You can set it outside of it to have the object, for example, rotate around another point.

Here we are changing the anchorPoint of the sprite to (0.5,0), which means it will be placed at the bottom-center part of the sprite. This makes the bar remain fixed at the bottom, regardless of its scaling.

Then we schedule the `drainBar` method to run each one fifth of a second. This method subtracts one unit form the `remainingTime` property, and checks its value. If it is 0, then Game Over!

The remaining code checks whether the player matched no stone, in which case we subtract 50 units of time, or if he made a group of four or more stones, in which case we add 50 units of time.

Changing a sprite's texture at runtime

Are you ready to continue? Great!

If you were paying attention to the previous example where we used the removed stones to make new ones, you may notice a method we hadn't used before.

```
[f.mySprite setTexture:[[CCTextureCache sharedTextureCache]
addImage:[NSString stringWithFormat:@"s%@.png",color]]];
```

Instead of creating a new sprite to replace the old one, we replaced the texture it is made from.

At any time you can call the sprite's `setTexture` method to change it without having to destroy and create a new sprite from another file.

Time for action – changing textures on the fly

Let's do a simple exercise to demonstrate the power of changing textures.

Right now, there is no feedback when the player groups any matching stones. Let's change that by changing the matching stone's texture to something else and then changing them back. Carry out the following steps:

1. Add the `sSmile.png` image to the project.
2. In the `checkgroups` method, make the following changes:

```
....
for (NSMutableSet * n in groupings)
   {
      if([n count]>=3)
      {
         for(Stone * c in n)
         {
            c.disappearing = YES;
            moveStones = YES;
            score += 100 * [n count];
            NSLog(Score: %d,score);

            //[c.mySprite setOpacity:0];
            [c.mySprite setTexture:[[CCTextureCache
            sharedTextureCache]addImage:@"sSmile.png"]];
         }

      }
   }
...

if(moveStones)
   {
      [self schedule:@selector(moveStonesDown) interval:0.5];
      //[self moveStonesDown];
   }
```

3. In the `moveStonesDown` method add the following line at the beginning:

   `[self unschedule:@selector(moveStonesDown)];`

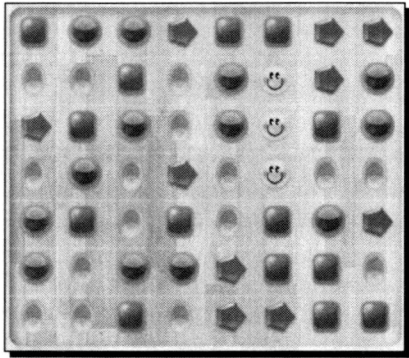

What just happened?

We are making use of the `setTexture` method to change the texture of any sprite at runtime. This method takes as its only parameter the `CCTexture2D` you wish to use. The `CCTexture2D` you pass to it can be one that you have around. For example, a texture of any other sprite. Alternatively, you can add an entirely new texture. In this case, we are adding a new texture to the `CCTextureCache` singleton class.

The CCTextureCache

The `CCTextureCache` is a singleton class that handles the loading of textures. You can add textures to it from image files, and if that image was previously loaded it will return a reference to it instead of creating it a new.

You can add a texture to `CCTextureCache` like we did before, by calling the `addImage` method which takes a file image as a parameter.

Pop Quiz – sprites

1. Which of the following statements is not true about CCSprites?
    a. You can add a CCSprite as a child of another CCSprite
    b. Their anchor Point are set to 0,0 by default
    c. You can change their texture at runtime
    d. All the above statements are true
2. Which one of the following pixel formats has the most quality but consumes the most resources?
    a. RGBA8888
    b. RGBA4444
    c. RGB5_A1
    d. RGB565
3. Which of the following is a property you can modify in a CSprite?
    a. Opacity
    b. Scale
    c. Anchor Point
    d. Tint
    e. All of the above

Using Spritesheets

Right now, our game has a few elements, but in real life your games could need to display a lot of images. This means that as you add more and more images, OpenGL will start having problems keeping up with the rendering of all those images.

Playing with Sprites

A **Spritesheet** or **Texture atlas** is a large image that contains other smaller images. The benefits of using a Spritesheet instead of lots of small images is reducing the texture memory and increasing performance. So now the OpenGL can draw all these elements in just one pass instead of a pass for each one.

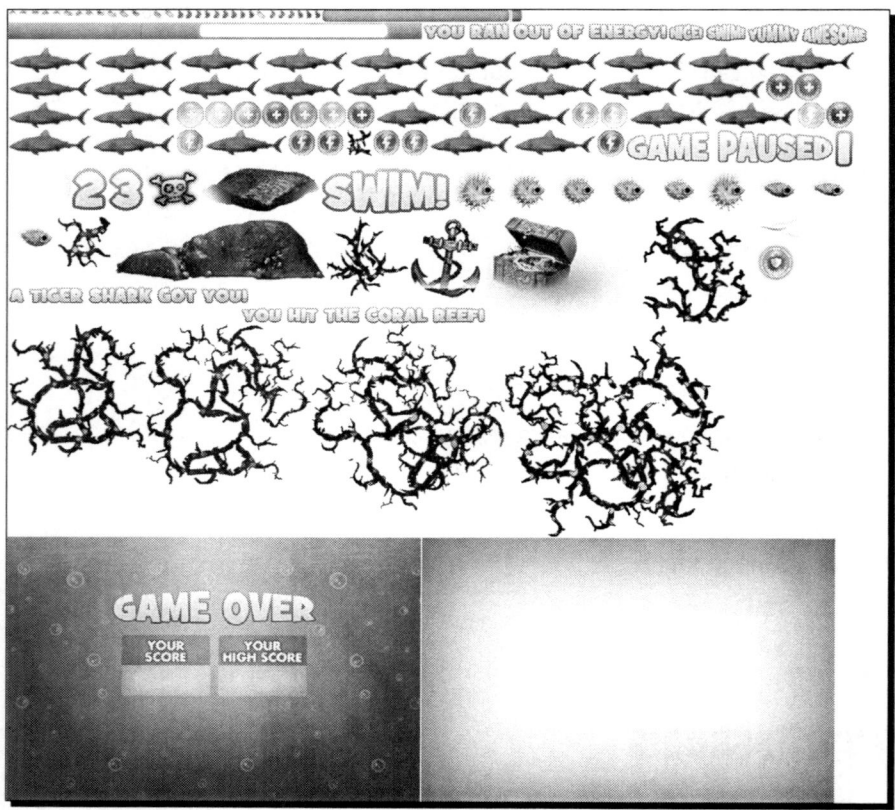

In the preceding image, you can see all the sample game's assets in just one image. All you have to do now to have a sprite use one of them is define the portion of the Spritesheet they occupy. For example, the green stone is contained inside the rectangle placed at coordinates (1,1) which has a width and height of 32 pixels.

Let's see how this is achieved in Cocos2d.

Chapter 2

Time for action – creating sprites from Spritesheets

To make our game perform better, we must change the CCSprites we have, so it can be loaded from a Spritesheet. Carry out the following steps:

1. Start by including the `colouredSheet.png` and `colouredSheet.plist` files from the companion files for Chapter 2. I have already arranged the images that we have been using until now into a Spritesheet.

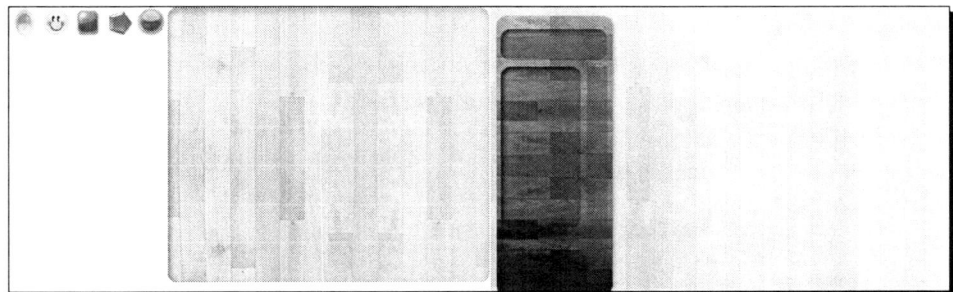

The first thing to do when using a Spritesheet is to create a `CCSpriteBatchNode` object. Let's do that in the GameLayer.

2. Before the line that creates the background image, add the following lines:

   ```
   CCSpriteBatchNode * sSheet = [CCSpriteBatchNode batchNodeWithFile:
   @"colouredSheet.png"];
   [self addChild:sSheet z:1 tag:kSSheet];
   ```

   Those lines instantiate a `CCSpriteBatchNode` object with the name `sSheet` and load it with the image `colouredSheet.png`. Then the newly created Spritesheet is added as a child of the layer with a tag. This tag will allow us to retrieve the Spritesheet from any other object.

   Remember to define `kSSheet` in your `GameScene.h` file as follows:

   ```
   #define kSSheet 1
   ```

   Now, we have to change the rest of the objects to get their images from a portion of the Spritesheet.

3. Open `Stone.m` file and make the following changes:

   ```
   -(void)placeInGrid:(CGPoint)place pt:(int)pt pl:(int)pl
   {
       int sType = arc4random() % 4;
       if(sType == pt || sType == pl)
       {   [self placeInGrid:place pt:pt pl:pl];
   ```

Playing with Sprites

```
            return;
        }else{
            //CGRect colorRect =[self setStoneColor:sType];
            
            CCSpriteBatchNode * s = (CCSpriteBatchNode *)[theGame
    getChildByTag:K_SSheet];
            
            mySprite = [CCSprite spriteWithBatchNode:s rect:[self
    setStoneColor:sType]];
            [s addChild:mySprite z:1];
            
            self.stoneType =sType;
            [self.mySprite setPosition:place];
        }
    }
    
    -(CGRect)setStoneColor:(int)stoneT
    {
        self.stoneType = stoneT;
        CGRect color;
        switch (self.stoneType) {
            case 0:
                color = CGRectMake(68,2,32,32);
                break;
            case 1:
                color =CGRectMake(132,2,32,32);
                break;
            case 2:
                color = CGRectMake(2,2,32,32);
                break;
            case 3:
                color = CGRectMake(100,2,32,32);
                break;
        }
        return color;
    }
```

Now, instead of selecting an image using their file names, we are selecting a rectangular portion of the Spritesheet.

```
mySprite = [CCSprite spriteWithBatchNode:s rect:[self
setStoneColor:sType]];
```

That line instantiates a sprite using the Spritesheet and a `CGRect` that contains the portion we want the sprite to render.

I have changed the `setStoneColor` method to return the corresponding `CGRect` instead of a `NSString` with the file name.

Also, the CCSprite is now added as a child of the Spritesheet instead of the layer, ensuring that all the sprites will be rendered in one go.

There is one more thing that we need to change in order for this to work. Remember, we were changing the sprites' textures when matching the stones and when making new ones appear. If a sprite is a child of a `SpriteBatchNode` we can no longer change the texture; we now have to change the `CGRect` to match another portion of the spriteSheet. So, let's do that where needed.

4. In the `checkGroups` method, where we were replacing the stones with nice smiling ones, we have to change the line:

```
[c.mySprite setTexture:[[CCTextureCache sharedTextureCache]addImage:@"sSmile.png"]];
```

Into the following:

```
[c.mySprite setTextureRect:CGRectMake(34,2,32,32)];
```

In the `moveStonesDown` method we have to change:

```
NSString * color =[f setStoneColor:stoneT];
[f.mySprite setTexture:[[CCTextureCache sharedTextureCache] addImage:[NSString stringWithFormat:@"s%@.png",color]]];
```

Into the following:

```
CGRect color =[f setStoneColor:stoneT];
[f.mySprite setTextureRect:color];
```

5. Now run the game. To tell you the truth, you will not see any difference right now, but as you start building your own games with hundreds of images going around, you will appreciate the benefits of using Spritesheets.

What just happened?

Spritesheets are really useful in game programming, even more so in iPhone games where the memory available is scarce. Even if you don't need the benefits it gives performance wise, you should accustom yourself to using them, as it is a good way to organize you image assets, and also when you learn how to do animations they will make your life easier.

Playing with Sprites

In the preceding example, we grabbed the Spritesheet I made and replaced the stones' images with images made from it. You should aim to do this every time you can. Although, using Spritesheets have some limitations, which are as follows:

- It only accepts CCSprites as a child, so you won't be able to add a menu item as a child of the Spritesheet, for instance.
- All its children are either *aliased* or *antialiased*.
- Spritesheets (as any other image in the iPhone) can be up to 1024 * 1024 pixels in 3G models and below and 2048 * 2048 pixels in newer models. This means you will sometimes need to create many Spritesheets to make all your images fit, which leads me to.
- Memory in the iPhone is scarce, so loading three or four Spritesheets into memory will probably cause you trouble. That is why you should try to compress the images you can into `pvrtc` files.
- The Z-order of each CCSprite inside a Spritesheet is relative to it. If your game needs many Spritesheets, ordering them correctly can be a pain.

In the previous example, I also made you include a file named `colouredSheet.plist`. This file contains the definitions for each image inside the spriteSheet we included.

Key	Type	Value
▼ Root	Dictionary	(2 items)
▼ texture	Dictionary	(2 items)
width	Number	1024
height	Number	1024
▼ frames	Dictionary	(7 items)
▼ background.png	Dictionary	(8 items)
x	Number	504
y	Number	1
width	Number	480
height	Number	320
offsetX	Number	0
offsetY	Number	0
originalWidth	Number	480
originalHeight	Number	320
▶ grid.png	Dictionary	(8 items)
▶ sBlue.png	Dictionary	(8 items)
▶ sGreen.png	Dictionary	(8 items)
▶ sRed.png	Dictionary	(8 items)
▶ sSmile.png	Dictionary	(8 items)
▶ sYellow.png	Dictionary	(8 items)

Select it inside Xcode to see its content. This plist contains the following two keys:

- Texture: Contains the width and height of the whole spriteSheet
- Frames: This has a key for each image included in the Spritesheet

This file is created by the software I used to create the Spritesheet, which you will learn how to use soon. It contains the data of the images included in the `colouredSheet.png` file, such as their positions and dimensions; this will prove to be very useful for making the rectangles that contain each image.

Have a go hero – changing the rest of the elements

The `colouredSheet.png` contains the background image and the grid image. Use what you have learned until know to have the background and grid sprites load their images from the Spritesheet.

Hint: Take a look at the `colouredSheet.plist` file to learn their positions and dimensions for the CGRects.

Creating Spritesheets with zwoptex

Now that you know how to use Spritesheets, let's see how to actually create them.

As you have seen, Spritesheets are just image files, so you can create them with whatever tool suits you. However, there is one tool that is compatible with Cocos2d that works perfectly.

Zwoptex was created by *Robert Payne* and there are currently two incarnations of it, which are as follows:

- A web version which is available at the following URL:
  `http://www.zwoptexapp.com/flashversion/`

- And a desktop version which you can download from:
  `http://www.zwoptexapp.com`

We will be using the Web version in this book, as it is more stable right now.

Playing with Sprites

Time for action – creating more colored stones with Spritesheets

Have you played our little game for a while? I know it is really boring right now, but soon we will try to make it better. You may have noticed that it is quite easy to match stones; that is because we have just a few types. Let's change that. What I propose here is to create three more types and add them to the Spritesheets that we used in the previous example, so you can then have seven different possible stones. Carry out the following steps:

1. Go ahead and open any graphics program that you have, and create your own stones. They should be 32 * 32 pixels to fit into the grid.

    If you are being lazy, I have included three more stones in the companion files for you to use.

2. Once you have the images that we will use, open the Zwoptex web application at `http://www.zwoptexapp.com/flashversion/`. This is a very simple application, and very straightforward to use. When it finishes loading, you can see a canvas where you will place all the images that you want to have in the Spritesheets. Then when you are ready, you can export the `.png` file and the `.plist` file like the ones we were using before.

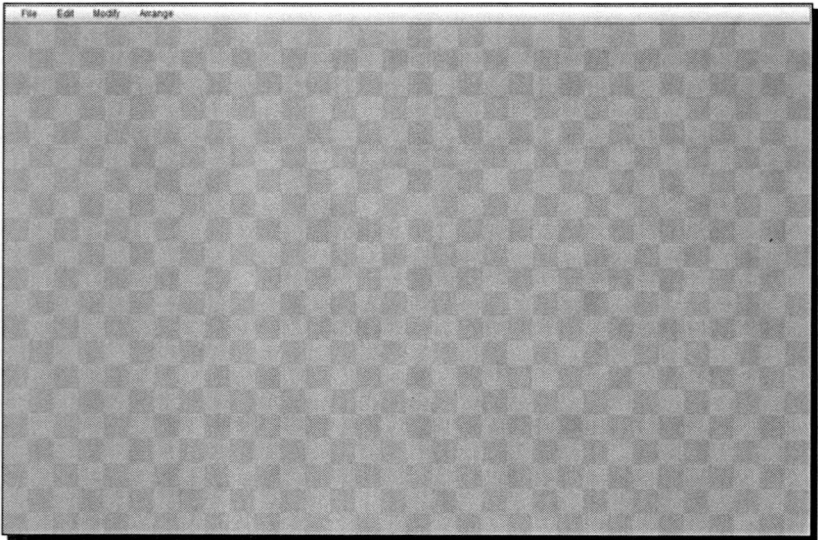

3. Let's add the new images to the existing project (the Spritesheets we were using before).

   Select **Project | Load Project** and search for the `colouredSheet.ztp` file in the `companion` folder. Zwoptex saves its projects with this format, allowing you to load the Spritesheet again to add new images if you need to.

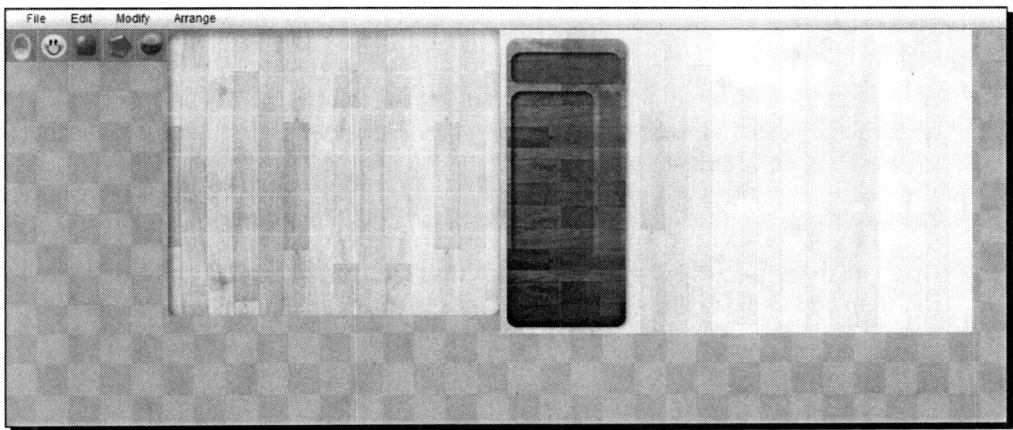

4. Now all we have to do is to add the new images. **Select file | Import Images** to load the three stones designs we created. Once you do so, they will appear at the top-left corner of the canvas.

   To place the images, you can either move them manually by selecting and moving them around with the mouse/keyboard. Alternatively you can arrange them automatically by selecting an option inside the **Arrange** menu. This allows you to arrange the images by their height, width, and name.

5. In this case, try to place them manually, so you don't change the previously loaded images' positions.

   If you change them, you will have to modify the code we used to load the other images to match the new image file.

    You should always arrange them in a way that there is at least 1 pixel of distance between the images to avoid artifacts. You can do this automatically by setting a minimum spacing in the **Arrange** menu.

Playing with Sprites

Another thing zwoptex does is trim your images to eliminate any transparent spaces. So if you had a 50 * 50 pixels image with a 20 pixel transparent border, zwoptex would trim it to a 30 * 30 pixels image. This is very useful to save space, but if you need it not to do that, just select the images that you want to untrim and select **Modify | Untrim selected images**.

In the modify menu, you can also change the canvas settings to be of a different size. So if you have a few images you should change the canvas size to a smaller one to save memory later.

6. When you have finished placing and arranging the images, go to **File | Export texture** and select a location for the `.png` file. Then select **File | Export** coordinates to save the `.plist` file to any location.

7. Save your project by selecting **Save project** from the file menu.

That's all there is to it. Now you can add those files to the project and use them. You can then add and use the new stone designs in your game just like we did before.

What just happened?

Zwoptex is a very useful application for making Spritesheets and it is compatible and fully supported by Cocos2d. When we see how to make animations you will learn other features of zwoptex that are very time saving in this case.

Preloading images

Image preloading is a very interesting feature that lets you know when you have finished loading a particular image into the cache. Thus you can call a method to respond to that.

For example, you can have a loading bar, and each time an image is loaded increment the loading bar's size until all images are done loading, then start the game. In big games where the loading times can take more than five seconds, it is very important to give the user feedback, so he doesn't think the application crashed; so, this technique really comes in handy.

We won't be doing a loading bar right now, but I will show you how to implement the preloading code and log the loading of images into the console.

Time for action – preloading your images

Let's see how an image is preloaded in Cocos2d. Open the project we have been working with and open the `ColouredStonesAppDelegate.m` file. We will be preloading the images here. You can do this in another part of your game if you want.

Add the following line in the `applicationDidFinishLaunching` method before `runWithScene` call:

```
[[CCTextureCache sharedTextureCache]addImageAsync:@"colouredSheet.png" target:self selector:@selector(imageLoaded:)];
```

Then we just have to create the callback method for when the texture is finished loading, as follows:

```
-(void)imageLoaded:(CCTexture2D *)texture
{
    NSLog(@"image loaded!");
}
```

What just happened?

That is all there is to image preloading!

First, we told the `CCTextureCache` to add an image to it asynchronously. This causes the image `colouredSheet.png` to be loaded in another thread behind the scenes.

The target parameter is the object that will be calling the callback method when the image finishes loading. `selector` is the name of the method that will be called when the image has finished loading.

So in this case, we are calling the `imageLoaded` method when it is ready, which just logs a message to the console. Inside these callback methods is where you should act in any way you want in response to an image being loaded; that might be by having a loading bar advance, messages shown, or whatever way you choose to show some feedback.

> Calling the `addImageAsync` method for various images in a particular order does not ensure they will be loaded in that order, so do not depend on the order to act in a particular way.

Playing with Sprites

Making OpenGl Calls

Let's talk about one more thing before moving on to the next chapter.

When using Cocos2d, you can still draw stuff using pure OpenGL. This is very useful for creating effects you can't do with just sprites.

Next, we will be adding a simple effect to our game.

Time for action – selecting a stone for swapping

Right now, when a stone is touched for swapping, there is no feedback whatsoever to let the player know which stone he/she touched. We will add a simple effect. Using OpenGL we will draw a square on top of the sprite to make it look selected.

1. First, add a new property to the `Stone` class. This will allow us to keep track of when the image is either selected and when it is not.

2. In the `CCTouchBegan` method, set new property to `YES` and change the opacity of `mySprite` to `100` (semi-transparent):
   ```
   self.isSelected = YES;
   [self.mySprite setOpacity:100];
   ```

3. In the `CCTouchEnded` method, set the new property to `NO` and change the opacity of `mySprite` to `255` (opaque):
   ```
   self.isSelected=NO;
   [self.mySprite setOpacity:255];
   ```

4. Then override the `draw` method:
   ```
   -(void)draw
   {
      if(isSelected)
      {
         glColor4ub(255, 0, 0, 100);
         glPointSize(30);
         ccDrawPoint( self.mySprite.position);
      }
   }
   ```

Now when you touch a stone it should be red colored and semi-transparent, and when released it should return to normal. An example is shown in the following screenshot:

Chapter 2

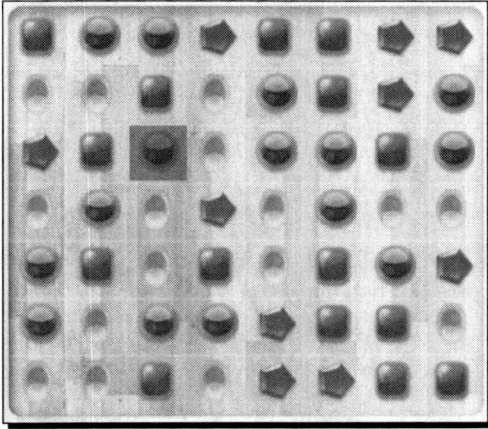

What just happened?

CCNodes use the draw method to render themselves into the screen. Inside the draw method if where you should make any drawing, like we just did. This method will be called each frame.

In our example, we are just drawing a 30 pixel red colored semi-translucent point, where the sprite is placed.

Cocos2d comes with a few methods that are just wrappers of OpenGL methods, ccDrawPoint is one of them.

You can see the other methods in action by opening the drawPrimitives text that comes in the Cocos2d test project.

>  This book is not an OpenGL primer so we won't be using any pure OpenGL code. However, bear in mind it is very important to know how to work with it in a lot of not so trivial situations.

As the draw method is a method from the CCNode class, any node can call it, so you are not just limited to drawing stuff in sprites. You can draw inside layers, labels, or any other custom class you create that inherits from CCNode.

Summary

Phew! This has been a very long chapter, but I hope you have learned a lot here.

In this chapter, we began working on our first game and learned a lot in the process.

- We saw how to create our own sprites, how to change their properties, and how to interact with them
- Then, you learned how to reduce memory usage by using Spritesheets, and how to preload them to speed things up
- Finally, you learned how to use pure OpenGL to your advantage

In the next chapter, we will take a look at the different actions you can apply to the elements in your game. Actions are a very powerful thing in Cocos2d, so be ready to be amazed!

3
Let's Do Some Actions

We covered a lot in the last chapter. We created sprites, we placed them, and we removed them from the screen. That was nice enough, but also quite uninteresting. Games need to be impressive to captivate the player, they need to show some life; you can't just have things move around in a dull way.

*In this chapter, we will be looking at **actions**, which can be applied to any CCNode in your game.*

These actions can be used for a wide range of applications. For example, moving text around, fading in and out sprites, applying many actions at once, calling methods after an action is completed, and lots of other stuff.

In this chapter, you shall:

- Explore different types of basic actions
- Use composition actions to give the user some nice feedback
- Learn how to make animations

Let's begin.

Let's Do Some Actions

Basic actions

The first group of actions we will be doing are basic actions. These so-called basic actions have the ability to change the node's properties we have been playing with, over time. This is particularly useful for animating some UI and feedback elements. Let's see how to use them.

Time for action – animating the stone falling

In the last chapter we wrote the code for eliminating stones and then made them fall instantaneously. This was fine for our purposes, but it looks pretty bad in practice. A distracted player may not notice what is happening onscreen. What we need to do now is use actions to move those stones from their location to the place where they are supposed to fall. You have to make the following changes to the existing code:

1. In the `moveStonesDown` method, change the code that sets the stones positions, to use actions as follows:

   ```
   if(nilCount >0 && !d.disappearing)
   {
     [d.mySprite runAction:[CCMoveTo actionWithDuration:
     (0.5 * nilCount)/3 position:ccp(42*i + GRID_OFFSET.x,42*
     (j-nilCount) + GRID_OFFSET.y)]];
   }
   ```

2. Below that, where we figured what to do with the removed stones do the same:

   ```
   for(Stone * f in removeds)
   {
     // code fragment...

     [f.mySprite runAction:[CCMoveTo actionWithDuration:0.5
      position:ccp(42*i + GRID_OFFSET.x,42*
      (GRID_HEIGHT -nilCount +q) + GRID_OFFSET.y)]];

     // code fragment...
   }
   ```

That will be all for now. Try running the game now and match some stones. You will see that now the stones are gracefully moving towards their destinations instead of instantly appearing in that place.

There are some problems we will solve soon, such as when you match five vertical stones, the stones falling from the sky get over the existing ones. It is just a matter of timing we will be able to correct when I talk about other time of actions.

What just happened?

You have just used your first action. Let's see what we have done here.

CCNodes, and by extension the classes that inherit from that, have the `runAction` method. This method takes a `CCAction` as the parameter that represents what action to apply to the node that ran it.

In the preceding example, we are calling the `runAction` method with the `CCMoveTo` class which makes the node move to a coordinate we choose over a period of time.

```
[d.mySprite runAction:[CCMoveTo actionWithDuration:(0.5 * nilCount)/3
    position:ccp(42*i + GRID_OFFSET.x,42*(j-nilCount) + GRID_OFFSET.y)]];
```

So, the `CCMoveTo` object, as well as the other actions that you can use, are created using a convenience method, so you don't have to worry about releasing them later.

This method takes the following two parameters:

- The duration of the action
- The place where you want the node to move to over that period of time

In our case, we are calculating the duration for the action of each stone, as we want them to move at the same speed to their destinations. The position where they must move is calculated like we did when placing them manually there.

Using other basic actions

Cocos2d comes packed with lots of basic actions and each new version adds more of them. The following are some of the actions that you can apply to your game elements:

- Position actions:
    - CCMoveTo: Moves the node to a point of the screen over a period of time. For example:

        ```
        [mySprite runAction:[CCMoveTo actionWithDuration:1
            position:ccp(100,100)]];
        ```

    - CCMoveBy: Moves the node by an amount of pixels from its position over a period of time. For example:

        ```
        [mySprite runAction:[CCMoveBy actionWithDuration:1
            position:ccp(10,0)]];
        ```

Let's Do Some Actions

- CCJumpTo: Moves the node in a parabolic fashion to a point of the screen over a period of time. For example:

  ```
  [mySprite runAction:[CCJumpTo actionWithDuration:1
      position:ccp(100,100) height:50 jumps:3]];
  ```

- CCJumpBy: This is the same as the preceding action, but it moves the node by an amount of pixels from its location. For example:

  ```
  [mySprite runAction:[CCJumpBy actionWithDuration:1
      position:ccp(100,100) height:50 jumps:3]];
  ```

- CCBezierTo: Moves the node with a cubic Bezier curve to a destination point over a period of time. For example:

  ```
  ccBezierConfig c = {ccp(300,300),ccp(50,50),ccp(-50,-50)};
  [mySprite runAction:[CCBezierTo actionWithDuration:1
      bezier:c]];
  ```

- CCBezierBy: Moves the node with a cubic Bezier curve by a certain distance over a period of time. For example:

  ```
  ccBezierConfig c = {ccp(50,300),ccp(20,30),ccp(-10,-20)};
  [mySprite runAction:[CCBezierBy actionWithDuration:1
      bezier:c]];
  ```

- CCPlace: Instantly places the node at the desired position. For example:

  ```
  [mySprite runAction:[CCPlace actionWithPosition:c
  cp(200,200)]];
  ```

◆ Scale actions:

- CCScaleTo: Changes the scaling of the node to a desired value over a period of time. For example:

  ```
  [mySprite runAction:[CCScaleTo actionWithDuration:2
      scale:2]];
  ```

- CCScaleBy: Changes the scaling of the node by a desired value over a period of time. For example:

  ```
  [mySprite runAction:[CCScaleBy actionWithDuration:1
      scale:0.1]];
  ```

- Rotation actions:
    - `CCRotateTo`: Sets the angle of the rotation of a node to a desired value over a period of time. For example:

        ```
        [mySprite runAction:[CCRotateTo actionWithDuration:2
            angle:180]];
        ```

    - `CCRotateBy`: Changes the angle of the rotation of a node by a desired value over a period of time. For example:

        ```
        [mySprite runAction:[CCRotateBy actionWithDuration:2
            angle:20]];
        ```

- Visible actions:
    - `CCShow`: Shows the node instantaneously. For example:

        ```
        [mySprite runAction:[CCShow action]];
        ```

    - `CCHide`: Shows the node instantaneously. For example:

        ```
        [mySprite runAction:[CCHide action]];
        ```

    - `CCToggleVisibility`: Toggles the visibility of a node. For example:

        ```
        [mySprite runAction:[CCToggleVisibility action]];
        ```

    - `CCBlink`: Blinks a node a desired amount of times over a period of time. For example:

        ```
        [mySprite runAction:[CCBlink actionWithDuration:2
            blinks:3]];
        ```

- Opacity actions:
    - `CCFadeIn`: Fades a node in over a period of time (changes its opacity from 0 to 255). For example:

        ```
        [mySprite runAction:[CCFadeIn actionWithDuration:1]];
        ```

    - `CCFadeOut`: Fades a node out over a period of time (changes its opacity from 255 to 0). For example:

        ```
        [mySprite runAction:[CCFadeOut actionWithDuration:1]];
        ```

    - `CCFadeTo`: Changes the node's opacity from its current value to the desired one over a period of time. For example:

        ```
        [mySprite runAction:[CCFadeTo actionWithDuration:1
            opacity:100]];
        ```

Let's Do Some Actions

- Colour actions:
  - `CCTintTo`: Tints the node to a desired RGB value over a period of time. For example:

    ```
    [mySprite runAction:[CCTintTo actionWithDuration:1 red:100
       green:120 blue:200]];
    ```

  - `CCTintBy`: Tints the node by a desired RGB value over a period of time. for example:

    ```
    [mySprite runAction:[CCTintBy actionWithDuration:1 red:255
       green:255 blue:200]];
    ```

These are all of the available basic actions. We will just apply a couple more of them, as we don't have much space here to explain them all. Once you learn how to use one or two of them, it will be easy for you to try out the other ones.

Hint: You can combine many actions to run at the same time or sequentially. We'll see how to do that later in this chapter.

Time for action – destroying stones with actions

I don't like how the stones are going away when matched right now. I propose we change that, so before they are eliminated they fade out. For that, we will use the `CCFadeOut` action which just needs to know how long it should take for the CCNode to completely fade out.

In the `GameScene.m` file, find the `checkGroups` method and where we were checking if three or more stones matched add the following code:

```
if([n count]>=3)
{
  for(Stone * c in n)
  {
     // not relevant code...
     [c.mySprite setTextureRect:CGRectMake(34,2,32, 32)];
     [c.mySprite runAction:[CCFadeOut actionWithDuration:0.5]];
  }
     // not relevant code...
}
```

Try the game out now. You should see the stones changing to the smile texture then fading out quickly, as shown in the following screenshot:

Chapter 3

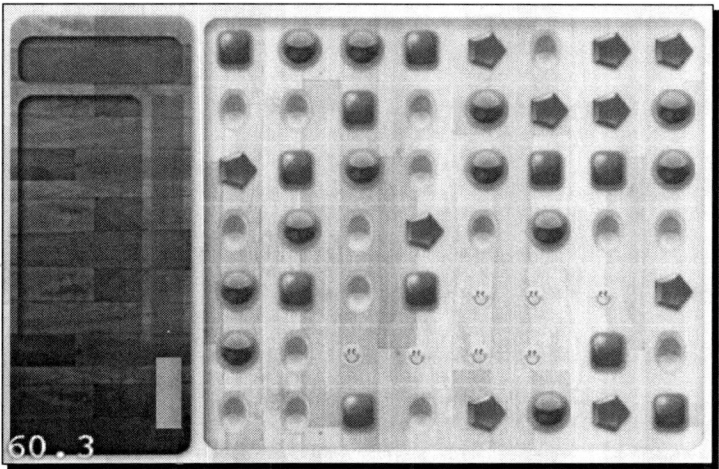

What just happened?

The `CCFadeOut` action just takes a parameter, the amount of time it should take the node to completely disappear. That is, reaching opacity of 0. In Cocos2d, 255 is the maximum opacity value.

As you can see, actions are very useful for making some nice, simple effects that add life to your game.

Let's see how to apply just one more action.

Time for action – tinting the time bar

I would like to let the player notice when he is running out of time. As he may be too focused on finding matching stones, he may not be able to see he has little time left. A good way to do this is making the time bar change its colour as time runs out.

The following is the code that accomplishes that. Add this to the `drainTime` method:

```
-(void)drainTime
{
  if (remainingTime>0)
    remainingTime--;
  [bar setScaleY:remainingTime];

  int currentTimeStatus = self.timeStatus;

  if (remainingTime < 100)
```

```
      self.timeStatus = 1;
   else
   {
      self.timeStatus = 0;
   }
   if(currentTimeStatus ==0 && timeStatus ==1)
   {
      [bar runAction:[CCTintTo actionWithDuration:1 red:255 green:0
         blue:0]];
   }
   else if(currentTimeStatus ==1 && timeStatus ==0)
   {
      [bar runAction:[CCTintTo actionWithDuration:1 red:255 green:255
         blue:255]];
   }

   if(remainingTime <=0)
   {
      score= 0;
      NSLog(@"You lost!");
      remainingTime = MAX_TIME;
   }
}
```

You must add the new instance variable `timeStatus`, which is an integer, to the interface of the GameLayer class for this to work. Also remember to make them a property and to synthesize them.

What just happened?

With this new code we are achieving the desired behavior, which is to change the colour of the time bar according to the state of the game.

Each time the `drainTime` method is called, what we do is check the previous `timeStatus` and compare it to the actual one (which changes if the timer is down to 100).

If we were doing good and now are running out of time, we run the `CCTintTo` action, which tints the time bar to red over a second. If we had little time left and then we got more time by matching many stones at once, then the time bar is tinted to its original colour again.

Good, so now you should have a basic understanding of how to use actions. You can check the samples to see them in action or start trying them in our game.

Have a go hero – applying actions all over the game

Why don't you practice what you have just learned here? Try adding all the actions you can to the existing game. You can do the following for example:

- Make the stones scale down instead of fading out
- Make the time bar blink when very little time remains
- When selecting a stone, rotate it and then when released rotate it back

Remember to consult the sample projects if you have any doubt on how to do this.

Composition actions

Composition actions are actions that let you chain other actions to perform one after another at the same time. This gives you endless possibilities when you want to create a nice effect for your game.

Let's see how to use them.

Time for action – making a nice disappear effect

Just a moment ago we made them disappear nicely, with a fade out action. That looks really good, but what would you do if you wanted it to fade out while scaling down?

This is a typical situation where you would want to use composition actions.

Change the code that ran the action that made the stones fade out into the following:

```
CCAction * action = [CCSpawn actions:
[CCFadeOut actionWithDuration:0.5],
[CCScaleTo actionWithDuration:0.5 scale:0.5],nil];
[c.mySprite runAction:action];
```

Let's Do Some Actions

Launch the game, and you should see that the stones are fading out and scaling at the same time, as shown in the following screenshot:

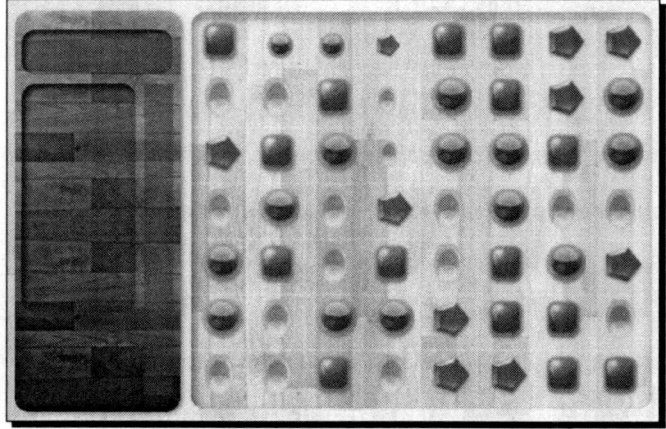

What just happened?

In the preceding example, we used the `CCSpawn` action which is one of the available composition actions. This action makes the actions passed along execute at the same time.

When initialized, we need to pass all the actions that we want it to compose. This list of actions can be as long as you want and you can even pass another composition action with more actions inside it.

In this case, we are passing two actions to it, the `CCFadeOut` and `CCScaleTo`, which will be applied at the same time.

More composition actions

There are four different composition actions you can use to combine other actions, which are as follows:

- `CCSpawn`: As we saw, it lets you run many actions at the same time
- `CCSequence`: It allows you to run several actions one after another
- `CCRepeat`: It lets you repeat an action a limited amount of times
- `CCRepeatForever`: It lets you repeat an action forever (this action cannot be used inside a `CCSequence` action)

Using these actions in combination with the basic actions and the actions we will see later, will be enough for you to make almost any kind of effect you can think of.

Let's see how to use the `CCSequence` action now.

Time for action – making stones fall and grow

In the previous example, we made the stones disappear while scaling down. If you played with the example, you may have noticed that when the new stones appear they are scaled down. We could solve this by setting the scale back to one before launching them, but let's use the opportunity to practise the usage of the CCSequence action. Let's make them fall and then, when correctly placed, grow back.

Replace the code that makes the new stones fall with the following one:

```
CCAction * action = [CCSequence actions:[CCMoveTo
actionWithDuration:0.5 position:ccp(42*i + GRID_OFFSET.x,42*(GRID_
HEIGHT -nilCount +q) + GRID_OFFSET.y)],[CCScaleTo
actionWithDuration:0.5 scale:1],nil];
[f.mySprite runAction:action];
```

When you run the game, you should now see the stones falling scaled down and after that, go back to their original size.

What just happened?

The CCSequence action is a very useful one. It allows very good effects that would be a pain to manually code.

As the CCSpawn action, it takes as arguments the actions you want to stack for running, and allows you to insert other composition actions inside it too.

Finally, let's take a look at how to use the CCRepeat action.

Time for action – animating the grid

Let's animate the grid's background a little when we make a matching group.

We will make the sprite scale down and up a couple of times when we match three or more stones. For this we will use the CCRepeat action.

In the place where we are checking how many stones are in each group, add the following lines:

```
for (NSMutableSet * n in groupings)
{
  if([n count] >=3)
  {
    // Irrelevant code...

    CCSprite * b = (CCSprite *)[self getChildByTag:K_GBACK];
```

Let's Do Some Actions

```
        CCAction * act = [CCSequence actions:[CCScaleTo
        actionWithDuration:0.2 scale:0.9],
        [CCScaleTo actionWithDuration:0.2 scale:1],nil];
        [b runAction:[CCRepeat actionWithAction:act times:3]];
    }
    // Irrelevant code...
}
```

Now run the game again, and you should see the grid scaling down and up three times when matching some stones. Ok, it doesn't look that good, but I hope it illustrates my point.

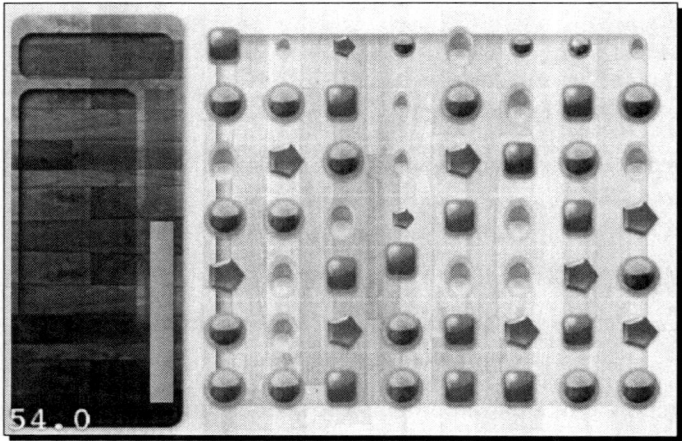

What just happened?

The `CCRepeat` action takes an action as argument and then repeats that action any number of times you tell it to.

As we saw here, you can repeat a `CCSequence` action that contains another set of actions inside, allowing really powerful animations.

On the other hand, you can also have a CCRepeat action inside another composition action. For example you could make a sequence where a sprite scales up and down three times and then fades out.

 Some actions are expensive to create, for example when making a CCSequence with a CCSpawn inside and another CCSequence, so you should try to reuse them when you can.

Pop quiz – actions

1. What do you think is the best way to make a sprite disappear and reappear many times in a second?
    a. By using a `CCRepeat` with a `CCSequence`, along with a pair of `CCHide` and `CCShow` actions
    b. By scheduling a method that sets the opacity of a sprite to 0 and another one that increases the opacity of that sprite to 255 and then calling them several times in a second
    c. By using the `CCBlink` action
    d. There is no possible way to do this in Cocos2d
2. What is a composition action?
    a. A kind of action that lets you do basic stuff, such as rotating a sprite over some time
    b. A kind of action that lets you compose layer elements together
    c. A kind of action that allows you to chain multiple actions together
3. Which one of the following elements of Cocos2d allows you to run actions on them?
    a. `CCSprite`
    b. `CCMenu`
    c. `CCLayer`
    d. None of them
    e. All of them, as they are all subclasses of `CCNode`

Ease actions

Ease actions are special composition actions that let you modify the time of the **inner** action. They modify the speed of the inner action, but not the time it takes to perform. So an action of one second will still last one second. These actions can give you a very good physics-like effect if used correctly.

For example, say you have a `CCMoveTo` action that moves an image from point a to b in five seconds. When the action is run, the sprite will move to its destination in a **linear** form, that is, uniformly, all the way at the same speed.

Now, if we apply an ease action, for example an `EaseInCubic` action, it will start moving slowly and then faster as it reaches the end of the movement.

Let's Do Some Actions

Cocos2d includes lots of ease actions for you to use. We will just take a look at how to use one of them. You can switch the one to be used later, to see the outcome of them.

The following is a diagram of how each function behaves over time:

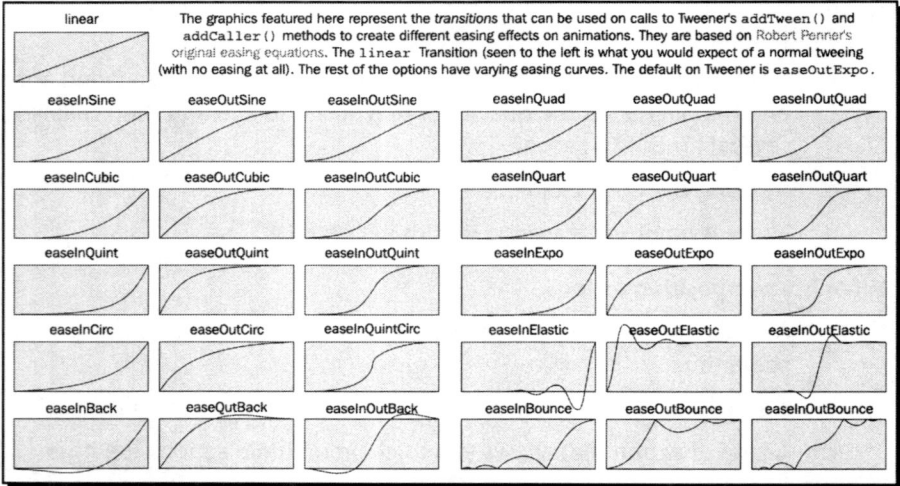

Let's try out one of the ease actions.

Time for action – modifying animations with ease actions

Let's make the stones fall with some style. We will change the actions we made before to use the CCEaseBounceOut ease action, which adds a nice bouncy effect.

Change the two parts we modified before to make use of the CCEaseBounceOut action.

```
if(nilCount >0 && !d.disappearing)
{
  CCAction * easeA = [CCEaseBounceOut actionWithAction:[CCMoveTo
    actionWithDuration:(0.5 * nilCount)/3 position:ccp(42*i +
    GRID_OFFSET.x,42*(j- nilCount) + GRID_OFFSET.y)]];
  [d.mySprite runAction:easeA];

}

for(Stone * f in removeds)
{
  //Not relevant....

  CCAction * easeA = [CCEaseBounceOut actionWithAction:[CCMoveTo
    actionWithDuration:0.5 position:ccp(42*i + GRID_OFFSET.x,42*
    (GRID_HEIGHT -nilCount +q) + GRID_OFFSET.y)]];
```

[106]

```
CCAction * action = [CCSequence actions:easeA, [CCScaleTo
    actionWithDuration:0.5 scale:1],nil];
[f.mySprite runAction:action];
```
}

When you run the game now, you should see the stones falling with a nice bounce effect.

What just happened?

We just used one of the many ease actions available. These actions let you modify the performance of other actions.

Using ease actions adds a lot of life to your animations. See how the falling of the stones drastically changed when we applied the ease action.

You can use them when applying any other basic action, not just a movement one. Try applying them to rotations or scaling actions too to see the effect!

Effect actions

These actions modify the node's **Grid**. This is a new property that divide's the node into smaller squares or tiles, allowing you to modify the node through them by moving the vertices that compose each square.

There are two types of grids, namely, tiled and non-tiled. The difference is that the non-tiled grid is composed by vertex, and the tiled one is composed of tiles, each with its individual vertex.

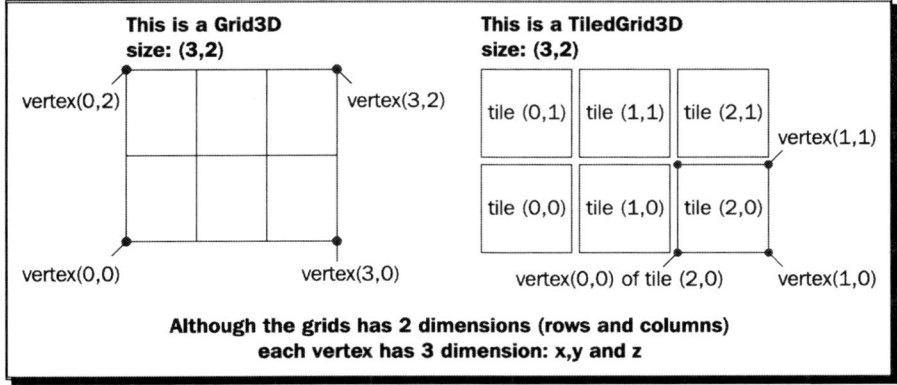

Let's Do Some Actions

Although the grid is two dimensional, each vertex has three components (x, y, z), allowing for three dimensional effects.

 Effect actions are capable of creating some very nice effects. The tradeoff is performance. Using effect actions can reduce your game's performance drastically, so use them with caution.

You can modify the grid's size. A bigger grid will make the effect look better, but will reduce the performance a lot. A smaller grid will have the opposite effect, a better performance but not such a good effect.

The following is a list of the available effects; you should try them to see how they behave:

- CCWaves
- CCWaves3D
- CCFlipX3D
- CCFlipY3D
- CCLens3D
- CCRipple3D
- CCShaky3D
- CCLiquid
- CCTwirl

Let's try one of them!

Time for action – making the background shake when matching five stones

Let's try one of these actions in our game. As these actions are very expensive, I don't want them running all the time, so I will have one play when the player matches five stones in a row.

In the `GameScene.m` file, add the following lines to the `checkGroups` method:

```
-(void)checkGroups:(bool)firstTime
{
   //Irrelevant code
   for (NSMutableSet * n in groupings)
   {
     if([n count]>=3)
```

```
    {
        //Irrelevant code
    }
    if([n count]>=4)
    {
        //Irrelevant code
    }
    if([n count]>=5)
    {
        CCSprite * back = (CCSprite *)[self getChildByTag:K_BACK];
        CCAction * effect = [CCWaves actionWithWaves:10 amplitude:10
          horizontal:YES vertical:YES grid:ccg(10,10) duration:3];
        [back runAction:effect];
    }
}

    //Irrelevant code
}
```

Running these actions, as with any other one, just requires a couple of lines of code.

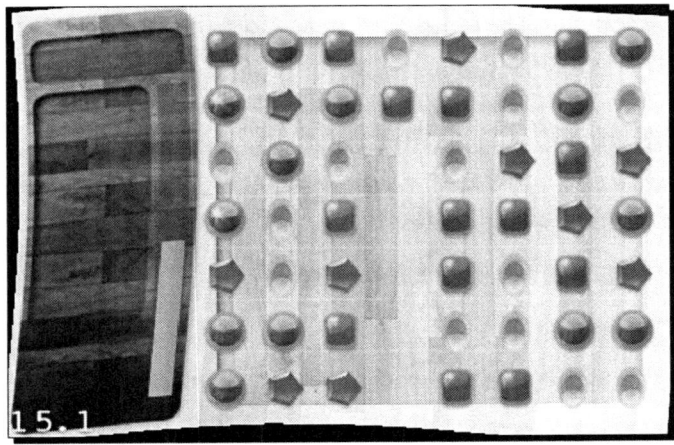

What just happened?

In the preceding example, we used a CCWaves action that makes the node wave.

For this action to run we initialize it with a few parameters, which are the amount of waves, their amplitude, their direction (whether these waves will run vertically or horizontally), the grid's size, and the duration of the effect.

Let's Do Some Actions

>  Notice we are using the helper function `ccg` to create the grid's dimensions. This is another Cocos2d helper function that creates a `CCGridBase` (the grid object) with that size.

There a lot of effect actions that you can use off the shelf. Each one is instantiated in a different way, so you should check the documentation or the samples to see how to use the one you would like to apply.

Some of these actions end in "3D", such as `CCShaky3D`, or `CCRipple3D`. These are effects that modify each vertex's *z* coordinate, giving a nice three dimensional effect.

You may have noticed that after the effect finishes playing the sprite does not return to its original form. In order to fix that, we have to run another action right after the `CCWaves` one. Change the effect to the following:

```
CCAction * effect = [CCSequence actions:[CCWaves actionWithWaves:10
amplitude:10 horizontal:YES vertical:YES grid:ccg(10,10)
duration:3],[CCStopGrid action],nil];
```

Now we are using a sequence to run the `CCWaves` action, and then we call the `CCStopGrid` action, which does not take any parameter. What it does is return every vertex of the grid to their original position, thus "restarting" the image to its original form before the effect is applied.

Applying a single action to multiple CCNodes

The effect action looks nice, but having it wave alone is not pretty; we must also have the bar wave along for the effect to look acceptable.

You first thought would be to just do the following:

```
[bar runAction:effect];
```

If you do so, you will notice it does not work as you expected.

Don't worry, it is not complicated at all to get it working right. What you just have to do is to copy the effect and then apply that one to the other sprite.

Just do the following:

```
CCAction * effect2 = [[effect copy]autorelease];
[bar runAction:effect2];
```

Now it should be working fine. We had to make a copy of the `CCAction` object because Cocos2d doesn't allow a single action to be run on multiple nodes at the same time.

Special actions

These are actions that let you perform stuff that doesn't directly modify the nodes you apply it to. As of this writing, there are three special actions you can use, and these are as follows:

- `CCCallFunc`
- `CCCallFuncN`
- `CCCallFuncND`

These three actions do almost the same, that is, call a method (in the form of a selector) from the action. The difference between them is that `CCCallFunc` just calls the method you wish, while `CCCallFuncN` calls the method and passes the node that called the action to it, and `CCCallFuncND` also passes another parameter you want along.

So, as you may guess, these are very important and useful actions. They are usually used at the end of a sequence to do something when the actions you called before end.

Let's see some examples.

Time for action – ready, set, go!

Right now when you launch the game, it just starts playing, and the time begins running out. Let's change it, so the player can prepare himself before the action begins.

We will just be adding a nice "ready, set, go!" message that will work as follows:

- A "Ready" sprite appears and disappears with a nice fadeout + scaling, and then we use `CCCallFuncN` to remove that sprite from the game
- The same for the "set" sprite
- The same for the "go!" sprite, and also we use `CCCallFuncN` to set a variable that allows the player to touch the stones and the time to start running out

So, let's put that into practice.

1. First, include the three images in the project like we have been doing. You can find them in the companion files for this chapter.

2. You will have to add a new property to the GameLayer. This new `BOOL` variable, `timerRunning`, will let us know whether the timer is supposed to be working or not.

3. In the `init` method, set this new variable to `NO` (so the time does not run out) and the `disallowTouch` variable to `YES` so the player can not touch the stones.

Let's Do Some Actions

4. Now, in the `drainTime` method, enclose all that code in an `if` clause:

   ```
   If(self.timerRunning)
   {
   //All the code
   }
   ```

5. If you run the game now, you will see nothing happens anymore; you cannot swap stones and the time bar is not moving. This is good. Now all we have to do is get the messages to appear and when the "Go!" sprite fades away, make the game start.

6. Add the following methods to the `GameLayer` class:

   ```
   -(void)startGame
   {
     CCSprite * ready = [CCSprite spriteWithFile:@"ready.png"];
     [self addChild:ready z:3];
     [ready setPosition:ccp(240,160)];
     [ready setOpacity:0];

     CCSprite * set =[CCSprite spriteWithFile:@"set.png"];
     [self addChild:set z:3];
     [set setPosition:ccp(240,160)];
     [set setOpacity:0];

     CCSprite * go = [CCSprite spriteWithFile:@"go.png"];
     [self addChild:go z:3];
     [go setPosition:ccp(240,160)];
     [go setOpacity:0];

     [ready runAction:[CCSequence actions:[CCDelayTime
     actionWithDuration:0.5],[CCSpawn actions:
     [CCFadeIn actionWithDuration:0.4],
     [CCScaleTo actionWithDuration:0.4 scale:1.2],nil],
     [CCDelayTime actionWithDuration:0.2],
     [CCFadeOut actionWithDuration:0.4],
     [CCCallFuncN actionWithTarget:self selector:
     @selector(removeSprite:)],nil]];
     [set runAction:[CCSequence actions:
     [CCDelayTime actionWithDuration:1.5],[CCSpawn actions:
     [CCFadeIn actionWithDuration:0.4],
     [CCScaleTo actionWithDuration:0.4 scale:1.2],nil],
     [CCDelayTime actionWithDuration:0.2],
     [CCFadeOut actionWithDuration:0.4],
     [CCCallFuncN actionWithTarget:self selector:
     @selector(removeSprite:)],nil]];
     [go runAction:[CCSequence actions:
     [CCDelayTime actionWithDuration:2.5],[CCSpawn actions:
     [CCFadeIn actionWithDuration:0.4],
     [CCScaleTo actionWithDuration:0.4 scale:1.2],nil],
   ```

```
      [CCDelayTime actionWithDuration:0.2],
      [CCFadeOut actionWithDuration:0.4],
      [CCCallFuncN actionWithTarget:self selector:
      @selector(removeSpriteAndBegin:)],nil]];
}

-(void)removeSprite:(CCNode *)n
{
   [self removeChild:n cleanup:YES];
}

-(void)removeSpriteAndBegin:(CCNode *)n
{
   [self removeChild:n cleanup:YES];
   self.disallowTouch = NO;
   self.timerRunning = YES;
}
```

7. Finally, call the `startGame` method just before the `init` method ends.

   ```
   [self startGame];
   ```

8. Now, when you run the game, you should see the "Ready, set, go!" sprites appearing and disappearing, and after that, the time should start running out and you should have the control to swap stones.

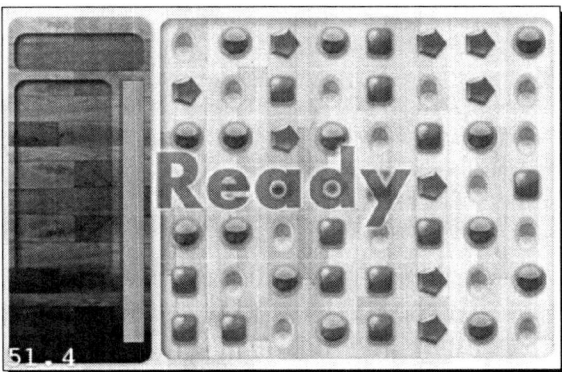

What just happened?

Special actions are very useful for creating callback functions for animations. They can let you know when an action has finished and act accordingly. In the preceding example, we did just that.

Let's Do Some Actions

First we created three sprites, one for each word, and then ran an action on them. Let's take a look at the actions we ran:

```
[ready runAction:[CCSequence actions:[CCDelayTime actionWithDurat
ion:0.5],[CCSpawn actions:[CCFadeIn actionWithDuration:0.4],[CCSc
aleTo actionWithDuration:0.4 scale:1.2],nil] ,[CCDelayTime action
WithDuration:0.2],[CCFadeOut actionWithDuration:0.4],[CCCallFuncN
actionWithTarget:self selector:@selector(removeSprite:)],nil]];
```

This action has a `CCSequence` which calls a `CCDelayAction`. This action does nothing but wait for the time it lasts, so it delays the action like it says.

Once the delay action finishes, we apply a `CCSpawn` action, which does the fade in + scaling animation. Then we delay a little more to leave the message onscreen for a little while, and then we fade it out.

Finally, the `CCCallFuncN` method is called, which calls the `removeSprite` method (which just removes the node passed from its parent, so it does not remain in the game with opacity 0).

The `CCCallFuncN` method takes two parameters—the selector that is the method that will be called, and the target, which is the object that will call the said method.

As you can see, special actions are very powerful and you will find yourself using them a lot.

Have a go hero – telling the player that he lost

I don't like giving bad news, so I will let you do it!

Right now, when the time runs out, a "You lost" message is logged into the console and the score and remaining time are reset. This has to be changed, so that the player can have a clue of what happened when the time reached 0.

As we just did for the starting message, you can do for the game over as well.

When the game is lost, place a sprite or label in the layer and run an action on it, anything you want! Just remember to use `CCCallFuncN` at the end of the sequence to remove the sprite and reset the score and timer after that.

Using CCCallFuncND

Let's now see an example of how to use the `CCCallFuncND` action.

Time for action – telling the player he lost

We'll see the `CCCallFuncND` action, with a very simple example to illustrate its usage.

I want to change the time bar behavior to animate itself when the player fails to match any stones or when he matches more than three. Once the animation is completed, add or subtract the time.

I will use a simple blink animation for this; once it finishes blinking the remaining time will be changed.

In order to do this, modify the `changeTime` method to look like the following:

```
-(void)changeTime:(int)time
{
  [bar runAction:[CCSequence actions:[CCBlink actionWithDuration:1
    blinks:10],[CCCallFuncND actionWithTarget:self
    selector:@selector(moveBar:data:) data:(void *)time],nil]];
}
```

And then create a new method with the previous content of the `changeTime` method:

```
-(void)moveBar:(CCSprite *)bar byAmount:(void *)amount
{
  remainingTime += (int)amount;
  if(remainingTime>=MAX_TIME)
    remainingTime = MAX_TIME;
  else if(remainingTime<=0)
    remainingTime =0;
}
```

That's it. Now when you fail to match any stones or match four or more, you should see the time bar blinking and then the time added or subtracted.

What just happened?

In the previous example, we illustrated the usage of the `CCCallFuncND` action.

Let's take a look at it:

```
[CCCallFuncND actionWithTarget:self selector:@selector(moveBar:data:)
data:(void *)time]
```

Let's Do Some Actions

The `CCCallFuncND` method takes three parameters, the target, which is the object that will execute the method, the selector that contains the name of the method we will call and the data we will pass along, and the actual data, which must be a pointer. As we are passing an `int` in this case, and those and the pointers have the same size we just cast it to `(void *)`. Remember, time is the amount of time we want to add or subtract to the time bar.

The new `moveBar` method does exactly the same we were doing before; the only change is that it now receives two arguments instead of one.

```
-(void)moveBar:(CCSprite *)bar byAmount:(void *)amount
```

Remember that the `CCCallFuncND` action, like the `CCCallFuncN`, also sends the node that called it; in this case we are not using it. The `(void *)` data argument is what we passed before; here we just cast it back to an `int` to avoid any compiler warning.

One more thing, how would you do if you had to send, for example, two `int` values? As you may have noticed there is no apparent way of doing so. Although the `CCCallFunc` method can take just one piece of data, it can be of any type. So, you can send an `NSArray` (or NSMutableArray or whatever you want) with all the data you need.

For example:

```
NSArray * letters = [NSArray arrayWithObjects:@"A",@"B",@"C",nil];
[mySprite runAction:[CCCallFuncND actionWithTarget:self selector:@selector(readLetters:data:) data:(void *)letters]];
-(void)readLetters(CCSprite *) mySprite  letters:(void *) letters
{
  NSLog(@"%@",[letters objectAtIndex:0]); //A
  NSLog(@"%@",[letters objectAtIndex:1]); //B
  NSLog(@"%@",[letters objectAtIndex:2]); //C
}
```

This is all there is to the `CCCallFuncND` action and special actions in general. There is just one more type of animations we have to see - the animation actions.

Animations

Animation actions are for doing... guess what? Animations!

To be a little more clear, to animate a sprite is to run a sequence of images fast enough to give the illusion of movement.

For example, if you had a sprite of a character standing and made him walk in any direction, just moving him would not suffice. You would also need to animate him in a way that looks like he is actually walking and not just floating around.

Animations are really easy to implement with Cocos2d; we just have to take a bunch of images from a spritesheet, put them in the order we want them to animate, and then run the action on the sprite.

Let's begin by arranging the images that will compose the frames of the animation.

Time for action – animating the stones

We are going to bring those stones to life. For that, we first have to put all the frames that will make our animations into a spritesheet, load them, and then use them to create a `CCAnimation` action, which we'll repeat over and over again.

You can find all the images for the frames in the Chapter 3 companion files or make your own. Just remember a couple things when doing your own animations:

- Whenever possible try to make all the frames the same size, as this will make life easier for you when running the animations. If you have different sized frames and the frames are not even centered, the animation will look jumpy and you would have to adjust their positions or offsets.

- Create the least possible number of frames for the animation to run smoothly; try to avoid animations of tens of frames. The more frames you use per animation, the more space you will need, and that means more spritesheets will have to be loaded in memory.

- If you want to animate a huge background, don't make lots of big, full screens; try to select some parts that you want animated and just create animations for those small things. For example, if you have a jungle with a waterfall and you just want the waterfall animated, create a static image for the background and the necessary frames just for the water falling.

- Give sequential names to your animation's images (that is: `redStone1.png`, `redStone2.png`, and so on). This will save you a lot of time when loading the frames into the cache. We will do this in a moment, but the basic idea is to load all the frames in a single `for` loop, naming them sequentially will make that step easier.

Let's Do Some Actions

First thing we'll do is import the `stonesSheet.png` spritesheet into the project. For this small project one spritesheet is more than enough, so begin by removing the one we were using and including this new one, which has all the elements we were using plus the animations for each stone.

Also include the `stonesSheet.plist` file into the project. This file was created by Zwoptex like we saw before and it will be necessary to be able to load all the frames easily without having to specify each one's coordinates in the spritesheet.

I will show you how to make one of the stones shine. Make the following changes to the code:

1. Add a new variable to Interface of your GameLayer class:

   ```
   NSMutableArray * blueFrames;
   ```

   Remember to make properties for them.

2. Then add the following code to the `init` method of the same class:

   ```
   -(id) init
   {
     if( (self=[super init] ))
     {
   
           self.disallowTouch = YES;
           self.timerRunning = NO;
   
           [[CCSpriteFrameCache sharedSpriteFrameCache]
              addSpriteFramesWithFile:@"colouredSheet.plist"];
   
           blueFrames = [[NSMutableArray alloc]init];
           for(int i = 1; i < 8; i++)
           {
   ```

```
            CCSpriteFrame *frame = [[CCSpriteFrameCache
              sharedSpriteFrameCache] spriteFrameByName:
              [NSString stringWithFormat:@"sBlue%d.png",i]];
            [blueFrames addObject:frame];
        }

        // Irrelevant code...
    }
    return self;
}
```

3. Now in the `moveStonesDown` method, where we were looping through the removed stones and giving them a new random color, call the following method:

```
for(Stone * f in removeds)
{
  [f.mySprite setOpacity:255];
  int stoneT = arc4random() % STONE_TYPES;
  CGRect color =[f setStoneColor:stoneT];
  [f.mySprite setTextureRect:color];

  [f setAnimation];

    //Irrelevant code
}
```

4. Open the `Stone.m` file and call the same method inside the `placeInGrid` one:

```
-(void)placeInGrid:(CGPoint)place pt:(int)pt pl:(int)pl
{

  int sType = arc4random() % 4;
  if(sType == pt || sType == pl)
  {  [self placeInGrid:place pt:pt pl:pl];
     return;
  }
  else
  {
     //CGRect colorRect =[self setStoneColor:sType];

     CCSpriteSheet * s = (CCSpriteSheet *)[theGame
       getChildByTag:K_SSheet];

     mySprite = [CCSprite spriteWithSpriteSheet:s rect:[self
         setStoneColor:sType]];
```

```
            [s addChild:mySprite z:1];
            [self setAnimation];

            self.stoneType =sType;
            [self.mySprite setPosition:place];

        }
    }
```

5. Finally, add the `setAnimation` method to the `Stone` class:

```
-(void)setAnimation
{
  [self.mySprite stopAllActions];
  CCAnimation *animation;
  switch (self.stoneType)
  {
    case 0:
    break;
    case 1:
    animation = [CCAnimation animationWithName:@"fBlue" delay:0.1f
      frames:theGame.blueFrames];
    [self.mySprite runAction:[CCRepeatForever actionWithAction:
    [CCSequence actions:[CCDelayTime actionWithDuration:arc4random
    ()%5],[CCAnimate actionWithAnimation:animation
    restoreOriginalFrame:NO],nil] ]];

      break;
      case 2:
      break;
      case 3:
      break;
    }
  }
```

6. Run the game now; you should see the blue stones shining at different time intervals, as shown in the following screenshot:

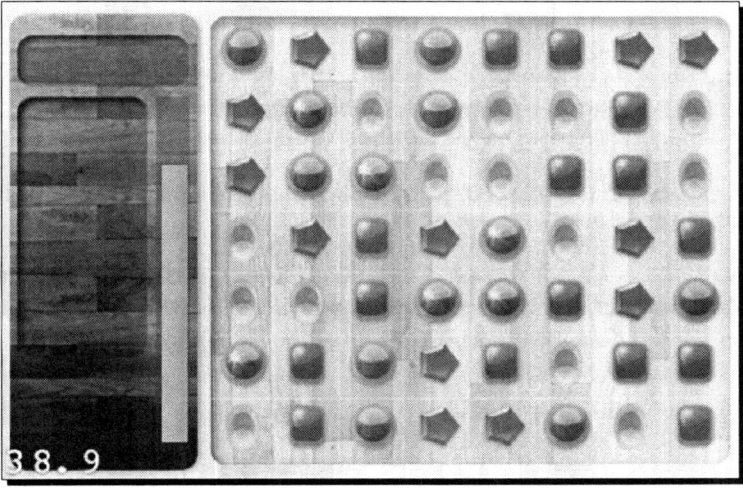

What just happened?

Great! Now we have our blue stones shining beautifully on the screen. I will explain what we did line by line, so that you can then go on and make the rest of the stones animated.

CCSpriteFrame and the CCSpriteFrameCache

Animations are made of multiple frames, each one displaying different images. The images used don't have to be necessarily "different". As we loaded sprites by taking a portion of a bigger image, we do so with frames.

CCSpriteFrames are just **NSObjects** that hold information about the CGRect that makes the frame from a Spritesheet. These frames will later be taken by the CCAnimation class to compose the animations.

The CCSpriteFrameCache class is a **singleton** that handles the loading of sprite frames and saves them in a cache for later use.

A singleton is a design pattern, which specifies that a class should be instantiated only once. In this case, we have a CCSpriteFrameCache singleton class that handles everything that has to do with the frame cache; only one of these objects is needed at a given time. You can find a lot of examples of this in Cocos2d. For example CCDirector is another singleton.

To find out more about design patterns you can take a look at the following URL:
http://en.wikipedia.org/wiki/Design_pattern_%28computer_science%29

It allows you to load one or multiple texture frames by using a dictionary or a .plist file.

Here is where the benefits of using Zwoptex for arranging your sprites become very obvious. You can use the `.plist` file generated by this tool to load all the frames in the Spritesheet and use them for your animations, and that is just what we are doing now.

```
[[CCSpriteFrameCache sharedSpriteFrameCache] addSpriteFramesWithFile:@
"colouredSheet.plist"];
```

This one line loads all the frames from the `colouredSheet.plist` file, allowing you to easily create animations later. If it wasn't for this, you would have to define the rectangle of each frame as we are doing with the sprites. Imagine having to manually define all the rectangles of a 100 frames animation!

 For this to work both `.png` and `.plist` files have to be named the same.

Once we have all the frames cached, we just have to select which ones we are going to use for each animation.

```
blueFrames = [[NSMutableArray alloc]init];
for(int i = 1; i < 5; i++)
{
  CCSpriteFrame *frame = [[CCSpriteFrameCache sharedSpriteFrameCache]
    spriteFrameByName:[NSString stringWithFormat:@"sBlue%d.png",i]];
  [blueFrames addObject:frame];
}
```

Here we are putting into the `blueFrames` array all the frames we would like to make an animation of.

The shining animation I intended to do was made of seven frames, so I created seven `CCSpriteFrame` objects by retrieving those frames from the cache using their names. The names of those frames are the names of your original images, so that is why I recommended naming them in a sequential way, so that you can retrieve them in an easy way like we did here.

The CCAnimation class

Now that we have an array with all the `CCSpriteFrames` that make the shining animation, we just have to play it. We do that in the `setAnimation` method:

```
animation = [CCAnimation animationWithName:@"fBlue" delay:0.1f
frames:theGame.blueFrames];
```

The `CCAnimation` class is the one responsible for joining all those separate frames and making an animation out of them. We initialize it with a name, the frames it will use (which is the array we created before), and a delay. This delay is the time that will pass between each frame is shown. The less time you set for the delay, the more fluid the animation will look. However, you will need a lot more frames to make it longer. The delay you set will depend on how you want your animation to look in each situation.

Now that we have the animation ready, we just have to play it. We do that using the `CCAnimate` action:

```
[self.mySprite runAction:[CCRepeatForever actionWithAction:
[CCSequence actions:[CCDelayTime actionWithDuration:arc4random()%5],
[CCAnimate actionWithAnimation:animation restoreOriginalFrame:NO],
nil]]];
```

The `CCAnimate` action takes the animation; we just did, as the parameter. And whether it should restore the original frame when it finishes, we don't need that here, as we will play the animation over and over again. For that I am using the `CCRepeatForever` action.

I also added a `CCDelayTime` action with a random delay, so we don't have all the stones shining at the same exact time.

Remember to add the animations for all the other stones if you want to. To do that, just create all the arrays for each stone and modify the `setAnimation` method for each case.

Before running the animations we call the `[self.mySprite stopAllActions];` method to stop all previous actions. So don't have all the animations running before stacking up.

Have a go hero – breaking the stones

You may have noticed I added another set of animations to the Spritesheet, those are the stones breaking. I propose you practice what you have learned here to apply those animations to your stones. When you are to remove the stones from the board, instead of fading them out I want you to apply an animation to them. The process is the same as before, but this time you don't have to make it repeat forever, just play once.

[123]

Let's Do Some Actions

Once you have done that, try combining the animation action with others, for example tinting or fading the sprite while playing the animation.

Summary

This chapter was about giving your game a lot of eye candy. If you compare this chapter with the previous one, you will realize that there weren't much changes game play wise, but a lot has changed visually, which, believe it or not, is very important especially for mobile casual games where the player has to be hooked in a really short time.

In this chapter, we learned:

- How to apply actions to any Cocos2d element
- How to combine those actions to achieve some powerful results
- How to animate your sprites

Actions are a very useful feature of Cocos2d, allowing you to move, change, and even animate things. We will be using them a lot through the rest of the game.

In the next chapter, we will take a look at Labels. You have already used them a little back in Chapter 1, but now we are going to see them in depth and, of course, apply actions to them!

4
Pasting Labels

In this chapter, we are going to add labels to our game. Labels are used to add text to your game that can be transformed and moved around as you please. You can even apply actions to them to animate them.

There are three ways to add text to your game through the different label classes. In this chapter, we will take a look at all of them with their advantages and drawbacks.

We'll also finish the Coloured Stones game, but there are lots of things you can add later to it, to make it a commercial game. We'll talk about that later!

So, in this chapter you shall:

- Learn how to use `CCLabels` to display tutorial messages
- Using `CCLabelAtlas` to display the score
- Create and use `CCBitmapFontAtlas` to display feedback and animate it with actions

So let's get started!

Pasting Labels

Using CCLabels

`CCLabels` are the most basic form of labels, which means they aren't useful for an array of things.

As they are very slow to render, you should use them with caution. Don't go around changing them in every frame because you will have some performance issues in the long run. You can use the other two types of labels for that.

So, why would you use `CCLabels` if they are slower as compared to their counterparts?

In the first place, `CCLabels` just need you to provide the font name and size and that is all. You can create your label with just that and add it to the scene, whereas with the other two label types you will need to have done some previous work to generate the files that will be used to create the text.

Another advantage `CCLabels` offer is that you can create blocks of text without much hassle, just having to define the `CGSize` that the text will occupy. The other label types don't allow this kind of freedom, at least not at this time.

So, let's begin by creating our `Tutorial` class that will handle the displaying of first time messages to our player, so he can learn how to play while playing.

Time for action – first time tutorials

We will start by creating the `Tutorial` class, which will display a message on the centre of the screen. This message can be in any text you want and can be displayed any time you want to display it. Once the player has read it, he can dismiss it by touching it.

1. The following is the `Tutorial.h` file:

```
#import <Foundation/Foundation.h>
#import "cocos2d.h"
#import "GameScene.h"


@interface Tutorial : CCNode {
    
    GameLayer * theGame;
    touchState state;
    CCSprite * back;
    CCLabel * label;
}

@property(readwrite,nonatomic) touchState state;
```

```
@property(nonatomic,retain) GameLayer * theGame;
@property(nonatomic,retain) CCSprite * back;
@property(nonatomic,retain) CCLabel * label;
-(id)initWithText:(NSString *)text theGame:(GameLayer *)game;
@end
```

2. The following is the `Tutorial.m` file:

```
#import "Tutorial.h"
@implementation Tutorial
@synthesize state,theGame,back,label;
-(id)initWithText:(NSString *)text theGame:(GameLayer *)game
{
  if ((self = [super init]))
  {
    self.theGame = game;
    [theGame addChild:self z:5];

    back = [CCSprite spriteWithFile:@"tutorialBackground.png"];
    [self addChild:back];
    [back setPosition:ccp(240,160)];
    [back setOpacity:0];

    label = [CCLabel labelWithString:text
    dimensions:CGSizeMake(270,110)
      alignment:UITextAlignmentCenter fontName:@"Verdana"
      fontSize:12];
    [self addChild:label];
    [label setPosition:ccp(240,160)];
    [label setColor:ccBLACK];
    [label setOpacity:0];

    [back runAction:[CCFadeIn actionWithDuration:1]];
    [label runAction:[CCFadeIn actionWithDuration:1]];

    [theGame unschedule:@selector(drainTime)];
    theGame.disallowTouch = YES;

    self.state = kStateUngrabbed;
  }
    return (self);
}
```

Pasting Labels

3. Now, let's handle the touches on the tutorial object.

```
- (CGRect)rect
{
  //CGSize s = [self.texture contentSize];
  CGRect r = CGRectMake(self.back.position.x-
  (self.back.textureRect.size.width/2) * self.back.scaleX ,back.
  position.y-(self.back.textureRect.size.height/2)* self.back.
  scaleY,self.back.textureRect.size.width* self.back.scaleX,self.
  back.textureRect.size.height * self.back.scaleY);
  return r;
}

- (void)onEnter
{
  [[CCTouchDispatcher sharedDispatcher] addTargetedDelegate:self
     priority:0 swallowsTouches:YES];
  [super onEnter];
}

- (void)onExit
{
  [[CCTouchDispatcher sharedDispatcher] removeDelegate:self];
  [super onExit];
}

- (BOOL)containsTouchLocation:(UITouch *)touch
{
  return CGRectContainsPoint(self.rect, [self
     convertTouchToNodeSpaceAR:touch]);
}

- (BOOL)ccTouchBegan:(UITouch *)touch withEvent:(UIEvent *)event
{
  if (state != kStateUngrabbed) return NO;
  if ( ![self containsTouchLocation:touch]) return NO;


  state = kStateGrabbed;
  return YES;
}

- (void)ccTouchEnded:(UITouch *)touch withEvent:(UIEvent *)event
{
```

```
    NSAssert(state == kStateGrabbed, @"error, it should always be
    grabbed when we get here.");

    [back runAction:[CCFadeOut actionWithDuration:1]];
    [label runAction:[CCFadeOut actionWithDuration:1]];
    [self schedule:@selector(removal) interval:1];

    state = kStateUngrabbed;
}

-(void)removal
{
    [self unschedule:@selector(removal)];

    [theGame schedule:@selector(drainTime) interval:0.20];
    theGame.disallowTouch = NO;

    [theGame removeChild:self cleanup:YES];

}

@end
```

Add these two files and the `tutorialBackground.png` file (which you can get from the Chapter 4 companion files) to your project. Also remember to import the `Tutorial.h` file in your `GameScene.h` file. All you have to do now is display a message wherever you want to. Let's display a welcome message when the game starts.

Add the following lines to the `removeSpriteAndBegin` method from the `GameLayer` class:

```
Tutorial * t = [[[Tutorial alloc]initWithText:@"Welcome to Coloured
Stones! \n To begin playing, touch an stone and drag it around to swap
it with an adjacent one. \n Match 3 or more stones to score points."
theGame:self]
 autorelease];
```

Pasting Labels

Now run the game. You should see a message fade in after the "ready, set, go!" sequence. When you are ready to dismiss it, touch it. Then the game will resume.

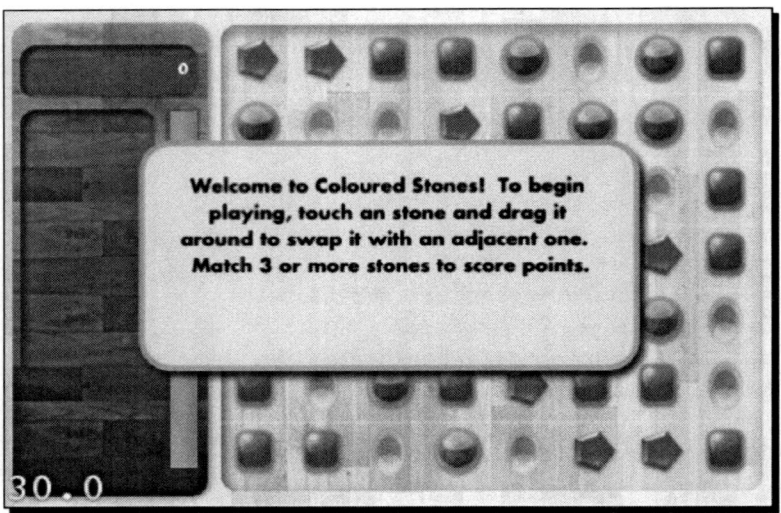

What just happened?

Now we have a simple tutorial system in place. Let's see how it works.

We created the `Tutorial` class which is initialized with an `NSString` object and the GameLayer instance to be able to reach it easily.

The `Tutorial` class takes this string and makes a label out of it with the following code:

```
label = [CCLabel labelWithString:text dimensions:CGSizeMake(270,110)
alignment:UITextAlignmentCenter fontName:@"Verdana" fontSize:12];
```

We pass the following parameters to it:

- `String`: The NSString that we wish to display
- `Dimensions`: A `CGSize` object which sets the width and height of the whole label, so if you write a long text the label will try to fit it in
- `Alignment`: If the text should be aligned left, center, or right within the box
- `FontName`: The name of the font that you wish to use to display the text
- `FontSize`: The size of the font in pixels

The font you use to display a text in a `CCLabel` can be any one of those that come included with **iOS**, or you can use any `.ttf` (TrueType) font. Just include the `.ttf` file in your project and use its name as FontName when initializing the `CCLabel`.

The following is a list of the available fonts in iOS:

- American Typewriter
- American Typewriter Condensed
- Arial
- Arial Rounded MT Bold
- Courier New
- Georgia
- Helvetica
- Marker Felt
- Times New Roman
- Trebuchet MS
- Verdana
- Zapfino

Most of them are also available in their bold and italics versions.

> Be careful when using fonts, as most of them are NOT free. This means that by including them in your application without the corresponding permits, you could be sued. Always check whether the font you are using is free for commercial use and check with the author to be sure. There lots of sites where you can get excellent, professional-looking font for free commercial use, for example, at http://www.dafont.com/

So, once we have our label created, we have to add it to the layer. `CCLabel` is a subclass of `CCSprite`. That means we can add them as a child of anything we could with CCSprites.

    [self addChild:label];

Here we are adding it as child of the `Tutorial` class, which by the way inherits from `CCNode`, so we are adding it to the layer.

Being a subclass of `CCSprite` means you can manipulate their properties as you would with sprites.

    [label setPosition:ccp(240,160)];
    [label setColor:ccBLACK];
    [label setOpacity:0];

Pasting Labels

As you may have noticed, we are changing quite a few properties of the label. You can also create your own colors by doing something like the following:

- For a ccColor3B:

  ```
  ccColor3B violetColor = ccc3(255,0,255);
  ```

- For a ccColor4B:

  ```
  ccColor4B transparentVioletColor = ccc4(255,0,255,100);
  ```

We can also run actions on `CCLabels` like the following line of code demonstrates:

```
[label runAction:[CCFadeIn actionWithDuration:1]];
```

The rest of the code handles some gameplay behavior. We don't want the time running out while the player is reading the text, neither do we want them to be able to swap stones in the background, so we do the following:

```
[theGame unschedule:@selector(drainTime)];
theGame.disallowTouch = YES;
```

Doing that allows the player to read the messages safely.

> See that `unschedule` call? Schedulers can be stopped at any time by calling this method and passing the scheduled selector that you want to stop from running.

The rest is just our usual touch-handling code that we saw back in chapter 2. Pay attention to the `CCTouchEnded` method. This is where we dismiss the message and return the game to normal:

```
[back runAction:[CCFadeOut actionWithDuration:1]];
[label runAction:[CCFadeOut actionWithDuration:1]];
[self schedule:@selector(removal) interval:1];
```

We fade out both the background and the label and then schedule the `removal` method to remove the Tutorial object from its parent:

```
-(void)removal
{
    [self unschedule:@selector(removal)];

    [theGame schedule:@selector(drainTime) interval:0.20];
    theGame.disallowTouch = NO;

    [theGame removeChild:self cleanup:YES];
}
```

We also re-schedule the `drainTime` method and allow the player to touch the stones again, so the gameplay is resumed.

Now each time you want to display a tutorial message, just initialize a Tutorial object with the message you want to show, as follows:

```
Tutorial * t = [[[Tutorial alloc]initWithText:@"Welcome to Coloured
Stones! \ To begin playing, touch an stone and drag it around to swap
it with an adjacent one. \n Match 3 or more stones to score points."
theGame:self]
  autorelease];
```

To sum up, `CCLabels` are the simplest way to display texts. However, they are slow to render, so use them with caution. You can use them to display simple blocks of text quite easily and with any font you have the permission to use. They are children of `CCSprite`, and so we can apply transformations or run actions on them.

Have a go hero – improving the Tutorial class

The `Tutorial` class is quite simple as it is, but allows a lot of room for improvement. You could make the following modifications:

- Create a label which displays a "Touch the box to dismiss it" message. It could be animated so it grows up and down until removed.
- Allow for two kinds of messages, those that occupy the whole screen and stop the game (like the one we did), and another smaller one that doesn't stop the game and can be used to give little hints.

That is all there is to `CCLabels`. Next we'll take a look at the `CCLAbelAtlas` class.

Displaying texts with CCLabelAtlas

`CCLabelAtlases` are labels that take their characters from an image file. This makes them a lot faster than normal `CCLabels`.

As the characters are taken from an image file, what you actually use as a character could be virtually any image, so if you want to draw your own font you can do so.

`CCLabelAtlases` have their limitations too. For starters, all characters must be of the same fixed size. Another problem you will encounter is that there isn't a flexible, easy-to-use tool to create your label atlases.

We will see a simple example of how to use `CCLabelAtlas` from an already created image, the same one used by Cocos2d to render the FPS.

Pasting Labels

Time for action – displaying and updating scores with CCLabelAtlas

It is time to create the label that will display the score. We already have everything in place since we are already displaying it on the console log. So now we just have to change that to update the label we will create.

The `fps_images.png` should already be in your project if you created it from the template. If it is not, you can get it from the Cocos2d sources folder.

Begin by creating the `CCLabelAtlas` in you `init` method of the `GameLayer` class:

```
CCLabelAtlas * scoreLabel = [CCLabelAtlas labelAtlasWithString:@"0"
charMapFile:@"fps_images.png" itemWidth:16 itemHeight:24
startCharMap:'.'];
[self addChild:scoreLabel z:2 tag:K_ScoreLabel];
[scoreLabel setPosition:ccp(115,280)];
[scoreLabel setAnchorPoint:ccp(1,0.5)];
```

Now that the label is in place, we just have to update it when needed.

In the `checkGroups` method, where we were logging the score, replace that line with the following one:

```
CCLabelAtlas * l = (CCLabelAtlas *)[self getChildByTag:K_ScoreLabel];
[l setString:[NSString stringWithFormat:@"%d",score]];
```

Also at those two lines in the `drainTime` method where you were telling the player he lost, so the score is reset to 0.

```
if(remainingTime <=0)
{
  score= 0;
  CCLabelAtlas * l = (CCLabelAtlas *)
  [self getChildByTag:K_ScoreLabel];
  [l setString:[NSString stringWithFormat:@"%d",score]];
  NSLog(@"You lost!");
  remainingTime = MAX_TIME;
}
```

Once you play the game again, you will see the score showing up right there at the upper left portion of the screen, as shown in the following screenshot:

[134]

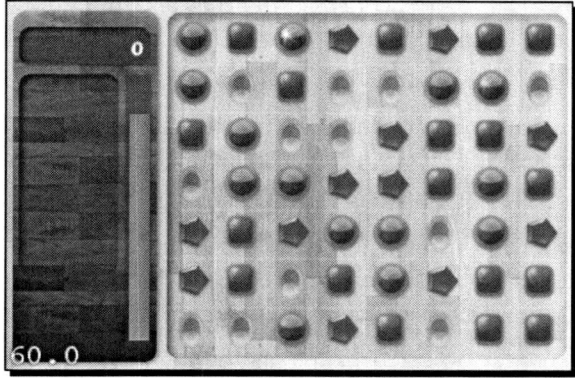

What just happened?

The most difficult part of using `CCLabelAtlas` is getting the image file right. Once you have that, the rest is pretty straightforward.

```
CCLabelAtlas * scoreLabel = [CCLabelAtlas labelAtlasWithString:@"0"
charMapFile:@"fps_images.png" itemWidth:16 itemHeight:24
startCharMap:'.'];
```

The preceding line creates the label. It takes the following parameters:

- `String`: The text you want to display
- `charMapFile`: The image you will be taking the characters from
- `itemWidth`: The width of the characters
- `itemHeight`: The height of the characters
- `startCharMap`: The first character in your image file

So, how does the `CCLabelAtlas` know where each character is? This is just like with Spritesheets. We can have inside a single image, a lot of smaller ones and then choose just a portion of it to display what we want.

Take a look at the actual `fps_image.png` file. See how we have all the characters being used in a single image, from where Cocos2d can take the needed portion to display the correct one.

Pasting Labels

The characters have to be placed in the same order they appear in the ASCII table. Then by using the `itemWidth` and `itemHeight` the `CCLabelAtlas` knows which portion of the image it has to retrieve.

Notice that in our example, we don't need the whole character set, just the numbers. So with the label that displays the FPS, we have an image with just the numbers and two more characters.

In order to be able to use such a small file, the `CCLabelAtlas` object takes a `startCharMap` parameter that indicates the position that it should start in the ASCII table. If you couldn't do that you would have to make an image file with the whole charset just for using some numbers.

Once we have the label created, we add it to the layer and modify some properties:

```
[self addChild:scoreLabel z:2 tag:K_ScoreLabel];
[scoreLabel setPosition:ccp(115,280)];
[scoreLabel setAnchorPoint:ccp(1,0.5)];
```

Of course, you can change the same things as in `CCLabels`, also apply actions to them.

Finally, when we need to change the text that the label displays we do the following:

```
CCLabelAtlas * l = (CCLabelAtlas *)[self getChildByTag:K_ScoreLabel];
[l setString:[NSString stringWithFormat:@"%d",score]];
```

We retrieve the `CCLabelAtlas` that we created in the `init` method by calling the layer's `getChildByTag` method and then call the `setString` method from the `CCLabelAtlas` to change the text.

As you may see, `CCLabelAtlas` is easy to display, but has its limitations. Next, we will take a look at the `CCBitmapFontAtlas`, which offers lots of improvements over its label brethren.

Creating texts with CCBitmapFontAtlas

We'll give now a try to `CCBitmapFontAtlas`. These labels have the flexibility of `CCLabels` and the speed of `CCLabelAtlas`. Also, there are some nice editors for creating your own `BitmapAtlases`. When in doubt, you should use this class to render your texts.

Yes, I left the best one for the end.

Another feature of `CCBitmapFontAtlas` is that it treats each character as an individual `CCSprite`, if you want to modify or apply actions to them individually or as a whole. The only limitation is that you shouldn't change the anchor point of the characters, as that might affect rendering (you still can change the anchor point of the whole label to align it). That is because the `CCLabel` is the parent of all the characters contained within it.

We'll begin by using a bitmap font I already made for you, and then I will show you how you can create them yourself, using one of the available tools.

Time for action – showing feedback

We want our game to tell the player when he is doing well, just a little something to make him feel like he is playing his best game. For that, we will show the score that was granted for matching a set of stones. Showing these encouraging messages are very important in a game, because they make the player feel rewarded for his ability, thus making him want to keep playing.

So what we want to do is, when a set is matched, find the center of that combination and place a label there (which we'll animate later). That label will obviously be a `CCBitmapFontAtlas` label.

For starters, go ahead and import the two files we will need for making the `CCBitmapFontAtlas` work. Those files are `feedbackFont.fnt` and `feedbackFont_0.png` and they can both be found in the Chapter 4 companion files.

Once you have imported those files, we are ready to display these new kinds of labels.

We have to make a few modifications in the `checkGroups` method of the GameLayer class. This is how it will look now. The new code is highlighted:

```
-(void)checkGroups:(bool)firstTime
{
  //Not relevant code

 for (NSMutableSet * n in groupings)
 {
  CGPoint averagePos = CGPointZero;
  if([n count]>=3)
   {
    for(Stone * c in n)
    {
     c.disappearing = YES;
     moveStones = YES;
     //[c.mySprite setOpacity:0];
     //[c.mySprite setTexture:[[CCTextureCache
         sharedTextureCache]addImage:@"sSmile.png"]];
     [c.mySprite setTextureRect:CGRectMake(34,2,32, 32)];
     CCAction * action = [CCSpawn actions:[CCFadeOut
       actionWithDuration:0.5],[CCScaleTo actionWithDuration:0.5
       scale:0.5],nil];
     [c.mySprite runAction:action];
```

Pasting Labels

```
    averagePos = cp(averagePos.x+c.mySprite.position.x,
       averagePos.y+c.mySprite.position.y);
}

averagePos = ccp(averagePos.x / [n count],averagePos.y /
[n count]);
```

With this, we know where to place the Label.

```
CCSprite * b  = (CCSprite *)[self getChildByTag:K_GBACK];
CCAction * act = [CCSequence actions:
                [CCScaleTo actionWithDuration:0.2
  scale:0.9],[CCScaleTo actionWithDuration:0.2 scale:1],nil];
[b runAction:[CCRepeat actionWithAction:act times:3]];

int newScore = 100 * [n count];
score += newScore;

CCBitmapFontAtlas * feedTxt = [CCBitmapFontAtlas
   bitmapFontAtlasWithString:[NSString stringWithFormat:@"%d",
                             newScore]
   fntFile:@"feedbackFont.fnt"];
[self addChild:feedTxt z:5];
[feedTxt setPosition:averagePos];
[feedTxt setColor:ccRED];

CCLabelAtlas * l = (CCLabelAtlas *)
[self getChildByTag:K_ScoreLabel];
[l setString:[NSString stringWithFormat:@"%d",score]];
}
   //Not relevant code
```

Now, when you run the game, you should see red numbers appear when some stones are matched (as shown in the following screenshot). For the time being they will remain there, which is really bad, but we will solve that soon when I show you how to animate these labels.

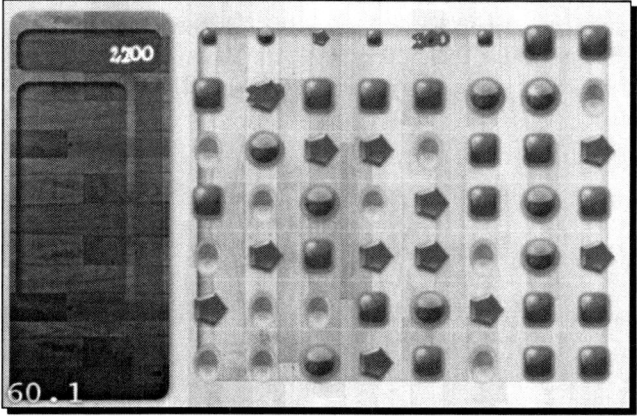

What just happened?

We are making a few modifications to the code we had, in order to be able to show the score just where the action occurred. For that, we create a CGPoint local variable, which we use to get the average position between all the eliminated stones. We achieved this just by adding all the positions of the stones that were removed and then dividing that number by the amount of stones removed.

Once we have the position where we want the text shown, we need to create our CCBitmapFontAtlas. We do that as follows:

```
CCBitmapFontAtlas * feedTxt = [CCBitmapFontAtlas bitmapFon
tAtlasWithString:[NSString stringWithFormat:@"%d",newScore]
fntFile:@"feedbackFont.fnt"];
```

We just need to pass the following two parameters for the CCBitmapFontAtlas object's initialization:

- string: Which is the text we are to show
- fntFile: The name of the file containing the font's definition.

Once created, we just need our usual code to actually add it and place it into the layer:

```
[self addChild:feedTxt z:5];
[feedTxt setPosition:averagePos];
[feedTxt setColor:ccRED];
```

We are also changing its color so it is noticeable.

Pasting Labels

 Cocos2d comes with a few colors already defined; they are named like the one above: ccRED, ccBLACK, ccBLUE, and so on. You can define your own colors without alpha (those are ccColor3B) and with alpha (ccColor4B).

Let's have a look at how `CCBitmapFontAtlas` works. Check out the `feedbackFont_0.png` file; you will notice that all the characters that compose this font are in there.

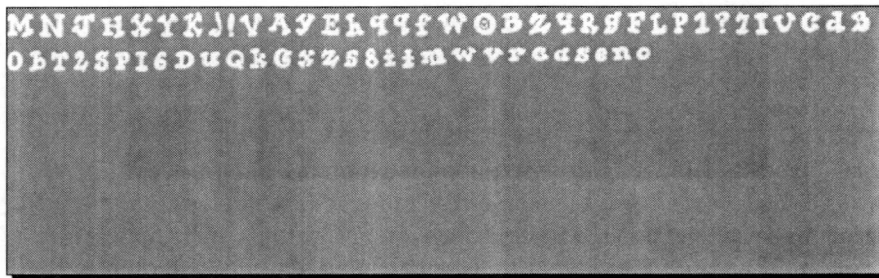

If you open the `feedbackFont.fnt` file, you will find some information about the font used and lots of coordinates and sizes which correspond to every character you had in the `.png` file. These are used internally by the `CCBitmapFontAtlas` class to determine the position of each character inside the `.png` file, where the images are stored.

One of the advantages of these labels is that they allow variable sized characters. So in order to do that it needs to store each character's position, size, and so on. Don't worry! All the data inside the `.fnt` file is put together by the software we use to create the font.

 Since retrieving all the definitions from the file takes a little while, sometimes it can get a little slowdown when creating your `CCBitmapFontAtlas` labels. So generally it is a good idea to have them precreated at the beginning of the scene and reuse them later.

`CCBitmapFontAtlas` labels can be animated just as any other label, but we can also animate each letter individually and that is what we are going to do next.

Time for action – running actions on texts

Having the feedback text appear and sit there doing nothing doesn't look good at all. What we want to do now is to make them fade in, animate each letter a little, and then fade it out. The following is the code that accomplishes that:

```
float dTime =0;
for(CCSprite * p in [feedTxt children])
```

```
{
  [p runAction:[CCSequence actions:[CCDelayTime 
     actionWithDuration:1+(dTime/3)],[CCMoveBy actionWithDuration:1 
     position:ccp(0,30)],nil]];
  dTime++;
}
[feedTxt runAction:[CCSequence actions:[CCFadeIn 
actionWithDuration:1],
   [CCDelayTime actionWithDuration:1],[CCFadeOut 
actionWithDuration:1],
   [CCCallFuncN actionWithTarget:self selector:@
selector(removeSprite:)],
   nil]];
```

Just add those lines after the `CCBitmapFontAtlas` label we created before.

Now, each time a score is shown, it will first fade in, then each letter will go up individually, then the whole label will fade out and be removed from the layer, as shown in the following screenshot:

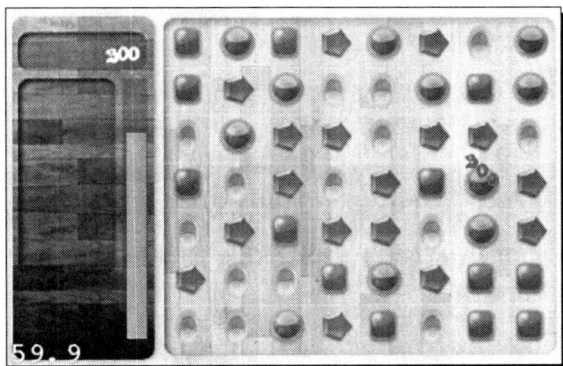

What just happened?

The code we just added demonstrates how you can run actions on the label or on each single `CCSprite` that composes the label.

```
float dTime =0;
for(CCSprite * p in [feedTxt children])
{
  [p runAction:[CCSequence actions:[CCDelayTime 
     actionWithDuration:1+(dTime/3)],[CCMoveBy actionWithDuration:1 
     position:ccp(0,30)],nil]];
  dTime++;
}
```

Pasting Labels

There we are looping through all the children of the label (which are the individual letters made from `CCSprites`) and applying an action to them which just waits a little and then moves the letter up.

```
[feedTxt runAction:[CCSequence actions:
[CCFadeIn actionWithDuration:1],[CCDelayTime actionWithDuration:1],
[CCFadeOut actionWithDuration:1],[CCCallFuncN actionWithTarget:
self selector:@selector(removeSprite:)], nil]];
```

At the same time we run an action that fades in the whole label, waits a moment so we can see the other animations run, and then fades out and calls the method that removes the `CCNode` from the layer.

Making your own BitmapFontAtlas with BM Font tool

Bitmap labels are really cool, they look nice and are easy to use. A little while ago I mentioned that they were also easy to make, and they are, thanks to a couple of free tools that are around.

You can use one of the following tools:

- **Hiero Bitmap Font Tool**: This one comes in the form of a Java Applet. You can run it directly by going to `http://www.n4te.com/hiero/hiero.jnlp`
- **Angelcode's Bitmap Font Generator**: This one is a `.exe` file for windows. You can find it at `http://www.angelcode.com/products/bmfont/`

Both are very good tools. They are good at what they do. However, Angelcode's tool has more features then the other one.

I will show you how to make your own bitmap fonts with the Hiero tool, as it can be run both on Windows and Mac OS. If you have a PC at hand, you should give it a try to the other tool later and see which one makes you more comfortable to work with.

Time for action – creating your own Bitmap font

Let's begin by downloading and running the Hiero Bitmap Font Tool.

Head to `http://slick.cokeandcode.com/demos/hiero.jnlp` to download the applet. You will be asked what you want to do with the file. Select **Open with: Java Web Start** and click on **OK**. This is shown in the following screenshot:

Chapter 4

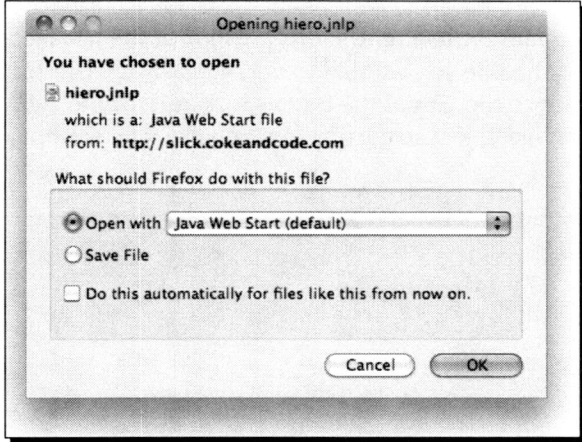

Once it has been downloaded and it is running, you will be presented with the following screen:

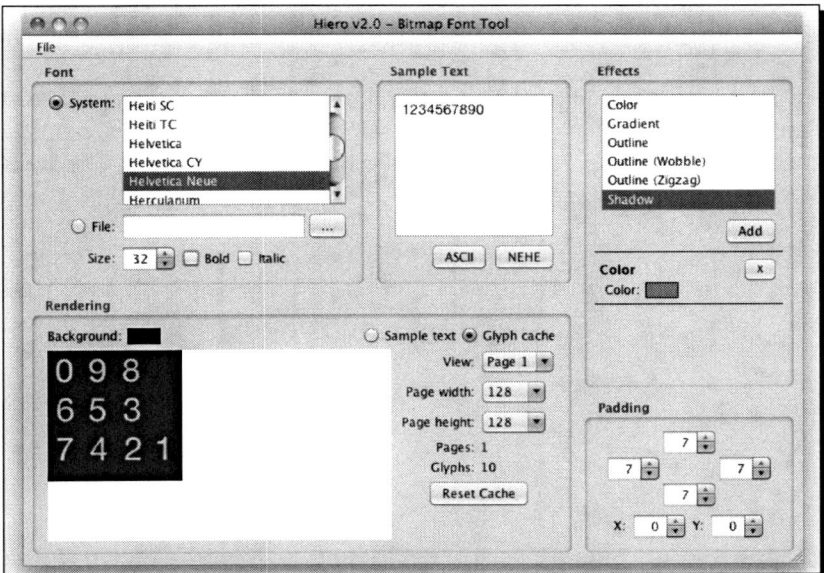

I will explain each section of it.

In the upper left section, you have the **Font** panel. Here you can select the TrueType font that you wish to use for your Bitmap font. Hiero will look at the installed fonts on your system. If you can't find the one you wanted to use, you can select it from a **File** just below. Down there you can choose the **Size** of the font as well as its **Style**. I will select the **Helvetica Neue** font, if you don't have it, just select any font you like. The **Font** panel is shown in the following screenshot:

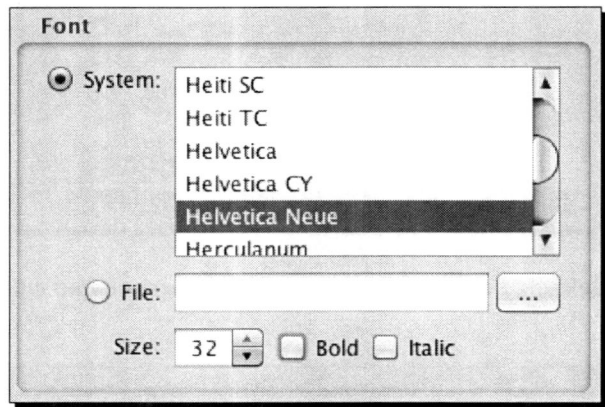

Next, to the right we have the **Sample Text** panel. Here you are shown the whole charset that will be rendered and used in your bitmap font. You can leave it as it is, or just write the characters that you want to use. I will write just the numbers from 0 to 9. The **Sample Text** panel is shown in the following screenshot:

Down there to the left, you have the **Rendering** panel. Here you are shown how the font is going to look. You should check the **Glyph cache** radio button. This will open more options and show you how the final .png file will really look. Once you check that button, you will see new options appear. If your characters are too big to fit into one image, Hiero will create more files, called pages, for your font. Cocos2d actually doesn't support more than just one page, so avoid using really big fonts with lots of spacing between characters. The **View** drop-down box lets you select the page you want to view. The **Page width** and **Page height** let you select the dimensions of the .png image. The bigger it is, the more the characters that will fit in there. As I only want to create 10 numbers, a 128 * 128 file is more than enough. Each time you change anything, remember to press the **Reset Cache** button to see the changes. The **Rendering** panel is shown in the following screenshot:

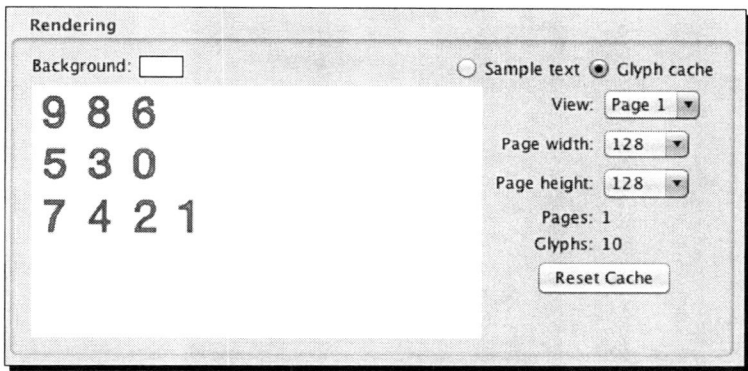

Just to the right, we have the **Padding** panel. Here you can change the spacing between each character and the spacing between the whole characters and the left and top borders. This is really useful if you later want to add some effect to your characters like a shadow or glow. I am going to add seven pixels to each side, as shown in the following screenshot:

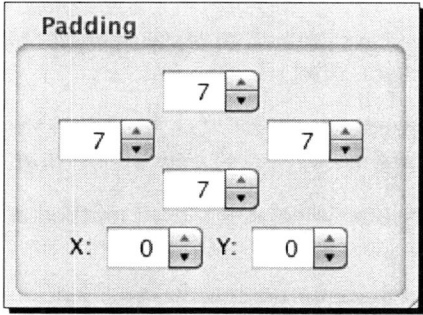

Up there we have the **Effects** panel. It allows you to apply some basic effects to the final font, such as shadow, outline, and gradient. Generally, they don't look as good as they would have, had you applied the effects using a graphic design software. However, for our basic needs it is more than enough. I will add a light blue color and a blue outline. To do that, select one of the effects from the list and click on the **Add** button. The added effects will appear below the list. Double click the **Color** box to change it. Then repeat the same process for the **Outline** effect.

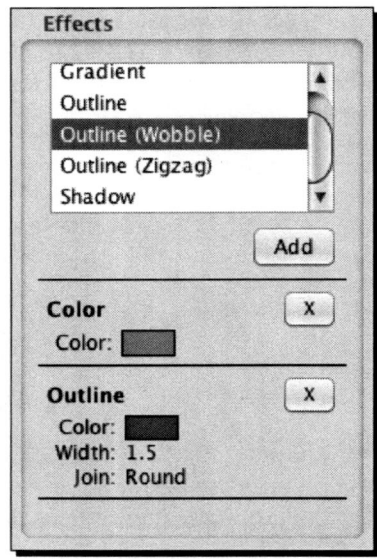

Once you have all that set, go to the **File** menu. There you can either load or save the configuration file, that is everything we have changed so far, or export the Bitmap font file. Save the configuration file in case you want to use it later, then save the bitmap font file. You will be asked for a name and a location. I will name it `newScore.fnt`.

Let's use this new font that we have created to replace the `CCLabelAtlas` for the score with this brand new custom-made `CCBitmapFontAtlas`.

First, check the location where you saved the `.fnt` file. Hiero should have created two files there: the `newScore.fnt` and the `newScore.png`. Import both of them to your project.

Once you have done so, go to your GameLayer's `init` method and replace the following line:

```
CCLabelAtlas * scoreLabel = [CCLabelAtlas labelAtlasWithString:@"0"
charMapFile:@"fps_images.png" itemWidth:16 itemHeight:24
startCharMap:'.'];
```

Chapter 4

With the following one:
```
CCBitmapFontAtlas * scoreLabel = [CCBitmapFontAtlas 
bitmapFontAtlasWithString:@"0" fntFile:@"newScore.fnt"];
```

Now run the project, and you will see the font you just created in place. If it looks too big, remember you can scale it by calling the `setScale` method of the label.

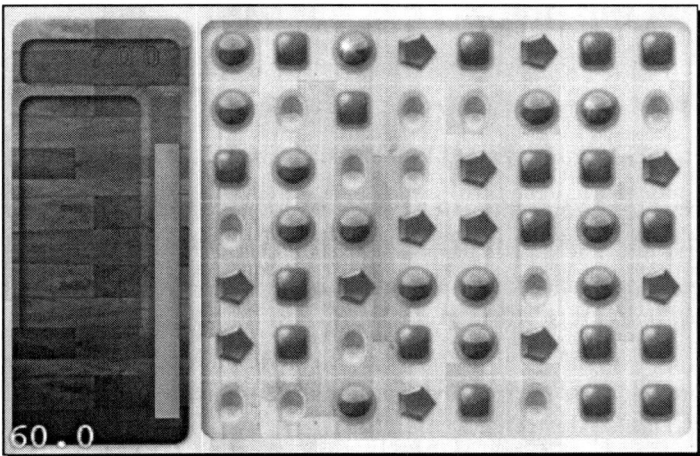

What just happened?

That pretty much covers the whole topic of how Bitmap fonts are created. Just remember Cocos2d only supports one image file (page) per font. So be careful with the size of your font when creating the bitmap file.

Pop Quiz

1. Which type of label is slow to update?
    a. CCLabel
    b. CCLabelAtlas
    c. CCBitmapFontAtlas

2. Which of the following is not true for `CCBitmapFontAtlas`?
    a. It has kerning support
    b. Each letter can be treated as a single CCSprite
    c. You can update it without suffering a performance drop
    d. You can create a block of text using many different fonts

3. Can you load any TTF font with `CCLabel`?
    a. Yes, if you import it into the project
    b. No, it is impossible
    c. Some TTF fonts can be used

Wrapping up the game

We have reached the end of the chapter, and also this is the last time we will talk about the Coloured Stones game.

There is a lot of room for improvement in this game. The following are a few ideas:

- A combo system: You can put into place a combo system, where the player is awarded more points by matching several sets of stones in one go.
- Multiple swapping: You could device a way for the player to keep matching stones while new ones are still falling.
- New stones with different properties: You could have some indestructible stones, other items, such as bombs that destroy all nearby stones, wildcard stones that can be used to match any other stones, and so on!
- Multiplayer: How about a hot seat mode where two players share the device and take turns to match stones?

In the following chapters, you will be learning lots of cool things, such as using particle effects and sounds. Feel free to come back to this game after you have learned that and put it into practice.

Summary

In this chapter we had a look at the following things:

- We saw how to use all the kinds of labels available in Cocos2D. Each type of label has its advantages and drawbacks that you must use in your favor in each situation.
- We also saw how to create our own bitmap fonts for using them in our projects.

This chapter marked the end of the game we have been creating since Chapter 2, although there are a lot of things you can change to make it a commercial game.

In the next chapter, we will start working on a new project while learning how to work with different scenes, layers, and lots of new stuff.

5
Surfing through Scenes

Scenes are an essential part of any Cocos2d game. Up until now we have been using just one scene which contained just one layer where we were putting all the game logic. In this chapter, we will look into the creation of many scenes to hold the different menus a game can have. Once we have a couple of scenes set up, you will learn how to go from one to another and with some nice transitions.

In this chapter, we will start working on a new game, which I called Aerial Gun. It is just another vertical shooter game, but I hope it serves its purpose of illustrating lots of new stuff.

So, by the end of the chapter you will understand how to:

- Create new scenes and move through them
- Build the base for an action game
- Handle accelerometer input
- Add more layers to your scenes
- Make a simple pause screen

We'll be doing a lot of things in this chapter, so let's get started.

Surfing through Scenes

Aerial Gun, a vertical shooter game

Let's talk about the game we will be making.

Aerial Gun, as I said earlier, is a vertical shooter game. That means you will be in control of an airship which will move vertically. Actually, the airship won't be moving anywhere (well except to the left and right); what is really going to move here is the background, giving the sense the airship is the one moving.

The player will be able to control the airship by using accelerometer controls. We'll also provide some areas where the player can touch to fire bullets or bombs to destroy the enemies.

Enemies will be appearing at different time intervals and will have some different behaviors attached to them. For example, some of them could just move towards the airship, others may stay there and shoot back, and so on. We'll do it in a way you can create more custom behaviors later.

In the following chapters, we will be adding particle effects for airships explosions, sounds, and tilemaps for the background, but right now let's focus on having the basics set up.

For this game we will be using the Cocos2d template again, just because it is the easier way to have a project properly set up, at least to begin our work.

So, follow the same steps as when we created the Coloured Stones game. Just open Xcode and go to the File menu, select to create a new project. Then choose the Cocos2d template (the simple one, without any physics engine) and give a name to the project. I will call it AerialGun. Once you do that, your new project should be opened.

Creating new scenes

We will begin this new game by first doing a couple of scenes other than the one that holds the actual game.

If you take a look at the class that the template generates, at first sight you won't find what would appear to be a scene. That is because the template handles that in a confusing fashion, at least for people who are just getting started with Cocos2d. Let's take a look at that. Open the newly generated `HelloWorldScene.m` file.

This is the same code in which we based our first game. This time we will analyze it so you understand what it is doing behind scenes. Take a look at the first method of the implementation of the HelloWorld Layer:

```
+(id) scene
{
```

```
    // 'scene' is an autorelease object.
    CCScene *scene = [CCScene node];

    // 'layer' is an autorelease object.
    HelloWorld *layer = [HelloWorld node];

    // add layer as a child to scene
    [scene addChild: layer];

    // return the scene
    return scene;
}
```

If you remember well, this is the method that get's called in the AppDelegate when the Director needs to start running with a scene. So why are we passing the method of a layer instead of an instance of a CCScene class?

If you pay attention to the `+ (id) scene` method of the layer, what it does is to instantiate a `CCScene` object, then it instantiates a `HelloWorld` object (the layer), and then it adds that layer to the scene and returns it.

This actually works as you have witnessed and is pretty quick to set up, and get you up and running. However, sometimes you will need to have you own custom scenes, that is a class that inherits from `CCScene` and extends it in some fashion.

Now we are going to create some of the scenes that we need for this game and add a layer to each one. Then when it is time to work with the game scene we will modify it to match our needs.

Before doing anything, please change the name of the `HelloWorld layer` to `GameLayer` and the name of the `HelloWorldScene` to `GameScene`, just as we did back then with our first game.

Time for action – creating the splash and main menu scene

We will begin with a simple scene, the **splash** screen. A splash screen is the first thing that appears as you launch a game. Well, the second if you count the `Default.png` image. The objective of this screen is to show the player some information about the developer, other companies that helped, and so on. Most times you will just show a couple and logos and move to the main menu.

So, what we will do now is put a new `Default.png` image, then create the SplashScene.

Surfing through Scenes

 The `Default.png` image is located in your project's `Resources` group folder and it is the first image that is shown when the application is launched. You should always have one, so that something is shown while the application is being launched. This happens before anything is initialized, so you can't do anything else other than show this image. Its dimensions must be 320 * 480 (when developing for older generation iPhones), so if your game is supposed to be in landscape mode, you should rotate the image with any graphics software before including it in your project.

The SplashScene is going to show a sprite for a moment, then fade it, show another one and then move to the GameScene.

Let's add a new file to the project. Select **New File** (*CMD + N*) from the File menu, then select **Objective-C** class (we are going to do it from scratch anyways) and name it `SplashScene`.

This file will hold both the `SplashScene` and the `SplashLayer` classes. The `SplashLayer` will be added as a child of the `SplashScene`, and inside the layer we will add the sprites.

Before writing any code, add to the project the three splash images I created for you. You can find them in the Chapter 5 `companion` files folder. Once you have them added into your project we can begin working on the `SplashScene`.

The following is the `SplashScene.h`:

```
#import <Foundation/Foundation.h>
#import "cocos2d.h"
#import "MainMenuScene.h"
@interface SplashScene : CCScene {

}
@end

@interface SplashLayer : CCLayer {

}
@end
```

And the `SplashScene.m` file:

```
#import "SplashScene.h"
//Here is the implementation of the SplashScene
@implementation SplashScene
- (id) init
{
```

```
  self = [super init];
  if (self != nil)
  {

    [self addChild:[SplashLayer node]];

  }
  return self;
}
-(void)dealloc
{
  [super dealloc];
}
@end

//And here is the implementation of the SplashLayer

@implementation SplashLayer
- (id) init
{
  if ((self = [super init]))
  {

    isTouchEnabled = YES;

    NSMutableArray * splashImages = [[NSMutableArray alloc]init];
    for(int i =1;i<=3;i++)
    {
      CCSprite * splashImage = [CCSprite spriteWithFile:[NSString
         stringWithFormat:@"splash%d.png",i]];
      [splashImage setPosition:ccp(240,160)];
      [self addChild:splashImage];
      if(i!=1)
      [splashImage setOpacity:0];

      [splashImages addObject:splashImage];
    }

    [self fadeAndShow:splashImages];


  }
  return self;
}
//Now we add the methods that handle the image switching
```

Surfing through Scenes

```objc
-(void)fadeAndShow:(NSMutableArray *)images
{
  if([images count]<=1)
  {
    [images release];
    [[CCDirector sharedDirector]replaceScene:[MainMenuScene node]];
  }
  else
  {

    CCSprite * actual = (CCSprite *)[images objectAtIndex:0];
    [images removeObjectAtIndex:0];

    CCSprite * next = (CCSprite *)[images objectAtIndex:0];


    [actual runAction:[CCSequence actions:[CCDelayTime
     actionWithDuration:2], [CCFadeOut actionWithDuration:1],
     [CCCallFuncN actionWithTarget:self
       selector:@selector(remove:)],nil]];
    [next runAction:[CCSequence actions:[CCDelayTime
     actionWithDuration:2], [CCFadeIn actionWithDuration:1],
     [CCDelayTime actionWithDuration:2],
       [CCCallFuncND actionWithTarget:self selector:@
         selector(cFadeAndShow:data:) data:images],nil]];

  }

}
-(void) cFadeAndShow:(id)sender data:(void*)data
{
  NSMutableArray * images = (NSMutableArray *)data;
  [self fadeAndShow:images];
}
-(void)remove:(CCSprite *)s
{
  [s.parent removeChild:s cleanup:YES];
}
-(void)dealloc
{
  [super dealloc];
}
@end
```

As you may notice, I have put together two classes in only one file. You can do this with any number of classes, as long you don't get lost in such a long file. Generally, you will create a pair of files (the .m and .h) for each class, but as the `SplashScene` class has very little code, I'd rather put it there.

For this to work properly, we need to make some other changes. First, open the `AerialGunAppDelegate.m` file and change the line where the the Director starts running the GameScene. We want it to start by running the SplashScene now. So replace that line with the following:

```
[[CCDirector sharedDirector] runWithScene:[SplashScene node]];
```

Also remember to import your `SplashScene.h` file in order for the project to properly compile.

Finally, we have to create the MainMenuScene, which is the scene the Director will run after the last image has faded out. So, let's create that one and leave it blank for now.

The following is the `MainMenuScene.h` file:

```
#import <Foundation/Foundation.h>
#import "cocos2d.h"

@interface MainMenuScene : CCScene {

}
@end

@interface MainMenuLayer : CCLayer {

}
@end
```

The following is the `MainMenuScene.m` file:

```
#import "MainMenuScene.h"

@implementation MainMenuScene
- (id) init
{
  self = [super init];
  if (self != nil)
  {
    [self addChild:[MainMenuLayer node]];
  }
```

```
    return self;
}
- (void)dealloc
{
    [super dealloc];
}
@end

@implementation MainMenuLayer
- (id) init
{
  if ((self = [super init]))
  {

    isTouchEnabled = YES;

  }
  return self;
}
- (void)dealloc
{
    [super dealloc];
}
@end
```

That would be all for now. Run the project and you should see the first image appear. Then fade to the next one after a while and continue till the last one. Once the last one has faded out, we move on to the MainMenuScene.

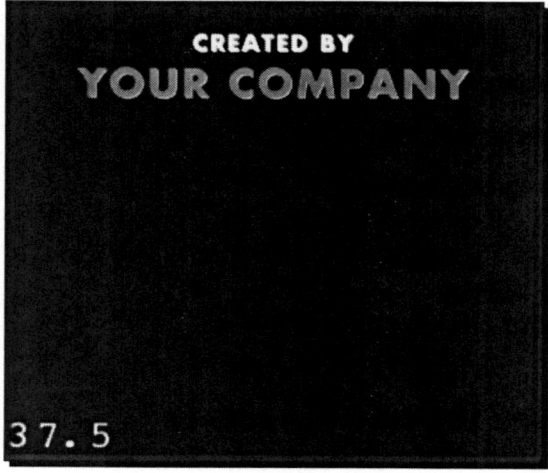

What just happened?

Creating a new scene is as easy as that. You can see from the MainMenuScene code that what we are doing is quite simple; when the MainMenuScene gets created we just instantiate the MainMenuLayer and add it to the scene. That layer is where we will later add all the necessary logic for the main menu.

The MainMenuScene as well as the SplashScene both inherit from the CCScene class. This class is just another CCNode.

Let's take a little look at the logic behind the SplashScene:

```
NSMutableArray * splashImages = [[NSMutableArray alloc]init];
for(int i =1;i<=3;i++)
{
  CCSprite * splashImage = [CCSprite spriteWithFile:
  [NSString stringWithFormat:@"splash%d.png",i]];
  [splashImage setPosition:ccp(240,160)];
  [self addChild:splashImage];
  if(i!=1)
    [splashImage setOpacity:0];

  [splashImages addObject:splashImage];
}

[self fadeAndShow:splashImages];
```

This piece of code is from the SplashLayer init method. What we are doing here is creating an array that will hold any amount of sprites (in this case, three of them). Then we create and add those sprites to it. Finally, the fadeAndShow method is called, passing that newly created array to it.

The fadeAndShow method is responsible for fading the images it has. It grabs the first image in the array (after that, the sprite is removed from the array). It then grabs the next one. Then it applies actions to both of them to fade them in and out.

The last action of the second sprite's action is a CCCallFuncND, which we use to call the fadeAndShow method again with the modified array. This occurs if there is more than one remaining sprite in the array. If there isn't, the fadeAndShow method calls the Director's replaceScene method with the MainMenuScene.

I have made the SplashLayer logic, so you can add more splash images to the array (or leave just one) if you like. Generally, just one or two images will be more than enough.

Transitioning through scenes

Did you notice how bad it looks when we go from the SplashScene into the MainMenuScene? We need to change the way we move from one scene to another, so the change is not so abrupt. In the previous example, we could have just faded out the last sprite and then replaced the scene to make the transition from one scene to another look smoother. However, what would happen if you had tens of sprites? Or what if you wanted to go from scene to scene by sliding them instead of doing a fade effect?

Fortunately, Cocos2d provides a variety of ways to *transition* from scene to scene. Cocos2d comes packed with more than 20 different transition classes for you to choose from; and of course, you are welcome to make your own if you find that none of them are suitable for your game style.

Time for action – moving through scenes in a nice way

Let's try a couple of transitions to move from the SplashScene to the MainMenuScene.

Open the `SplashScene.m` file and in the `fadeAndShow` method change the line:

```
[[CCDirector sharedDirector] replaceScene:[MainMenuScene node]];
```

Change it to the following:

```
[[CCDirector sharedDirector] replaceScene:[CCFadeTransition
transitionWithDuration:2 scene:[MainMenuScene node]
withColor:ccBLUE]];
```

Run the project again, and now you should see a nice fade out to blue, and then a nice fade in to the new scene.

Let's try some more interesting transitions. Change the preceding line to the following:

```
[[CCDirector sharedDirector] replaceScene:[CCZoomFlipAngularTransition
transitionWithDuration:2 scene:[MainMenuScene node] orientation:kOrien
tationLeftOver]];
```

Run the project one more time and take a look now. Did you like that one?

Chapter 5

Cocos2d has lots of transitions that you can try, so take a look at the documentation and the transitions test to see all the options you have.

What just happened?

Transitions are really easy to apply and they look really good, adding a little production value to your game.

Every transition is an individual class that extends the `CCTransitionScene` class. This class defines a duration and the scene that we want to transit to. So those two parameters will always be needed, then each class may add another extra parameter. For example, the `CCFadeTransition` takes a `color` as an extra parameter and the `CCZoomFlipAngularTransition` takes an orientation.

Implementing the game logic

Now that we have the SplashScene and the MainMenuScene, we can start working on the game. In the next chapter, we will revisit the main menu and add content to it. For now, change the `AerialGunAppDelegate` to run the `GameScene` directly, so you can test the game quickly without having to wait for the splash to run each time you want to see the changes made in the game.

Let's begin by making some preparations for the game. Then we will start making each component of the game and then we'll put it all together.

Preparing for the game

AerialGun is a vertical shooter game, so let's begin by changing the orientation of the device. By default, the template sets the orientation to landscape, but we need it to be in portrait mode this time. So, open the `AerialGunAppDelegate` and search for the following line:

```
[[CCDirector sharedDirector] setDeviceOrientation:CCDeviceOrientationLandscapeLeft];
```

Then, change it to:

```
[[CCDirector sharedDirector] setDeviceOrientation:CCDeviceOrientationPortrait];
```

Good, now if you didn't do this before, take some time to change the `HelloWorld` files and classes that are created automatically by the template to a more descriptive name. Let's name the game scene `GameScene` and make the proper changes. Remember, you have to change the file names, the class names, and any imports that were lying around to match the new names. Also remove the label that is created by the template.

Finally, let's create the `GameScene` class as we did with the other scenes.

The following shows how your `GameScene` should look:

GameScene.h:

```
#import "cocos2d.h"
@interface GameScene : CCScene {

}
@end
@interface GameLayer : CCLayer
{
  Hero * hero;

  NSMutableArray * bullets;
  bool playerFiring;

  NSMutableArray * enemies;
  float lastTimeEnemyLaunched;
  float enemyInterval;

  int score;
  int lives;
  int bombs;
  int level;
```

```objc
}
@property (nonatomic,retain) Hero * hero;
@property (nonatomic,readwrite) bool playerFiring;
@property (nonatomic,readwrite) float lastTimeEnemyLaunched;
@property (nonatomic,readwrite) float enemyInterval;
@property (nonatomic,retain) NSMutableArray * enemies;
@property (nonatomic,retain) NSMutableArray * bullets;
@property (assign,readwrite) int score;
@property (assign,readwrite) int lives;
@property (assign,readwrite) int level;
@property (assign,readwrite) int bombs;
@end
```

GameScene.m:

```objc
#import "GameScene.h"
@implementation GameScene
- (id) init
{
  self = [super init];
  if (self != nil)
  {

    [self addChild:[GameLayer node]];

  }
  return self;
}
-(void)dealloc
{
   [super dealloc];
}
@end
@implementation GameLayer
// on "init" you need to initialize your instance
-(id) init
{
  if((self=[super init]))
  {


  }
```

```
    return self;
}
// on "dealloc" you need to release all your retained objects
- (void) dealloc
{
    [super dealloc];
}
@end
```

If you run the game you should see a black screen, no more, no less. That is good for now; we have a blank slate to start our work.

Now we are ready to start making the game's components such as the main character, the enemies, and so on.

Let's begin with our hero.

Making a hero

This is the airplane that the user will control. It will be pretty simple for now, and then we will make it more and more complex as we advance through the chapter. Then, the `Hero` class should do the following things:

- Render the image of the airship into the screen
- Receive accelerometer feedback to update its position
- Check collisions against enemies and the bullets fired by them
- Get destroyed

Let's begin by creating the `Hero` class and getting it to display the airship image on the screen.

Time for action – creating the hero class

We will represent the hero with a single sprite which we'll later move around using the device's accelerometer. The following code is not new at all. We will create a sprite just as we have been doing it all this time:

1. First, create a new class and add it to the project. Name it `Hero`.

2. Now, change the `Hero.h` file to look like the following:

   ```
   #import <Foundation/Foundation.h>
   #import "cocos2d.h"
   #import "GameScene.h"
   ```

```
@class GameLayer;
@interface Hero : CCNode
{
  CCSprite * mySprite;
  GameLayer * theGame;
  float lastTimeFired;
  float fireInterval;
  float firingSpeed;
  float movementSpeed;

}
@property (nonatomic,retain) CCSprite * mySprite;
@property (nonatomic,retain) GameLayer * theGame;
@property (nonatomic,readwrite) float lastTimeFired;
@property (nonatomic,readwrite) float fireInterval;
@property (nonatomic,readwrite) float firingSpeed;
@property (nonatomic,readwrite) float movementSpeed;

@end
```

3. Next, change the `Hero.m` file as follows:

```
#import "Hero.h"

@implementation Hero

@synthesize theGame,mySprite;

- (id) initWithGame:(GameLayer *)game
{
  self = [super init];
  if (self != nil) {

  self.theGame = game;
  mySprite = [CCSprite spriteWithFile:@"hero.png"];
  [theGame addChild:mySprite z:2];
  [mySprite setPosition:ccp(160,50)];

  self.lastTimeFired =0;
  self.fireInterval = 3;
  self.firingSpeed = 10;
  self.movementSpeed = 5;

  }
```

```
    return self;
}

-(void)dealloc
{
    [super dealloc];
}

@end
```

4. Finally, create an instance of the `Hero` class in your `GameLayer`.

    In your `GameLayer` interface, add the following ivar:
    ```
    Hero * hero;
    ```

    In the `GameLayer` implementation, add the following line to the `init` method:
    ```
    hero = [[Hero alloc] initWithGame:self];
    ```

5. Now, run the game. You should see your airship right there at the bottom of the screen, as shown in the following screenshot:

What just happened?

We just laid the foundations for our `Hero` class. It does not have much content right now, but as the chapter progresses we will be adding more stuff to it.

The preceding code just creates a `CCSprite` object with an image of the airship and places it on the screen. The rest of the properties that we added will be used later for handling the movement and fire rate of the hero.

Making yourself some enemies

What would a hero be without enemies?

We are now going to make enemies appear, we will start simple and later work a little more on this. For the time being, we will just have enemies appear one after another in order to get us going. We will be making four types of enemies, which will behave the same way except for their movement speed, their fire rate, and their endurance.

Time for action – throwing enemies at your hero

To make it simple, we will just make the simplest, dumbest enemies; those would be the ones that just move forward no matter what. They are slow and easy to shoot down and some of them will shoot back. For the time being, we will have them appear at regular time intervals. The following are the steps involved in the creation of the `Enemy` class:

1. Add a new class to your project named `Enemy`.

2. Replace the `Enemy.h` file's content with the following code:

    ```
    #import <Foundation/Foundation.h>
    #import "cocos2d.h"
    #import "GameScene.h"

    @interface Enemy : CCNode
    {
      CCSprite * mySprite;
      GameLayer * theGame;
      float lastTimeFired;
      float fireInterval;
      float firingSpeed;
      float movementSpeed;
      bool launched;
      int hp;
      int maxHp;

    }

    @property (nonatomic,retain) CCSprite * mySprite;
    @property (nonatomic,retain) GameLayer * theGame;
    @property (nonatomic,readwrite) float lastTimeFired;
    @property (nonatomic,readwrite) float fireInterval;
    @property (nonatomic,readwrite) float firingSpeed;
    @property (nonatomic,readwrite) float movementSpeed;
    ```

```
@property (nonatomic,readwrite) bool launched;
@property (nonatomic,readwrite) int hp;
@property (nonatomic,readwrite) int maxHp;

-(CGRect)myRecta;

@end
```

3. Do the same with the `Enemy.m` file. The following is the code that should go in there:

```
#import "Enemy.h"

@implementation Enemy

@synthesize theGame,mySprite,lastTimeFired,fireInterval,firingSpeed,movementSpeed,launched,hp,maxHp;

//The following method will create an enemy airplane with a random configuration
- (id) initWithGame:(GameLayer *)game
{
  self = [super init];
  if (self != nil)
  {

    self.theGame = game;
    self.lastTimeFired =0;

    int enType= arc4random() %4 + 1;

    mySprite = [CCSprite spriteWithFile:[NSString
       stringWithFormat:@"enemy%d.png",enType]];
    [theGame addChild:mySprite z:2];
    [mySprite setPosition:ccp(-500,200)];

    switch (enType)
    {
      case 1:
      self.movementSpeed = 5;
      self.fireInterval = -1;
      self.hp = self.maxHp = 1;
      break;
      case 2:
      self.movementSpeed = 3;
      self.fireInterval = 6;
      self.hp = self.maxHp= 1;
      break;
      case 3:
```

```
          self.movementSpeed = 1;
          self.fireInterval = 9;
          self.hp = self.maxHp= 2;
          break;
          case 4:
          self.movementSpeed = 1;
          self.fireInterval = 8;
          self.hp = self.maxHp= 2;
          break;
          default:
          self.movementSpeed = 5;
          self.fireInterval = -1;
          self.hp = self.maxHp= 1;
          break;

      }

      self.firingSpeed = -3- self.movementSpeed;

  }
  return self;
}

//We'll call the update method each frame, changing the enemy
position

-(void)update
{
  [self.mySprite
     setPosition:ccp(self.mySprite.position.x,self.mySprite.
     position.y - self.movementSpeed)];

  if(self.mySprite.position.y <-20)
  {
    [self reset];
  }
}

-(void)launch
{
  self.launched = YES;
  [self.mySprite setPosition:ccp(arc4random()% 260 + 30,520)];
}
```

Surfing through Scenes

```
-(void)reset
{
  self.hp = self.maxHp;
  self.launched =NO;
  [self.mySprite setPosition:ccp(-500,200)];
}

@end
```

Now we have to make some changes in the `GameLayer` class.

4. Add the following properties to the `GameLayer` interface:

```
NSMutableArray * enemies;
    float lastTimeEnemyLaunched;
    float enemyInterval;
```

5. Now, add the following lines to the `init` method of the `GameLayer` class:

```
enemies = [[NSMutableArray alloc]initWithCapacity:10];
for(int i=0;i<10;i++)
{
  Enemy * e = [[Enemy alloc]initWithGame:self];
  [enemies addObject:e];
  [e release];
}

lastTimeEnemyLaunched =0;
enemyInterval = 20;
self.lives = STARTING_LIVES; //#define STARTING_LIVES 3 at the top
of the file.
[self schedule:@selector(step:)];
```

6. Finally, create the `step` method that we are scheduling above:

```
-(void)step:(ccTime *)dt
{
  for(Enemy * e in enemies)
  {
    if(e.launched)
    [e update];
  }

  if(self.lastTimeEnemyLaunched > self.enemyInterval)
  {
```

```
        Enemy * n = (Enemy *)[enemies objectAtIndex:arc4random()
        % [enemies count]];
        if(!n.launched)
        {
          [n launch];
          self.lastTimeEnemyLaunched=0;
        }
      }
    }

    lastTimeEnemyLaunched +=0.1;
}
```

7. That is all. Now run the game, and you will be able to see enemies coming down at regular time intervals, as shown in the following screenshot:

What just happened?

We began by creating the Enemy class, which at first sight is similar to the Hero class. As a matter of fact, we could have made a general Airship class and have both of them inherit from that, but let's keep it simple for now.

So, the Enemy class has a couple more properties to handle its hp. That is the amount of bullets required to take that airship down.

Surfing through Scenes

In the `init` method of this class, we are defining the behavior of each different type of enemy. They will be initialized at random and each will have different speeds, hp, and fire rates. Notice this could also be broken up into several subclasses if you wanted.

The rest of the properties are the same that we placed in our `Hero` class. The one we are using for now is the `movementSpeed`, which, as the name suggests, controls the speed of the enemies. Try changing it if you'd like to have them fly faster or slower.

The `Enemy` class has a `reset` and a `launch` method. These methods control the position of the enemies when they are to be removed and placed on the screen.

We also added an `update` method to it, which will be called from the `GameLayer` constantly, that is as fast as the game is able to do it, while the Enemy object is launched. What it does is update the position of the enemy's sprite.

The logic that makes the enemies appear at regular intervals is in the `GameLayer` class. First we allocate a reasonable amount of enemies in the `init` method and add them to an array. There we also set two important variables to control the apparition interval: `lastTimeEnemyLaunched` and `enemyInterval`, which handle the time separation between one enemy and the next one. You can change that number to make them appear more or less regularly.

The `step` method is the method that does the magic; this method will be used a lot, not just for updating the enemies but also for the hero, the bullets, checking collisions, and so on.

Right now, what we do is loop through the enemies array and check whether they have launched. If they are, we call the `update` method, which makes the active planes move downwards. If we have not launched any enemy in a while, we activate one of them.

That was pretty simple but it is more than enough for us to continue working with the rest of the elements.

Have a go hero – enhancing the enemies behavior

The AI for the enemies is really simple as you can see. There are a lot of things you could do to improve that. For example, instead of having the enemies come at you one by one at regular time intervals, you could create a system that allows you to send wave after wave of them. You could customize the types of enemies that come in each wave as well.

One way to do that would be something like the following:

- Create a `.plist` file. This file would hold an array of "waves". Each wave would contain an array of enemies, which would be an `NSDictionary`.
- That `NSDictionary` would hold the types of enemies you want to send and their positions. For example, wave1 could be made of five fast enemies.

- Now in the `GameLayer`, you would have to initialize an array which will hold one of the wave arrays at a time.
- When the game starts, load the array with one of the arrays in the `.plist`.
- When the last of those enemies is off screen, load the array again and send those enemies.

Forging some bullets

Our hero and enemies need something to defend themselves. Let's create some bullets for them to shoot!

We'll do something similar to what we did with enemies; we have to create a pool of bullets which we will use and reuse at the request of an airship requests.

Time for action – creating and reusing bullets

The logic behind the `Bullet` class is quite similar to that of the `Enemy` class. We'll create a bunch of bullets outside of the screen, and use them when needed. If they are activated, that is on screen, we update their position depending on who fired them. Let's do that and have our enemies fire first.

1. The following should go in the `Bullet.h` file:

```
#import <Foundation/Foundation.h>
#import "cocos2d.h"
#import "GameScene.h"

@class GameLayer;

@interface Bullet : CCNode
{
  CCSprite * mySprite;
  GameLayer * theGame;
  bool fired;
  int whoFired;
  int firingSpeed;
}

@property (nonatomic,retain) CCSprite * mySprite;
@property (nonatomic,retain) GameLayer * theGame;
@property (nonatomic,readwrite) bool fired;
@property (nonatomic,readwrite) int whoFired;
@property (nonatomic,readwrite) int firingSpeed;
```

```
-(void)fire:(int)who position:(CGPoint)position fspeed:(int)
fspeed;
@end
```

2. The following should go in the `Bullet.m` file:

```
#import "Bullet.h"

@implementation Bullet

@synthesize theGame,mySprite,fired,whoFired,firingSpeed;

- (id) initWithGame:(GameLayer *)game
{
  self = [super init];
  if (self != nil)
  {

    self.theGame = game;
    mySprite = [CCSprite spriteWithFile:@"bullet1.png"];
    [theGame addChild:mySprite z:1];
    [mySprite setPosition:ccp(-100,-100)];
    [mySprite setVisible:NO];

  }
  return self;
}

-(void)update
{
  switch (self.whoFired)
  {
    case 1:
     [self.mySprite
       setPosition:ccp(self.mySprite.position.x,self.mySprite.
       position.y + self.firingSpeed)];

     break;

    case 2:
     [self.mySprite
       setPosition:ccp(self.mySprite.position.x,self.mySprite.
       position.y + self.firingSpeed)];

     break;
  }
```

```
    if(self.mySprite.position.y >500 || self.mySprite.position.y
<-20)
    {
      [self reset];
    }
}

-(void)reset
{
  self.fired =NO;
  [self.mySprite setPosition:ccp(-100,-100)];
}

-(void)fire:(int)who position:(CGPoint)position fspeed:(int)
fspeed;
{
  self.firingSpeed = fspeed;
  self.whoFired = who;
  self.fired = YES;
  [self.mySprite setPosition:position];
}

-(void)dealloc
{
  [super dealloc];
}

@end
```

Also don't forget to add the bullet's image to your project.

Once you have those files, we have to create the pool of bullets in our GameScene.

3. Add a new property to the GameLayer, `NSMutableArray *` enemies. This array will hold the bullets.

4. Now in the `init` method of the `GameLayer` class, initialize that array with some `Bullet` objects:

```
bullets = [[NSMutableArray alloc]initWithCapacity:50];
  for(int i=0;i<50;i++)
  {
    Bullet * c = [[Bullet alloc]initWithGame:self];
    [bullets addObject:c];
    [c release];
  }
```

Surfing through Scenes

5. We have to tell all the bullets to update their positions if they were fired, so in the `step` method add the following lines of code:

   ```
   for(Bullet * b in bullets)
   {
      if(b.fired)
      {
         [b update];
      }
   }
   ```

   That would be all the code needed for creating the bullets and updating their positions when fired. If you run your project now you won't see any change, as we didn't define a way for them to appear. Let's give our enemies the ability to fire those bullets.

6. Open the `Enemy.m` file and change the `update` method to look like the following:

   ```
   -(void)update
   {
      [self.mySprite
         setPosition:ccp(self.mySprite.position.x,self.mySprite.
         position.y - self.movementSpeed)];

      for(Bullet * b in theGame.bullets)
      {
         if(self.fireInterval>0 && !b.fired && self.lastTimeFired >
            self.fireInterval)
         {
            [b fire:2 position:self.mySprite.position fspeed:self.
            firingSpeed]; self.lastTimeFired=0;
         }
      }

      self.lastTimeFired +=0.1;

      if(self.mySprite.position.y <-20)
      {
         [self reset];
      }
   }
   ```

7. That's all, so run the project and wait. You should see some enemies firing at the hero as shown in the following screenshot:

What just happened?

That was all the code involved in the creation and manipulation of bullets as of now. Let's take a look at what we did.

The implementation of the `Bullet` class is quite simple. The `init` method just creates a sprite which gets added to the `GameLayer`.

We have the `update` method which checks who shot the bullet, and updates its position accordingly. Right now, we have only two possible behaviors: if the player shoots, the bullet has to move upwards, but if the enemies shoot, the bullets go downwards.

The `fire` and `reset` methods manage the state of the bullet and its position, so it is placed correctly when fired and when being removed from the screen.

In the `GameLayer` we made quite a few changes. First we created the `NSMutableArray` that holds the bullets just like we did with the enemies, then we added the required code to the `step` method to have the bullets update themselves.

The important part is in the `update` method of the `Enemy` class. There, we loop through all the bullets and if that particular enemy is allowed to shoot, he does so by calling the bullet's `fire` method, which places a bullet where the enemy is and has it start updating its position.

Have a go hero – upgrading your firepower

The way I devised for bullets to be shot is very simple and uninteresting. The following are a few ideas to enhance it:

- Powerful enemies would be able to shoot in different ways, for example three-way shots, double shots, shots to their sides, and so on.
- The hero might be able to like that too, once he has acquired some powerups.
- Bullets don't necessarily have to move in the same direction all the time. They could be shot in curved paths, or have some advanced behavior, such as following the nearest target.

As you can see, there is a lot of room for improvement and if you desire to develop a real game of this type, you should do all this and more.

Handling accelerometer input

Now that we have our three basic elements roughly defined, let's focus on the player's interaction with the hero. We will start by allowing the player to move the hero using the device's built-in accelerometer.

The accelerometer opens a new world of interaction between the user and the device, allowing for a lot of interesting uses.

There are already lots of applications and games that use this feature in innovative ways. For example, in the game Rolando, players have to roll the main character around using the accelerometer, and here we will be doing something similar to that.

The accelerometer gives you data of the current tilting of the device in the three axes, that is the x, y, and z axes. Depending on the game you are making, you will be needing all that data or just the values for one or two of the axis.

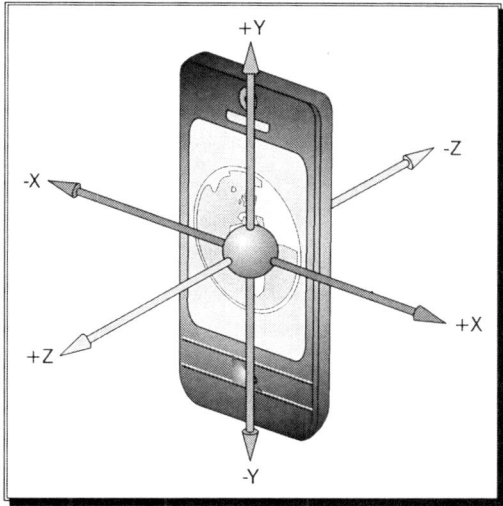

Fortunately, Apple has made it very easy for developers to access the data provided by the accelerometer hardware.

Time for action – moving your hero with the accelerometer

We have to add a few lines of code in order to have our hero move. The end result will be the hero moving horizontally when the user tilts the device to the left or to the right. We will also do some checkovers, in order to avoid the hero moving out of the screen.

1. The first step involved in using the accelerometer is to enable it for the CCLayers that want to receive its input. Add the following line of code to the GameLayer's init method:

   ```
   self.isAccelerometerEnabled = YES;
   ```

   Then we have to set the update interval for the accelerometer. This will set the interval at which the hardware delivers the data to the GameLayer.

2. Add the following line afterwards:

   ```
   [[UIAccelerometer sharedAccelerometer] setUpdateInterval:
   (1.0 / 60)];
   ```

   Now that our GameLayer is prepared to receive accelerometer input, we just have to implement the method that receives and handles it.

Surfing through Scenes

3. The following is the method that receives the input and makes our hero move. Add it to the `GameLayer` class:

```
- (void)accelerometer:(UIAccelerometer*)accelerometer
didAccelerate:(UIAcceleration*)acceleration
{
  static float prevX=0, prevY=0;

#define kFilterFactor 0.05f

  float accelX = (float) acceleration.x * kFilterFactor + (1-
    kFilterFactor)*prevX;

  prevX = accelX;

//If the hero object exists, we use the calculated accelerometer
values to move him

  if(hero)
  {
//We calculate the speed it will have and constrain it so it
doesn't move faster than he is allowed to

    float speed = -20 * -accelX;
    if(speed > hero.movementSpeed)
      speed = hero.movementSpeed;
    else if(speed < -hero.movementSpeed)
      speed = -hero.movementSpeed;

//We also check that the hero won't go past the borders of the
screen, if he would exit the screen we don't move it

    if((accelX >0 || hero.mySprite.position.x
      >hero.mySprite.textureRect.size.width / 2) && ( accelX <0
      ||hero.mySprite.position.x <320-
      hero.mySprite.textureRect.size.width / 2))
      [hero.mySprite setPosition:ccp(hero.mySprite.position.x
        +speed,hero.mySprite.position.y)];
  }
}
```

4. Run the game now. You should be able to move the hero by tilting you device, as shown in the following screenshot:

[178]

Chapter 5

 The iPhone simulator does not provide a way to simulate accelerometer input, so you won't be able to test it in there; it won't move at all.

What just happened?

Accelerometer input can be achieved quite easily and fast. In our example, we just used the *x* component of the accelerometer input to handle the hero's position.

The `accelX` variable holds the current value of the *x* component. This value ranges from -1 to 1, so we multiply it by the speed of the hero, then we just add that result to the current position of the hero, giving the sense of motion.

We are also checking to make sure that the hero is not going off the screen before applying that movement.

Now that we finally made our hero move, let's give him more power. Let's make him shoot back at the enemies!

Handling touches on layers

Handling touches on layers with Cocos2d is pretty straightforward. As a matter of fact, it works just as it does in regular Cocoa applications. So if you have already worked on other applications, handling touches on iPhone won't be anything new.

Surfing through Scenes

We have already seen how to handle touches back in Chapter 2, but remember there were two ways of doing that. Either by giving your `CCNodes` the ability to capture touches on themselves or by having the whole layer process them.

Here we are going to explore the second method. What we are going to do is make the `GameLayer` touchable, so it can receive and process touches on it.

There are four possible methods to handle the touches over a CCLayer. They are as follows:

- `ccTouchesBegan`: Called when the user puts a finger over the layer
- `ccTouchesMoved`: Called when the user moves that finger over the layer without lifting it
- `ccTouchesEnded`: Called when the user lifts that finger
- `ccTouchesCancelled`: Called when a system event occurs (for example, a low memory warning) and the touch is cancelled

Those four methods alone are enough to create any kind of touching logic.

Cocos2d does not offer any kind of off-the-shelve gestures. So if you want to implement pinching or swiping, you will have to come up with a way to do it for yourself.

Time for action – firing the bullets

What we'll do now is create the methods for handling touches on the layer. In our example, we will make the hero fire bullets while the player holds a finger on the screen. When he releases it, we will stop firing bullets. In order to do that, we need to define the methods which get fired when the user puts a finger over the screen and when the user lifts that finger.

Back when we used the other touching method, we needed to do some previous work of registering the nodes to receive the events, set their boundaries, and so on. With this other method, we don't need to do all that.

So, let's add those methods to the `GameLayer`, as follows:

1. Before you do anything, you have to tell the layer that you want to receive the touches to enable them. To do that, add the following line to the `init` method of the GameLayer class:

   `self.isTouchEnabled = YES;`

From now on, the methods that handle touches on the layer will be called (if they are there, of course).

2. In order to register when the user touches the layer, we need to create the ccTouchesBegan method. The following is the code involved:

```
- (void)ccTouchesBegan:(NSSet *)touches withEvent:(UIEvent *)event
{
  for( UITouch *touch in touches )
  {
    CGPoint location = [touch locationInView: [touch view]];

    location = [[CCDirector sharedDirector]
    convertToGL: location];

    [self setPlayerFiring:YES];
  }
}
```

The only part important for the task at hand is the last line, where we set the playerFiring variable to YES. While that value is true, the hero will fire bullets as fast as he can.

3. Now we need to tell the hero to stop firing. In order to do that we need to know when the player stopped touching the screen. That means, we need to use the ccTouchesEnded method:

```
- (void)ccTouchesEnded:(NSSet *)touches withEvent:(UIEvent *)event
{
  for( UITouch *touch in touches )
  {
    CGPoint location = [touch locationInView: [touch view]];

    location = [[CCDirector sharedDirector] convertToGL:
    location];

    [self setPlayerFiring:NO];
  }
}
```

Again, the only thing important for the game right now is setting the playerFiring variable to NO, to let the game know it has to stop firing bullets.

Let's make the corresponding changes to the GameLayer in order to allow the hero to shoot bullets.

Surfing through Scenes

4. Add the following lines to the `step` method of the `GameLayer` class:

```
-(void)step:(ccTime *)dt
{
  [hero update];

  for(Bullet * b in bullets)
  {
    if(b.fired)
    {
      [b update];
    }
    else
    {
      if(self.playerFiring && hero.lastTimeFired >
      hero.fireInterval)
      {
        [b fire:1 position:hero.mySprite.position
          fspeed:hero.firingSpeed];
        hero.lastTimeFired=0;
      }
    }
  }

  ...
  //enemy updating code
}
```

5. Finally, add the `update` method to the `Hero` class:

```
-(void)update
{
  self.lastTimeFired +=0.1;
}
```

6. Launch the game. Now, when you touch anywhere on the screen, you should see bullets going upwards from the hero's position, as shown in the following screenshot:

What just happened?

After all that work, we now have a moving, shooting hero. The last example showed how to handle the touching over layers. For doing that, we used the CCTouchesBegan and the CCtouchesEnded methods.

All four touches methods can handle multiple touches at once. That is why they receive an NSSet which you can travel to get all those touches. In the preceding examples we were doing that, although we weren't doing anything with them.

As for the firing logic, we added a little code to the step method. What it does is check whether this playerFiring ivar is true or false. If it is true, it makes a bullet get fired. Also we are checking when the hero last fired a bullet, so he does not fire a continuous stream of bullets. You can change the fireInterval of the hero, so he fires more (or less) bullets per second, turning him into a flying machinegun.

Detecting collisions

Great! Now we have a moving hero, enemies flying towards him, bullets flying everywhere, but nothing is happening! Enemies collide with the hero and they don't crash, bullets hit enemies and they don't get destroyed. "What is going on?", you may ask. Well, we need to do a little more work in order to get those done.

The first thing to do is to detect the collisions, and then act in response to them. We are going to have the following possible collisions for now:

- Hero collides with enemy
- Bullet fired by the hero collides with enemy
- Bullet fired by the enemy collides with hero.

Each of those collisions will have an outcome which we have to define. For example, when the bullet fired by the hero hits an enemy, both that bullet and said enemy must be removed from the screen, points must be summed up, and an explosion should be triggered. Except for the explosion, which we will analyze in Chapter 7, we will do all that now.

Time for action – shooting down your enemies

We need to know when a bullet is touching an enemy. In order to do that we need to check the intersection between the bullet's sprite and the enemy's sprite. If the rectangles defined by both of those sprites are intersecting, then we have a collision.

A simple way of achieving that is using the `CGRectIntersectsRect` method, which receives two CGRects and returns either `YES` or `NO` depending on whether those two CGRects are intersecting or not.

At first sight it seems easy to detect a collision between two rectangles, and it is. However, if you need more advanced collision detection, like when those rectangles are rotated or just detecting collisions between non-transparent pixels, then you will be in trouble. You can either use a Physics system to handle the collision detection or research the different algorithms for collision detection. Which method you use will depend on the game's particular needs.

1. The first step is to create a method that will return the CGRect of each sprite. Add the following method to the `GameLayer` class:

```
-(CGRect)myRect:(CCSprite *)sp
{
  CGRect rect = CGRectMake(sp.position.x-sp.textureRect.size.width/2,
      sp.position.y-sp.textureRect.size.height/2,sp.textureRect.size.width,
      sp.textureRect.size.height);
  return rect;
}
```

This method will return the CGRect of any given CCSprite that requests it.

Now that we can get the CGRects of each element, we must check if any of those collide.

2. Add the following lines to the `update` method of the `Bullet` class:

```
-(void)update
{
  switch (self.whoFired)
  {
    case 1:


      for(Enemy * s in theGame.enemies)
      {
        if(ccpDistance(self.mySprite.position,s.mySprite.position)
        <30)
        {
          if([self checkCollisions:[theGame myRect:s.mySprite]])
          {
            [s damage];
          }
        }
      }

     break;

       ...
  }

   ...
}
```

This will make each bullet check whether they are colliding with any enemy. If they do we call that enemy's damage method.

3. Add the `checkCollisions` method to the `Bullet` class:

```
-(BOOL)checkCollisions:(CGRect)r
{
  BOOL x = NO;

  if(CGRectIntersectsRect([theGame myRect:self.mySprite],r))
  {
    x=YES;
    [self reset];
  }

  return x;
}
```

4. The following is the damage method from the `Enemy` class that gets called if an enemy is hit:

```
-(void)damage
{
  self.hp--;
  [self.mySprite runAction:[CCSequence actions:
    [CCTintTo actionWithDuration:0.5 red:255 green:0 blue:0],
    [CCTintTo actionWithDuration:0.5 red:255 green:255
    blue:255],nil ]];
  if(hp<=0)
    [self destroy];
}
```

5. Finally, add the `destroy` method to the `Enemy` class. It will be called when an enemies hp is down to 0:

```
-(void)destroy
{
  [self reset];
  [theGame setScore:theGame.score+100];
  NSLog(@"%d",theGame.score);
}
```

6. Run the game now. Try shooting at enemies. If everything went well, they should flash red when hit and disappear when their hp is 0, as shown in the following screenshot:

Chapter 5

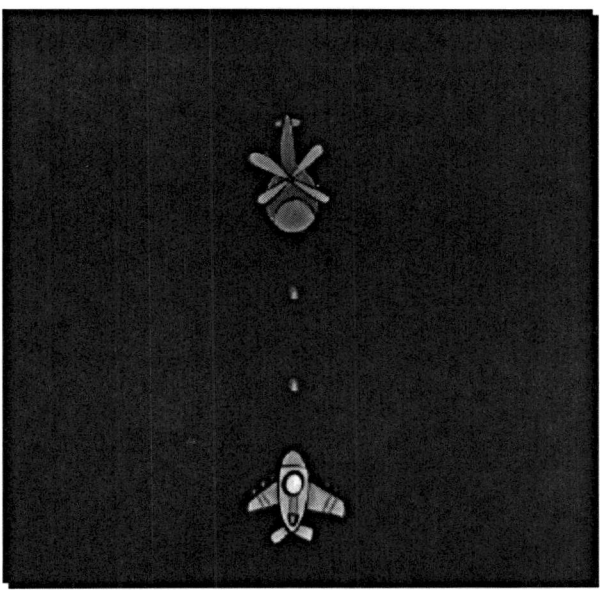

What just happened?

After inserting this new code, your bullets and enemies were able to interact with each other. For doing that, we created a method that returns a CGRect that represents the boundaries of those objects at any time. Every time we call the update method of the Bullet objects, they check if they are close enough to any of the Enemy objects. If they are, then we call the checkCollision method that checks the intersection between those two seemingly colliding objects.

Once the checkCollision returns YES, we are sure that the objects are colliding and we can act accordingly. In this case when a bullet hits an enemy, we subtract a point from its hp ivar and play an action. When hit many times and the hp reaches 0, the enemy is destroyed (removed from screen and reset).

Surfing through Scenes

Time for action – losing your life

We have to create a couple of more collisions and their responses. Those would be when a bullet hits the hero and when an enemy touches the hero, but cases make the player lose a life, the hero disappear and then reappear. We are going to do the same thing as before, but this time the response to the collision will be different. Let's get this done now.

1. Begin by making some changes to the `Hero` class. Add the following lines of code to it:

```
-(void)update
{
 self.lastTimeFired +=0.1;
 
 for(Enemy * s in theGame.enemies)
 {
 if(ccpDistance(self.mySprite.position,s.mySprite.position) <30)
 {
  //CGRect rect =  CGRectMake(s.mySprite.position.x-
    s.mySprite.textureRect.size.width/2,s.mySprite.position.y-
    s.mySprite.textureRect.size.height/2,s.mySprite.textureRect.
    size.width,  s.mySprite.textureRect.size.height);
    
   if([self checkCollisions:[theGame myRect:s.mySprite]])
   {
    [s reset];
    [self destroy];
   }
  }
 }
}

-(BOOL)checkCollisions:(CGRect)tam
{
   BOOL x = NO;
   
   if(CGRectIntersectsRect([theGame myRect:self.mySprite],tam))
   {
     x=YES;
   }
   
   }
```

```
    return x;
}
```

By adding that, the Hero is now aware of the surrounding enemies and it can check if it is colliding with any of them.

2. Also add these two other methods to the `Hero` class:

```
-(void)destroy
{
  //EXPLODE
  if(!self.reviving)
  {
    self.reviving = YES;
    [self.mySprite setPosition:ccp(160,-200)];
    [self.mySprite runAction:[CCSequence actions:[CCDelayTime
      actionWithDuration:1],
    [CCEaseOut actionWithAction:[CCMoveTo actionWithDuration:1
      position:ccp(160,50)] rate:5],
    [CCCallFunc actionWithTarget:self selector:@
    selector(finishReviving)], nil]];

    [theGame loseLive];
  }

}

-(void)finishReviving
{
  self.reviving = NO;
}
```

These two methods handle what happens when the collision between the hero and any enemy is detected.

3. Move to the Bullet class and modify the update method to look like this:

```
-(void)update
{
  switch (self.whoFired)
  {
    case 1:
    [self.mySprite
      setPosition:ccp(self.mySprite.position.x,self.mySprite.
      position.y + self.firingSpeed)];
```

```
        for(Enemy * s in theGame.enemies)
        {
         if(ccpDistance(self.mySprite.position,s.mySprite.position)
         <30)
         {
          if([self checkCollisions:[theGame myRect:s.mySprite]])
          {
            [s damage];
          }
         }
       }

      break;

        case 2:
        [self.mySprite
          setPosition:ccp(self.mySprite.position.x,self.mySprite.
          position.y + self.firingSpeed)];

        if(ccpDistance(self.mySprite.position,
          theGame.hero.mySprite.position) < 30)
        {
          if([self checkCollisions:[theGame myRect:theGame.hero.
          mySprite]])
          {
             [theGame.hero destroy];
          }
        }


      break;
      }

      if(self.mySprite.position.y >500 || self.mySprite.position.y
      <-20)
      {
         [self reset];
      }
   }
```

That will check for a collision between the hero and the bullets fired by enemies.

4. When the hero is hit, we call the GameLayer's `loseLife` method, and add it:

   ```
   -(void)loseLife
   {
     self.lives--;

     if(self.lives ==0)
     {
       //LOSE THE GAME
       //GO TO GAME OVER LAYER
     }
   }
   ```

5. Run the game now. Try getting hit by a bullet shot from an enemy and by enemies themselves. When one of those collisions is triggered you should see the hero disappear and reappear a moment later as shown in the following screenshot:

What just happened?

Just as we made the bullets collide with enemies, we made them collide with the hero. We check whether it is close to the surrounding objects, then, if it is, we check their boundaries and if they are intersecting, we act accordingly. In the case of the hero, we make it go away and then run an action to make it return to the screen gracefully.

When the hero is hit, we call the `loseLife` method, which takes a life from the player, but nothing else happens. We will fix this when we make a Game Over screen.

That's all we would need to do for now regarding collisions. Now that we have something like a game set up, let's begin doing some new stuff.

Adding more layers to scenes

As we have discussed before, a scene can contain any number of layers you want. Well, as long as performance is not an issue. As `CCLayer` inherits from `CCNode`, it can be added as the child of `CCScenes` or other CCLayers, allowing you to organize your content in a nice fashion.

There are three types of CCLayers that you can use and combine in your games. They are as follows:

- `CCLayer`: We have been using them forever. Besides all the features inherited from `CCNodes`, they can receive touches and accelerometer input.
- `CCColorLayer`: They inherit from `CCLayer` so besides being able to receive touches and accelerometer input, their opacity and RGB colors can be changed.
- `CCMultiplexLayer`: It inherits from `CCLayer` and can have many children, but only one will be active at any given time. You can switch between those children.

In the following examples, we will be creating some CCLayers in different ways to achieve different results.

Time for action – creating a HUD to display lives and the score

We will begin by building a simple Heads Up Display (HUD) for our game. Its purpose is to show some useful data about the current state of the game to the player. The idea behind making the HUD into a new layer is to simplify the logic of the GameLayer. This way, the GameLayer will only handle stuff of the game itself while leaving the HUD logic to the HUDLayer.

In our game, the HUD will display the remaining lives, score, remaining bombs, and anything you want to display later. Once it is done, all we need to do in the GameLayer is send a message so the HUDLayer gets updated.

1. The first step in creating the HUD is to add a new file to the project. In the Xcode project, select **File | New file** and add a new **Objective-C** class. Rename it as `HUDLayer`.

2. Replace the contents of the `HudLayer.h` with the following lines:

   ```
   #import <Foundation/Foundation.h>
   #import "cocos2d.h"
   ```

```
#import "GameScene.h"
@interface HudLayer : CCLayer
{

  CCBitmapFontAtlas * level;
  CCBitmapFontAtlas * score;
  CCBitmapFontAtlas * bombs;
  NSMutableArray * lives;
}

@property (nonatomic,retain) CCBitmapFontAtlas * level;
@property (nonatomic,retain) CCBitmapFontAtlas * score;
@property (nonatomic,retain) CCBitmapFontAtlas * bombs;
@property (nonatomic,retain) NSMutableArray * lives;

@end
```

3. Do the same with the contents of the HudLayer.m file:

```
#import "HudLayer.h"

@implementation HudLayer

@synthesize lives,bombs,score,level;

- (id) init
{
  if ((self = [super init])) {

  CCSprite * background = [CCSprite spriteWithFile:@
  "hud_background.png"];
  [background setPosition:ccp(160,455)];
  [self addChild:background];

  lives = [[NSMutableArray arrayWithCapacity:3]retain];
  for(int i=0;i<3;i++)
  {
    CCSprite * life = [CCSprite spriteWithFile:@"hud_life.png"];
    [life setPosition:ccp(18+ 28*i,465)];
    [self addChild:life];
    [lives addObject:life];
  }

  CCSprite * bomb = [CCSprite spriteWithFile:@"hud_bomb.png"];
  [bomb setPosition:ccp(18,445)];
```

```
    [self addChild:bomb];
    
    GameLayer * gl = (GameLayer *)[self.parent
      getChildByTag:KGameLayer];
    
    level = [CCBitmapFontAtlas bitmapFontAtlasWithString:@"Level 1"
       fntFile:@"hud_font.fnt"];
    [level setAnchorPoint:ccp(1,0.5)];
    [level setPosition:ccp(310,465)];
    [level setColor:ccBLACK];
    [self addChild:level];
    
    score = [CCBitmapFontAtlas bitmapFontAtlasWithString:@"Score 0"
       fntFile:@"hud_font.fnt"];
    [score setAnchorPoint:ccp(1,0.5)];
    [score setPosition:ccp(310,445)];
    [score setColor:ccBLACK];
    [self addChild:score];
    
    bombs = [CCBitmapFontAtlas bitmapFontAtlasWithString:@"X3"
       fntFile:@"hud_font.fnt"];
    [bombs setAnchorPoint:ccp(1,0.5)];
    [bombs setPosition:ccp(47,440)];
    [bombs setColor:ccBLACK];
    [self addChild:bombs];
    
    }
    return self;
}

- (void) dealloc
{
    [super dealloc];
    [lives release];
}
@end
```

You can find the images and the font used above in the Chapter 5 companion files.

4. What we have to do now is load this new layer and add it as a child of the GameScene. Change the `init` method of the GameScene class to look like the following:

```
- (id) init
{
```

```
    self = [super init];
    if (self != nil)
    {

        [self addChild:[GameLayer node] z:0 tag:KGameLayer];
        //kGameLayer defined in the GameScene.h file.
        #define kGameLayer 1
        [self addChild:[HudLayer node] z:1 tag:KHudLayer];
        //kHudLayer defined in the GameScene.h file. #define
        kHudLayer 2

    }
    return self;
}
```

The only thing missing now is to make some changes here and there to be able to update the HUDLayer with the actual state of the game. Let's update the score and remaining lives, for now.

5. Change the `loseLife` method of the `GameLayer` class:

```
-(void)loseLife
{
    self.lives--;

    HudLayer * hl = (HudLayer *)[self.parent
    getChildByTag:KHudLayer];
    CCSprite * live = [hl.lives objectAtIndex:self.lives];
    [live setVisible:NO];

    if(self.lives ==0)
    {
        [self resetGame];

        //LOSE THE GAME
        //GO TO GAME OVER LAYER
    }
}
```

6. Add the `resetGame` method:

```
-(void)resetGame
{
    HudLayer * hl = (HudLayer *)[self.parent
    getChildByTag:KHudLayer];
    for(CCSprite * c in hl.lives)
```

```
      {
         [c setVisible:YES];
      }
      self.level=1;
      [hl.level setString:@"Level 1"];
      self.score=0;
      [hl.score setString:@"Score 0"];
      self.bombs =3;
      [hl.bombs setString:@"X3"];
      lives = STARTING_LIVES;
   }
```

   These methods will handle the displaying of the remaining lives.

7. Finally, modify the `Enemy` class's `destroy` method, so it updates the score label instead of logging the score to the console:

```
-(void)destroy
{
   [self reset];
   [theGame setScore:theGame.score+100];
   HudLayer * hl = (HudLayer *)[theGame.parent
      getChildByTag:KHudLayer];
   [hl.score setString:[NSString stringWithFormat:@"Score
      %d",theGame.score]];
}
```

8. Run the game. You should see a HUD at the top of the screen (as shown in the following screenshot) with all the actual information about the state of the game. Destroy some enemies to see the score updated and lose some lives to see the "lives" icons disappear.

Chapter 5

What just happened?

We just went through the steps needed to create a new layer, adding it to the scene and updating its contents.

Our new layer just holds some information of the game state and displays it to the player. In order to achieve that we just added a few CCSprites and `CCBitmapFontAtlases` which get updated when needed.

Once the `HudLayer` class was created we added it to the GameScene over the GameLayer, so its contents are always shown on top of the GameLayer's ones. We also provided a tag for both layers, as we will need to access them from other places. We could also have added a reference to the other layer inside them.

That is all what we need to do in order to add more layers to a scene. The rest of the code just handles the updating of the contents of the `HudLayer`. When the player hits an enemy, a score is awarded. Then the label placed in the HUD is updated like we have already seen in previous chapters.

Surfing through Scenes

When the hero is hit and a life is lost, we just turn the corresponding icon's visibility off, then when the game is reset we turn all of them on.

Have a go hero – creating a Game Over screen

I will let you put into practise what you have just learnt.

Our game needs a Game Over screen. It should be a new layer that appears when the lives variable reaches 0. Right now we are just resetting the corresponding variables, but a proper way to do this would be as follows:

- When lives reaches 0, stop updating the game elements, just unschedule the `step` method.
- Create and add to the scene a `GameoverLayer` which could have anything you want to display. Maybe a background image, the final score, and a tap to restart message.
- When the layer is tapped, remove it from the scene. Call the `resetGame` method from the `GameLayer`, and re-schedule the `step` method.

Once you have that working you can later display high scores, add a menu to go to the main menu screen, or anything else you can think of!

Time for action – creating a pause menu

Now we will see how to create a `CCColorLayer` and use it to display a pause screen. Along with that I will teach you a way to actually pause the game. So when you press the pause button, or press the lock button, or receive a call, the elements of the game stop moving and then when you wish to, gameplay is resumed.

Actually, the template already created some helpful code for handling the pausing, when the game stops/resumes activity. Check the `AerialGunAppDelegate`, and you will find the following two methods:

```
-(void) applicationWillResignActive:(UIApplication *)application
{
   [[CCDirector sharedDirector] pause];
}

- (void)applicationDidBecomeActive:(UIApplication *)application
{
   [[CCDirector sharedDirector] resume];
}
```

Chapter 5

If you run the game and press the lock button, then unlock the screen, your game keeps playing. Although execution was really paused while you left, the game is resumed abruptly. So we should have the game still paused when you unlock the screen and give a chance to the player to resume it when he is ready.

Pausing the CCDirector stops all movement in your game and sets the fps to four, so very little battery is consumed. The drawback of doing this is that you are not able to show any custom screen while you are in this state. If you want to just call the CCDirector's `pause` method, you should show a UIAlert, for example, with a resume button that calls the CCDirector's `resume` method when touched. That's easy, but looks pretty awful for a game you spent so much time designing a nice coherent UI for.

Don't worry; there is another way to solve this! Let me guide you through the process of making a custom pause screen now.

1. First, create the `PauseLayer` class, which should inherit from `CCColorLayer`. The following is the `PauseLayer.h` contents:

    ```
    #import <Foundation/Foundation.h>
    #import "cocos2d.h"
    #import "GameScene.h"

    @interface PauseLayer : CCColorLayer {

    }

    @end
    ```

2. Now replace the contents of the `PauseLayer.m` with the following lines:

    ```
    #import "PauseLayer.h"

    @implementation PauseLayer


    - (id) initWithColor:(ccColor4B)color
    {
      if ((self = [super initWithColor:color]))
      {

        self.isTouchEnabled=YES;

        CCSprite * paused = [CCSprite spriteWithFile:@"paused.png"];
        [paused setPosition:ccp(160,240)];
        [self addChild:paused];
    ```

[199]

Surfing through Scenes

```
   }
   return self;
}

- (void)ccTouchesBegan:(NSSet *)touches withEvent:(UIEvent *)event
{
   for( UITouch *touch in touches )
   {
      CGPoint location = [touch locationInView: [touch view]];

      location = [[CCDirector sharedDirector] convertToGL:
      location];

      GameLayer * gl = (GameLayer *)[self.parent
      getChildByTag:KGameLayer];
      [gl resume];
      [self.parent removeChild:self cleanup:YES];
   }
}
- (void) dealloc
{
   [super dealloc];
}
@end
```

Remember to add the paused.png image to the project, which can be found in the *Chapter 5* companion files.

3. Let's first handle the manual pausing. For now, we will pause the game when the player touches the HUD bar, at the top. Add the ccTouchesBegan method to the HudLayer to handle that, as follows:

```
- (void)ccTouchesBegan:(NSSet *)touches withEvent:(UIEvent *)event
{
  GameLayer * gl = (GameLayer *)[self.parent getChildByTag:KGameLayer];

   for( UITouch *touch in touches )
   {
      CGPoint location = [touch locationInView: [touch view]];

      location = [[CCDirector sharedDirector] convertToGL:
      location];
```

[200]

```
      if(location.y>400)
      {
        [gl pauseGame];
      }
    }
  }
}
```

From now on, when you touch over there, the GameLayer's `pauseGame` method will be called. Let's check what that method does.

4. Add the following methods to the `GameLayer` class:

```
-(void)pauseGame
{
  ccColor4B c = {100,100,0,100};
  PauseLayer * p = [[[PauseLayer alloc]initWithColor:c] autorelease];
  [self.parent addChild:p z:10];
  [self onExit];
}
```

The preceding method will be called when we decide to pause the game. It will create a new PauseLayer, add it to the GameScene, and place it on top of the GameLayer.

```
- (void) resume
{
  if(![AerialGunAppDelegate get].paused)
  {
    return;
  }
  [AerialGunAppDelegate get].paused =NO;
  [self onEnter];
}
```

The Resume method will be called when the player dismisses the PauseLayer.

```
- (void) onExit
{
  if(![AerialGunAppDelegate get].paused)
  {
    [AerialGunAppDelegate get].paused = YES;
    [super onExit];
  }
}

- (void) onEnter
{
```

```
    if(![AerialGunAppDelegate get].paused )
    {
      [super onEnter];
    }
}
```

These are the two methods that do the magic of stopping and resuming the execution of that layer and its contents.

5. As you can see, we are calling a method on the `AppDelegate` and retrieving one of its variables, so we need to add those to the `AerialGunAppDelegate`:

```
+(AerialGunAppDelegate *) get
{

  return (AerialGunAppDelegate *) [[UIApplication
  sharedApplication] delegate];
}
```

That method will allow you to reach the `AppDelegate` from anywhere. We can use that to hold some "global" variables, such as whether the game is paused, or sounds that should be loaded and be available from the beginning of the execution.

6. Add the paused `Bool` variable to the `AerialGunAppDelegate` class.

7. Run the game now and touch the top portion of the screen. You should see a yellowish layer appear on top and the game getting paused below. When you want to resume gameplay, just touch the screen again. This is shown in the following screenshot:

What just happened?

Well, we just did a lot of things. Let's go over them one at a time, starting with the actual `PauseLayer` code.

Take a look at the `PauseLayer.h` file. It has just a few lines of code, but there is a difference there when compared to the previous layers we have made. The difference is that it inherits from CCColorLayer instead.

`CCColorLayer` allows you to set a color and opacity to it, so it is ideal for overlaying it on another layer. You could use it to show some kind of modal alert, hints, and varied information. Also, doing this takes practically no memory compared to using a full screen background image.

The code inside this new class should not be new to you. It just overrides the CCColorLayer's `initWithColor` method, so when initialized an image is placed in the middle. Then the `ccTouchesBegan` makes the layer be removed from its parent when touched, and calls the GameLayer's `resumeGame` method, which we will analyze in a moment.

The `pauseGame` method instantiates a new `PauseLayer` object with a color of our liking. The interesting part here is the call to the layer's `onExit` method, which we are overriding below. So if the game is not already paused, we pause it and call the `onExit` method of the layer's super class.

If you remember well, `onEnter` and `onExit` methods are called when a `CCNode` enters and leaves the stage respectively. Well, here we are calling them directly when pausing and resuming the game. Why do that? We do that because when a CCLayer's `onExit` method is called, it stops the layer from receiving touches and accelerometer events. Also its super class's `onExit` is called (CCNode), which in turn deactivates timers of that layer and its children.

When we call the `resumeGame` method we do the opposite, which is calling the layer's `onEnter` method.

If you receive a call or lock the screen and then return to the game, you will notice that it is not working as expected; we are still resuming the game instantly without letting the player get ready. Let's solve that little issue.

Time for action – pausing the game while inactive

In the previous part, we created a pause layer and had it shown when you touched a part of the screen. We now have to have it shown when the game stops playing by an external event like a call. We have almost everything done, so this should be quick to implement. We just have to work a little with the `AppDelegate`.

In order to make the game be still paused after returning from a call, just replace the contents of the `applicationWillResignActive` method with the following:

```
-(void) applicationWillResignActive:(UIApplication *)application
{
  CCScene * current = [[CCDirector sharedDirector] runningScene];
  if([current isKindOfClass:[GameScene class]])
  {
    if(![AerialGunAppDelegate get].paused)
    {
      GameLayer * layer = (GameLayer *)[current
      getChildByTag:KGameLayer];
      [layer pauseGame];
    }
  }
  [[CCDirector sharedDirector] pause];
}
```

That's all! Run the game now, press the lock button, unlock the screen, and you should see the same PauseLayer as when you touched the screen.

What just happened?

The preceding code calls the layer's `pauseGame` when the application is about to stop being active, just as we did when we paused the game by touching the screen.

There is a little noticeable difference here that is we are using the CDirector's `runningScene` method that gives us the scene that is currently running. Why do we do this? For starters, we need to know which scene is running, so we call the `pauseGame` method on the correct layer.

For this game, it makes no sense adding the PauseLayer in the main menu or splash screen. We just need to show it during the actual gameplay, so, that is why before doing all that we check whether we are running the GameScene.

One more thing; just as I placed a single image on the PauseLayer, you can do whatever you want. You are free to add menus, run actions on the PauseLayer's elements, and so on.

Pop quiz – scenes and layers

1. Which one of the following is not a touch handling method?
   a. `ccTouchesBegan`
   b. `ccTouchesEnded`
   c. `ccTouchesDragged`
   d. `ccTouchesMoved`
   e. `ccTouchesCancelled`

2. Which one of the following statements is false about CCLayers?
   a. There are three types of `CCLayer`: `CCLayer`, `CCColorLayer`, `CCMultiplexLayer`
   b. `CCLayers` add the ability to handle touches and accelerometer input
   c. You can have just one `CCLayer` per scene

3. Which one of the following statements is true about `CCScenes`?
   a. You can have more than one scene running at the same time
   b. The only thing you can add as a child to a scene is a `CCLayer`
   c. You can transition through different scenes using transition classes, such as `CCFadeTransition`

Summary

This chapter is officially over! We really made a lot of advancements here, as follows:

- We started a new game, a vertical-shooter action game; no more, no less
- You learnt how to create new scenes and use transitions for going from one to another
- You learnt how to receive touches and accelerometer input on your layers
- We used several layers in a single scene
- You learnt how to pause your game and show a custom screen.

In the next chapter, you will finally learn how to make menus. We will make the main menu screen, an option menu with texts, images, and all kinds of buttons. We will also see how to animate them. Finally, we will take a look at how to save some preferences in order to persist the chosen options.

6
Menu Design

Menus are a necessary thing in every game, whether it is just a couple of buttons or a more complex hierarchy of option screens.

Cocos2d makes it easy to make menus and assign behaviors to them, so you will be using them in no time.

In this chapter you shall:

- Go over the different configurations of menus
- Implement all the possible menu items
- Learn how to animate menu items
- Create an options menu
- Save the selected preferences

Are you ready to begin working?

Creating a simple menu

In order to create menus you are going to use the `CCMenu` menu class. This class is a subclass of `CCLayer` and provides a way to change its color and opacity. Its main purpose is to attach CCMenuItems to it.

These CCMenuItems are the actual buttons of a menu and they come in many flavors, which are as follows:

- `CCMenuItemLabel`: **Creates a menu item from any kind of label**

Menu Design

- `CCMenuItemSprite`: Creates a menu item from a sprite
- `CCMenuItemImage`: Creates a menu item from an image
- `CCMenuItemToogle`: Creates a menu item that can toggle between the items it contains, which can be any CCMenuItem

You also have the possibility of creating your own CCMenuItems by subclassing this class when you feel the need to do so.

CCMenuItems have a few useful properties to let you know if they are enabled or not, or if they were selected. Also, being made from CCNodes allows you to control their position, opacity, color, and anything that you could with CCNodes.

`CCMenu` provides some methods to allow you to initialize them using an array of these CCMenuItems, or you can add them to the menu at runtime. Also you can tell a `CCMenu` to align its menu items automatically in rows/columns or vertically/horizontally with some padding. Of course, you are free to manually set the positions at any time.

Throughout this chapter, we will see how to do all the stuff described earlier and even more while we enhance our current game.

Time for action – adding a menu with texts to the main scene

We will start by making a very simple menu for the main menu. If you remember well, we already made this scene at the beginning of the previous chapter. Although, we left it blank and skipped over it so we could focus on the game itself. Well, now we are going to go back to this scene and we are going to complete it this time.

What we want to accomplish here is to have this scene present the player with a menu from which he can choose some options. In this case he will be able to choose from: Starting a new game, going to the options menu, and going to the "About" screen.

1. Placing menus is quite tedious, if you want them to be positioned correctly. So let's make the main menu our first scene so we can see what we are doing quickly. In order to do that we have to tell the `CCDirector` to start running with the `MainMenuScene` instead of the `GameScene`. Change the corresponding line in the `AerialGunAppDelegate` to the following:

   `[[CCDirector sharedDirector] runWithScene:[MainMenuScene node]];`

   You should now see an empty screen when running the game. That is our MainMenuScene. Let's fill it up.

2. Let's add a background image to the main menu screen and, of course, a menu. Add the following code to the init method of the MainMenuLayer class:

```
- (id) init
{
 if ((self = [super init]))
 {

    isTouchEnabled = YES;

    CCSprite * background = 
    [CCSprite spriteWithFile:@"menuBackground.png"];
    [background setPosition:ccp(160,240)];
    [self addChild:background];

    CCBitmapFontAtlas * newgameLabel = [CCBitmapFontAtlas 
       bitmapFontAtlasWithString:@"NEW GAME" fntFile:@"hud_font.
       fnt"];
    CCBitmapFontAtlas * optionsLabel = [CCBitmapFontAtlas 
       bitmapFontAtlasWithString:@"OPTIONS" fntFile:@"hud_font.fnt"];
    CCBitmapFontAtlas * aboutLabel = [CCBitmapFontAtlas 
       bitmapFontAtlasWithString:@"ABOUT" fntFile:@"hud_font.fnt"];

    [newgameLabel setColor:ccRED];
    [optionsLabel setColor:ccRED];
    [aboutLabel setColor:ccRED];

    CCMenuItemLabel * newgame = [CCMenuItemLabel 
    itemWithLabel:newgameLabel target:self selector:
    @selector(newGame:)];
    CCMenuItemLabel * options = [CCMenuItemLabel 
    itemWithLabel:optionsLabel target:self selector:
    @selector(options:)];
    CCMenuItemLabel * about = [CCMenuItemLabel 
    itemWithLabel:aboutLabel target:self selector:
    @selector(about:)];

    CCMenu * menu = [CCMenu menuWithItems:newgame,options, 
    about,nil];
    [menu alignItemsVerticallyWithPadding:5];
    [self addChild:menu];
    [menu setPosition:ccp(240,120)];

 }
 return self;
}
```

Menu Design

The preceding code adds a background sprite and then creates a couple of menu items which get added to the CCMenu. Each menu item calls a different method when pressed. We now have to implement those.

3. Create the methods that get called when a menu item is touched:

```
-(void)newGame:(id)sender
{
   GameScene * gs = [GameScene node];
   [[CCDirector sharedDirector] replaceScene:gs];
}
-(void)options:(id)sender
{

}
-(void)about:(id)sender
{

}
```

> Even if for the time being the options and about method don't do anything, you must have them defined. If they are not there, when the application runs, it will crash.

4. Run the game. Now you should see the main menu loaded when the application starts. It should have the new background and the menu. If you touch the **New Game** option, the game begins, as shown in the following screenshot:

What just happened?

We have just created the first menu of the game. Let's go over the creation of the `MainMenuScene`.

The first part should be simple to understand by now. We are creating and adding a sprite for the background and initializing three labels from the same font that we use for the HUD text. Since that font has a white color, we change its color to red.

Instead of adding those labels as children of the layer, we use them to create a `CCMenuItemLabel`, which is a menu item made from a label, as the name implies.

```
CCMenuItemLabel * newgame = [CCMenuItemLabel
itemWithLabel:newgameLabel target:self selector:@selector(newGame:)];
```

The preceding line is what gets the job done. The convenience constructor for the `CCMenuItemLabel` takes as parameters the wanted label, the target (which class is responsible for handling the touch event), and the method that should be invoked when the item is touched.

Once we have all the CCMenuItemLabels we want in a menu, we initialize a `CCMenu` with those items, position that menu, and add it as a child of the layer.

You can manually place menu items by changing each one's position, or use some `CCMenu` methods to automatically align them.

In this case, we are using the CCMenu's `alignItemsVerticallyWithPadding` method, which aligns the items one over the other with the desired padding (separation).

In order for all this to work, we must create the methods that will be called when the menu items are touched.

Have a go hero – moving CCMenuItems around

Try playing a little with the position of the menu items; you can do one of the following things:

- Remove the CCmenu's method that aligns the items and instead place each one yourself by setting their positions. If you do it this way, you should place the menu at position (0,0).
- Try aligning them horizontally with the following CCMenu's method:

    `alignItemsHorizontallyWithPadding:`
- Align them in rows or columns with the corresponding CCMenu's methods.

Menu Design

Using image menu items

We will now take a look at how to use images for your menu items. You can do that by using one of the following `CCMenuItem` variants:

- `CCMenuItemSprite`: This makes a menu item from an existing sprite
- `CCMenuItemImage`: This makes a menu item from an image file you want

Both CCMenuItems accept an image for each state (normal, selected, and disabled) and you should try to have all three of them of the same size, so the item looks ok when it is touched and it does not look like it is moving around.

Adding this kind of CCMenuItems is as simple as what we did before. We just need to create the instances of each item and add them to the menu, and then display the menu.

Time for action – adding a difficulty selection screen

Let's create a simple layer that asks the player to select a difficulty level. He will be able to choose from easy, normal, and extreme, where the last option will be disabled. We will show this layer when the player selects "New game" from the main menu and it will show a menu with those three menu items.

When one of them is touched, we will pass the selected difficulty to the `GameScene` which in turn will pass the value to the `GameLayer` to adjust the difficulty level. You may do this in other ways like storing the selected value in a variable in the `AppDelegate` or saving this to the user preferences. I will do it by passing the values around scenes and layers so I can show you how to do that. However, you are free to do it the way you want or you feel is the cleanest way.

We won't be creating a new class for this layer because it is very simple. We will just create an instance of `CCColorLayer` at runtime, add the needed buttons, and set their behaviors. Let's get this done.

1. The first thing to do is to create the method that will create the layer with the menu. We will do all this in the `MainMenuLayer` class:

    ```
    -(void)showDifficultySelection
    {
      ccColor4B c = {0,0,0,180};
      CCColorLayer * difficulty = [CCColorLayer layerWithColor:c];
      [self addChild:difficulty];

      CCMenuItemImage * easyBtn = [CCMenuItemImage
        itemFromNormalImage:@"easy.png"
    ```

```
      selectedImage:@"easy_dwn.png"
      disabledImage:@"easy_dis.png"
         target:self

  selector:@selector(selectMode:)];

  CCMenuItemImage * normalBtn = [CCMenuItemImage
    itemFromNormalImage:@"normal.png"
      selectedImage:@"normal_dwn.png"
      disabledImage:@"normal_dis.png"
         target:self

  selector:@selector(selectMode:)];

  CCMenuItemImage * extremeBtn = [CCMenuItemImage
    itemFromNormalImage:@"extreme.png"
      selectedImage:@"extreme_dwn.png"
      disabledImage:@"extreme_dis.png"
         target:self

  selector:@selector(selectMode:)];

  [extremeBtn setIsEnabled:NO];

  [easyBtn setTag:1];
  [normalBtn setTag:2];
  [extremeBtn setTag:3];

  CCMenu * dMenu = [CCMenu menuWithItems:easyBtn,normalBtn,
  extremeBtn,nil];
  [dMenu alignItemsVerticallyWithPadding:10];
  [difficulty addChild:dMenu];
}
```

2. Now we have to call this new method instead of moving away to the next scene directly. Change the `newGame` method to do that:

```
-(void)newGame:(id)sender
{
  [self showDifficultySelection];
}
```

Menu Design

3. When any of the CCMenuItems are touched we call the `selectMode` method, as follows:

```
-(void)selectMode:(CCMenuItemImage *)btn
{
  int mode = btn.tag;
  GameScene * gs = [[[GameScene
     alloc]initWithDifficulty:mode]autorelease];
  [[CCDirector sharedDirector]replaceScene:gs];

}
```

4. Since now we are initializing the `GameScene` with a parameter, we must change its `init` method to reflect that. Open the `GameScene.m` file and make the following changes:

```
- (id) initWithDifficulty:(int)mode
{
  self = [super init];
  if (self != nil)
  {

    GameLayer * gameLayer = [[[GameLayer
       alloc]initWithDifficulty:mode]autorelease];
    [self addChild:gameLayer z:0 tag:KGameLayer];
    [self addChild:[HudLayer node] z:1 tag:KHudLayer];

  }
  return self;
}
```

5. We must change the GameLayer's `init` method to receive the same parameter we passed to the `gameScene`, so let's do that:

```
-(id) initWithDifficulty:(int)mode
{
  if( (self=[super init] ))
  {

    self.difficulty = mode;

    //Rest of the code

  }
  return self;
}
```

Also add the difficulty property to the GameLayer class. We will use this int value to modify the speed of enemies.

6. All we have to do now is use this new difficulty variable to modify some things in our game. In the GameLayer's `initWithDifficulty` method, change the `enemyInterval` variable from 20 to 20/self.difficulty.

7. In the enemy's `init` method, change each type of enemy's movementSpeed by multiplying the actual value and the Game.difficulty.

   What we are doing here is affecting the variables by multiplying them by the difficulty value, which in easy mode is 1. So they remain like they are in the original version, but when we select normal mode those values get doubled up, making the enemies faster.

8. Run the game. When you select "New game", you should see a new layer appear with the buttons we created. The extreme menu item should be greyed out to show it is disabled (locked). Try selecting both available modes to see the difference in the gameplay difficulty. This is shown in the following screenshot:

Menu Design

What just happened?

Creating a menu with images is as easy as doing it with labels.

All you have to do is to provide each item with the needed images for each state. Also as with any other `CCMenuItem`, we must provide the method which will be called and the target (the class responsible for calling said method).

We also have a couple of new things. First, the usage of the CCMenuItem's tag property.

Instead of having each menu item call a different method, we are making them call the same one and figuring out which one was pressed by their tags. We assigned each `CCMenuItem` with a different tag value and passed a reference of the menu item touched to the `selectMode` method. This method uses that tag to set the difficulty level. You can do this with any `CCMenuItem`, not just `CCMenuItemImages`.

The other new stuff here is the disabling of CCMenuItems. Here we added the extremeBtn menu item which we disable by calling the `setIsEnabled:NO` method. Doing that prevents the menu item from receiving any touches and also makes it display the disabled image we provided for it.

The rest of the code just takes the difficulty value passed around and uses it to modify the speed of the enemies.

Animating menu items

`CCMenuItem` and `CCMenu` are subclasses of `CCNode`, so guess what? You can do whatever you would do with CCNodes. You can control their opacity, position, rotation, tint, and a lot more; and of course, you can run actions on them to animate them. Let's take a look at a simple example.

Time for action – animating the main menu

What we'll do now to demonstrate the ability of the CCMenuItems to be animated, is run some actions on the Main menu's items. We'll have them appear from outside the screen and then scale up and down forever.

All you have to do is, in the MainMenuLayer's `init` method, change the position of the `CCMenu` to be outside of the screen to the right. Place it at coordinates (480,120).

Then, just add the following lines of code after that:

```
[newgame runAction:[CCSequence actions:
    [CCEaseOut actionWithAction:[CCMoveBy actionWithDuration:1
        position:ccp(-240,0)]   rate:2],
```

```
[CCRepeat actionWithAction:[CCSequence actions:
   [CCScaleTo actionWithDuration:1 scale:1.3],
[CCScaleTo actionWithDuration:1 scale:1],nil] times:9000], nil]];
[options runAction:[CCSequence actions:
[CCDelayTime actionWithDuration:0.5],
 [CCEaseOut actionWithAction:[CCMoveBy actionWithDuration:1
   position:ccp(-240,0)] rate:2],
[CCRepeat actionWithAction:[CCSequence actions:
   [CCScaleTo actionWithDuration:1 scale:1.3],
[CCScaleTo actionWithDuration:1 scale:1],nil] times:9000], nil]];
 [about runAction:[CCSequence actions:
 [CCDelayTime actionWithDuration:1],[CCEaseOut actionWithAction:
   [CCMoveBy actionWithDuration:1 position:ccp(-240,0)]  rate:2],
[CCRepeat actionWithAction:[CCSequence actions:
  [CCScaleTo actionWithDuration:1 scale:1.3],
   [CCScaleTo actionWithDuration:1 scale:1],nil] times:9000],
   nil]];
```

 Notice that we are using a CCRepeat action with a really high value for the times parameter. That is because Cocos2d does not allow us to place a CCRepeatForever action inside a CCSequence action. That can be solved using a very high value for the times parameter. No one is going to spend so much time in this scene to allow the CCRepeat action to end!

That's it. Run the game now, and you should see each CCMenuItem entering the screen one at a time and then start scaling up and down. This is shown in the following screenshot:

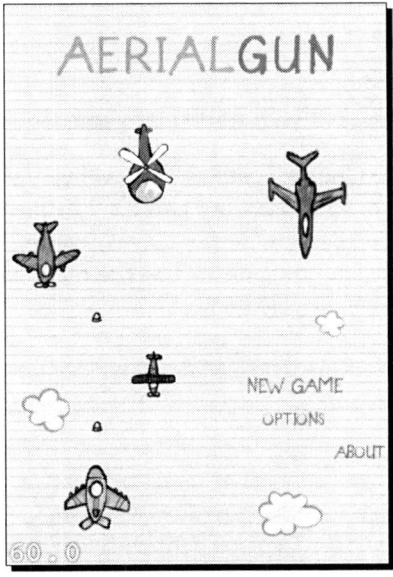

Menu Design

What just happened?

We didn't do anything really new here. In order to demonstrate that CCMenuItems can be manipulated just like any other CCNode, we ran some actions on them. As you can see, you can achieve lots of interesting effects by applying actions and effects even to menu items.

Using toggle menu items

We have to take a look at one more `CCMenuItem`. This one is the `CCMenuItemToggle`.

This type of `CCMenuItem` can hold any number of elements and when touched, cycle through them. Those elements can be any type of CCMenuItem.

For example, you can create a CCMenuItemToggle and add three CCMenuItemImage to it. Now when the scene loads, you will see the first element; when touched you will see the second element, and touch again and the third element will appear. The next time you touch it, the first element will be shown again, and so on.

So, this type of CCMenuItem is ideal for showing many options in a small space, or for making some checkboxes.

Time for action – creating the options menu

Let's create our game's options menu. This menu will hold all the preferences the player might want to change. For example, here you would allow him to:

- Turn the music on/off
- Turn the sounds on/off
- Choose a difficulty level
- Change any other settings of your particular game

We are now going to create the OptionsScene, which will contain some of these options. We'll start by allowing the player to choose the game's difficulty from the options menu. However, first things first. We have to create the corresponding scene and layer, make it appear when touching the corresponding button on the main menu, and then we can start playing with our new `CCMenuItemToggle` toy.

1. Make the options menu item in the MainMenuScene launch the options screen when touched:

    ```
    -(void)options:(id)sender
    {
      OptionsScene * gs = [OptionsScene node];
      [[CCDirector sharedDirector] replaceScene:gs];
    }
    ```

2. Now, create the new `OptionsScene` and `OptionsLayer`. These will hold all the menu items:

```
OptionsScene.h:
#import <Foundation/Foundation.h>
#import "cocos2d.h"
#import "GameScene.h"

@interface OptionsScene : CCScene {

}
@end

@interface OptionsLayer : CCLayer {

}
@end
OptionsScene.m:
#import "OptionsScene.h"

@implementation OptionsScene
- (id) init
{
  self = [super init];
  if (self != nil)
  {

    [self addChild:[OptionsLayer node]];

  }
  return self;
}
-(void)dealloc
{
  [super dealloc];
}
@end
```

Next, we have the `OptionsLayer` class:

```
@implementation OptionsLayer
- (id) init
{
 if ((self = [super init]))
 {
```

Menu Design

```
isTouchEnabled = YES;

//First, we create the Bitmap fonts we'll use for the menu item
labels

    CCSprite * background = [CCSprite
      spriteWithFile:@"options_background.png"];
    [background setPosition:ccp(160,240)];
    [self addChild:background];

    CCBitmapFontAtlas * difficultyLabel = [CCBitmapFontAtlas
      bitmapFontAtlasWithString:@"DIFFICULTY" fntFile:@"hud_font.
      fnt"];
    [difficultyLabel setColor:ccRED];
    [self addChild:difficultyLabel];
    [difficultyLabel setPosition:ccp(80,350)];

    CCBitmapFontAtlas * musicLabel = [CCBitmapFontAtlas
      bitmapFontAtlasWithString:@"MUSIC" fntFile:@"hud_font.fnt"];
    [musicLabel setColor:ccRED];
    [self addChild:musicLabel];
    [musicLabel setPosition:ccp(80,250)];

    CCBitmapFontAtlas * soundLabel = [CCBitmapFontAtlas
     bitmapFontAtlasWithString:@"SOUND" fntFile:@"hud_font.fnt"];
    [soundLabel setColor:ccRED];
    [self addChild:soundLabel];
    [soundLabel setPosition:ccp(80,150)];

//Then, we create the menu items

    CCMenuItemImage * easyBtn = [CCMenuItemImage
      itemFromNormalImage:@"easy.png"
      selectedImage:@"easy_dwn.png"];

    CCMenuItemImage * normalBtn = [CCMenuItemImage
      itemFromNormalImage:@"normal.png"
      selectedImage:@"normal_dwn.png" ];

    CCMenuItemToggle * difficulty = [CCMenuItemToggle
    itemWithTarget:self
      selector:@selector(changeDifficulty:)
      items:easyBtn,normalBtn,nil];
```

```
    CCMenuItemImage * unchecked1 = [CCMenuItemImage
      itemFromNormalImage:@"options_check_d.png"
      selectedImage:@"options_check.png"];

    CCMenuItemImage * checked1 = [CCMenuItemImage
      itemFromNormalImage:@"options_check.png"
      selectedImage:@"options_check_d.png" ];

    CCMenuItemToggle * music = [CCMenuItemToggle itemWithTarget:
    self selector:@selector(changeMusic:)
    items:checked1,unchecked1,nil];

    CCMenuItemImage * unchecked2 = [CCMenuItemImage
      itemFromNormalImage:@"options_check_d.png"
      selectedImage:@"options_check.png"];

    CCMenuItemImage * checked2 = [CCMenuItemImage
      itemFromNormalImage:@"options_check.png"
      selectedImage:@"options_check_d.png" ];

    CCMenuItemToggle * sound = [CCMenuItemToggle itemWithTarget:self
      selector:@selector(changeSound:)
      items:checked2,unchecked2,nil];

//Then, we create the menu which will hold those menu items

    CCMenuItemImage * goback = [CCMenuItemImage
      itemFromNormalImage:@"options_goback.png"
      selectedImage:@"options_goback.png"
      disabledImage:@"options_goback.png"
      target:self

      selector:@selector(goBack:)];

    [difficulty setPosition:ccp(220,350)];
    [music setPosition:ccp(220,260)];
    [sound setPosition:ccp(220,160)];
    [goback setPosition:ccp(160,30)];

    CCMenu * menu = [CCMenu
      menuWithItems:difficulty,music,sound,goback,nil];
    [self addChild:menu];
    [menu setPosition:ccp(0,0)];

    }
```

Menu Design

```objc
    return self;
}
//Here are the methods that will be called when menu items are pressed
-(void)changeDifficulty:(CCMenuItemToggle *)sender
{
   NSLog(@"%d",sender.selectedIndex);
}
-(void)changeSound:(CCMenuItemToggle *)sender
{
}
-(void)changeMusic:(CCMenuItemToggle *)sender
{
}

-(void)goBack:(id)sender
{
   MainMenuScene * gs = [MainMenuScene node];
   [[CCDirector sharedDirector]replaceScene:gs];

}
-(void)dealloc
{
   [super dealloc];
}
@end
```

3. Launch the game and go into the newly created OptionsScene. You will be able to touch the difficulty CCMenuItemToggle, and cycle between its items.

Chapter 6

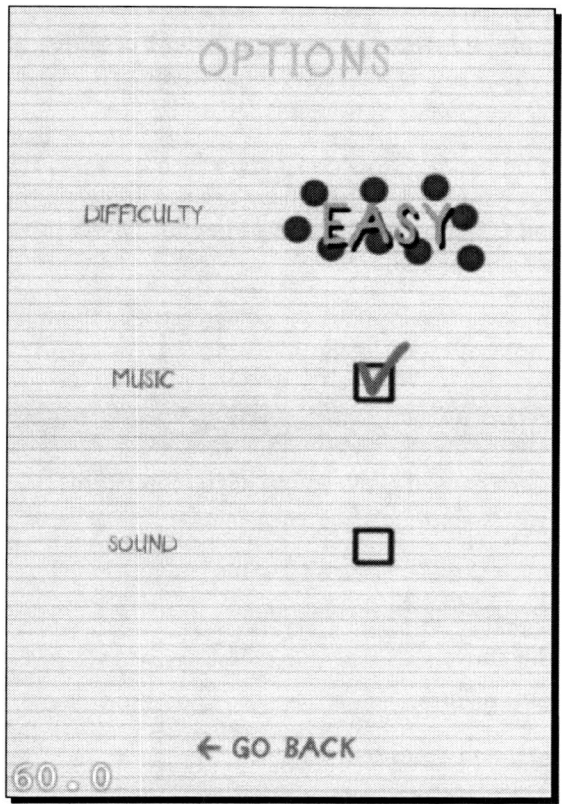

What just happened?

We just worked on a simple usage of CCMenuItemToggle. What we did here is, create a new scene which will display some options. Right now we just added a difficulty selection item.

This item was made from a CCMenuItemToggle, which works by cycling between the CCMenuItems that you give to it.

```
CCMenuItemImage * easyBtn = [CCMenuItemImage
    itemFromNormalImage:@"easy.png"
    selectedImage:@"easy_dwn.png"];

CCMenuItemImage * normalBtn = [CCMenuItemImage
    itemFromNormalImage:@"normal.png"
    selectedImage:@"normal_dwn.png" ];

CCMenuItemToggle * difficulty = [CCMenuItemToggle itemWithTarget:self
    selector:@selector(changeDifficulty:) items:easyBtn,normalBtn,nil];
```

Menu Design

This is what we just did. As you can see, we are initializing two `CCMenuItemImage` with just two images for the normal and selected states, and instead of adding those to the menu we create a `CCMenuItemToggle` object, and pass those items to it. We are also telling it to call the `changeDifficulty` method each time it is pressed.

That's nice, but you may be asking: "How do I know which item was selected?". Take a look at the `changeDifficulty` method. Although we are not doing anything useful with it (yet), we are logging the passed CCMenuItemToggle's `selectedIndex` property, which returns the index of the currently shown item.

Next, we will see how to save these options so we can retrieve them later in the game and each time we enter the options menu again.

Pop Quiz – menu items

1. In which way does Cocos2d allow you to align menu items?
    a. By calling `alignItemsVertically`
    b. By calling `alignItemsInColumns`
    c. By setting their positions manually
    d. All of the above
    e. None of the above

2. How do you add menu items to a layer?
    a. By adding them as a child of the layer
    b. By adding them as a child of a CCMenu object and then adding that menu to the layer
    c. They are added automatically upon creation

3. Which of the following is not a valid Cocos2d MenuItem?
    a. `CCMenuItemLabel`
    b. `CCMenuItemFont`
    c. `CCMenuItemImage`
    d. `CCMenuItemCheckbox`
    e. `CCMenuItemToggle`

Saving and loading preferences

We have finished creating our options menu. However, as you can see, if you change one of those options and then you exit and go back to the options screen again, the selected options will return to its default values.

What is happening here is not right. However, it is the expected behavior, as we are not doing anything to actually save what we change.

There are several ways to save data in the iPhone, and as this is not an Objective-C/iPhone programming primer, I won't go into detail about them. We are just going to see how to use some of these available methods when needed.

In the case of saving these little preferences, using `NSUserDefaults` will be enough. The `NSUserDefaults` class provides a way for developers to change the application behavior to match the user's preferences.

Saving and loading data using `NSUserDefaults` is quite easy, and it let's you store a good variety of data types. You can use it to save integers, arrays, dictionaries, and strings, among other data types.

`NSUserDefaults` is very useful to store a lot of your game's data. For example you could use it to store the following:

- Your options preferences
- Simple high scores
- Whether the player has unlocked a new level, weapon, and so on

Let's give it a go by saving our OptionsScene's data.

Time for action – persisting options data

What we'll do now is save what the player selects in the options menu. Then we will load that data again each time we reenter this scene. Using this base you will be able to save and retrieve any other simple data you wish, when you wish to.

1. Open the `OptionsScene.m` file and modify the three methods that get called when the player touches the `CCMenuItemToggle` buttons:

   ```
   -(void)changeDifficulty:(CCMenuItemToggle *)sender
   {
     NSUserDefaults *usrDef = [NSUserDefaults standardUserDefaults];
     
     if(sender.selectedIndex ==1)
       [usrDef setInteger:1 forKey:@"difficulty"];
   ```

Menu Design

```objc
    if(sender.selectedIndex ==0)
        [usrDef setInteger:0 forKey:@"difficulty"];
}

-(void)changeSound:(CCMenuItemToggle *)sender
{
    NSUserDefaults *usrDef = [NSUserDefaults standardUserDefaults];

    if(sender.selectedIndex ==1)
        [usrDef setBool:NO forKey:@"sound"];
    if(sender.selectedIndex ==0)
        [usrDef setBool:YES forKey:@"sound"];
}

-(void)changeMusic:(CCMenuItemToggle *)sender
{
    NSUserDefaults *usrDef = [NSUserDefaults standardUserDefaults];

    if(sender.selectedIndex ==1)
        [usrDef setBool:NO forKey:@"music"];
    if(sender.selectedIndex ==0)
        [usrDef setBool:YES forKey:@"music"];
}
```

2. Now add the following lines at the end of the `init` method of the `OptionsLayer` class:

```objc
NSUserDefaults *usrDef = [NSUserDefaults standardUserDefaults];
if([usrDef boolForKey:@"sound"] == NO)
    sound.selectedIndex = 1;
if([usrDef boolForKey:@"music"] == NO)
    music.selectedIndex = 1;
if([usrDef integerForKey:@"difficulty"] == 0)
    difficulty.selectedIndex =0;
else if([usrDef integerForKey:@"difficulty"] == 1)
    difficulty.selectedIndex =1;
```

3. Run the game. Change some options, then exit and reenter the scene or even the game. You will see the options you selected, remain the same.

What just happened?

We just implemented a simple options menu with persisting data.

Let's take a look at the `changeDifficulty` method. What we do when the player touches the corresponding menu item is, to check its value, so we know what is the current state of the button (whether the user selected easy or normal). Based on that value we use the `NSUserDefaults` object to store an integer value with the key "difficulty"; we will be able to retrieve that saved data using that same key name later.

As you can see, saving a value using `NSUserDefaults` just takes two lines of code! Notice that if you want to store another data type, you have to use the corresponding method. For example, we can use the NSUserDefault's `setBool` method if we want to save the status of music (that is on or off).

What we need to do now is to reflect these changes when loading the scene, so in the `init` method of the layer we load the saved data using the NSUserDefault's `integerForKey` method and use that value to set the `CCMenuItemToggle` selected index.

Have a go hero – loading and using your saved data

Now that we can select the game's difficulty through the option's menu, we don't need to show the difficulty selection screen anymore, each time we start a new game. You can delete this layer and the code that makes it appear, or use your new found data loading skills to make it better.

What you can do is to show it only the first time the game is played. In order to do that, just save a `firstTime` value to the `NSUserDefaults` when the game starts. The first time it is played, it will be set to `YES`. You can then use this value to check whether to show the difficulty selection layer or not.

Summary

This chapter is officially over. I hope you have learned a lot about creating menus for you game.

In this chapter, we did the following:

- We built a few menus using the different menu items available in Cocos2D
- We ran actions on those items, animating them
- We learnt how to save the selected settings

In the next chapter, we are finally going to add some eye candy to our game. It is time to use particles!

7
Implementing Particle Systems

A particle system is a graphic technique used to represent some elements that otherwise would be very difficult to get right. These systems can easily generate effects such as fire, explosions, magic, snow, smoke, trails, and lots of other really cool effects.

A particle system consists of an emitter which is the source of the system; the place where the particles will come from. Each particle in a given system is represented by a single image and has a set of properties that affect how the system will look as a whole.

There are many parameters that you can tweak in order to achieve all kinds of different effects; for example, you can change the size of the particles over time, their emission rate, their color, the speed, and so on.

In this chapter, you will learn how to integrate lots of custom-made particle systems in order to enhance the look of your games. The following is a list of things we will do:

- Take a look at premade particle systems that come included with Cocos2d
- Learn how to use the two types of particle systems included in Cocos2d
- Learn how to use the two modes of particle systems
- Learn how to create and reuse particles systems
- Take a look at 71squared's particle designer tool for generating particles

Let's begin.

Taking a look at the prebuilt particle systems

If you have already taken a look at all of the samples that come with Cocos2d source code, you must have passed through this one, and if you are like most people and you like flashy, good looking effects, you must have been really eager to get to use this.

Using particles in Cocos2d is like everything we have seen so far, very easy and straight forward. You just create the system, tweak a few parameters, and then you see nice effects come to life. In reality, the most difficult part of making a good particle effect is tweaking the tens of available parameters and choosing the right image for the particles. This requires a lot of patience, some imagination, and sometimes luck. After trying and trying to achieve a nice effect you might come to an unexpected result that just looks better than what you wanted! Later in this chapter, I will show you how to use a nice tool that lets you previsualize your particles and even export the result in a format that Cocos2d can load. (Doing this requires the paid version of the tool).

For now, let's take a look at the premade particle systems that come with Cocos2d, so you can get a feeling of what you can achieve using particles.

The following is a list of premade particle systems that ship with Cocos2d:

- `CCParticleFire`
- `CCParticleFireworks`
- `CCParticleSun`
- `CCParticleGalaxy`
- `CCParticleFlower`
- `CCParticleMeteor`
- `CCParticleSpiral`
- `CCParticleExplosion`
- `CCParticleSmoke`
- `CCParticleSnow`
- `CCParticleRain`

Let's take a closer look at them by seeing them in action.

Time for action – running the particle test

The particle test is one the few tests that we ran at the beginning of the book.

1. Open the Cocos2d project that contains all of the tests.
2. In the overview dropdown box, select the `particleTest` in both Active target and Active Executable.
3. Build and run the project.
4. If everything is ok, you will be able to cycle through different particle system examples.

What just happened?

Running the Cocos2d test is a good way to get a preview of what you can expect from the framework. In this case, you can see how some already made particle systems will look on the device, what frame rate to expect (if you are testing on the device), how the particles and the emitter behave, and so on.

Time for action – analyzing the ParticleMeteor system

Let's take a look at how the ParticleMeteor system works. I chose this one over all the other ones just because I think it looks really cool.

In order to see how these particle systems look, do the following:

1. In the Cocos2d source folder, there is a `CCParticleExamples.m` file. Open it.

   This file contains many example classes of premade particle systems.
2. Search for the ParticleMeteor class.
3. There just two methods to this class, and the important one is the `initWithTotalParticles`.

   Inside this method the entire configuration for the ParticleMeteor occurs. Setting all those properties is what makes this system unique.

4. Try changing some of those properties to see how that affects the existing test.

What just happened?

Setting the different properties of the particle system is what makes each one of them unique. Changing some little value might make the whole system look totally different from what you had before, giving you infinite possibilities when it comes to making nice looking effects.

I recommend you to start playing with the existing particle systems and tweaking them to see what each property does. Most of them are very self explanatory such as `Gravity`, `startSize`, `endSize`, `start`, and `endColor`.

Particle system properties

Particle systems have many properties that you can tweak in order to behave in different ways. If you took a look at the sample code you may have already seen them. The following is a list of those properties:

Property name	Behavior	Mode
Duration	How much does the system last? If you set it to -1 it will last forever	Both
centerOfGravity	The initial position of the particles	Both
posVar	The variance of that initial position	Both
Angle	The direction of those particles	Both
angleVar	The variance of that angle	Both
startSize	Initial size of the particles	Both
startSizeVar	The variance of that starting size	Both
endSize	Final size of the particles	Both
endSizeVar	The variance of that ending size	Both
Life	How many seconds the particles live	Both
liveVar	The variance of that time	Both
startColor	The starting color of the particles	Both
startColorVar	The variance of that starting color	Both
endColor	The ending color of the particles	Both
endColorVar	The variance of that ending color	Both
startSpin	The start angle of the particles	Both
startSpinVar	The variance of that starting angle	Both
endSpin	The end angle of the particles	Both
endSpinVar	The variance of that end angle	Both
Texture	The image of the particles	Both
Gravity	The gravity applied to the particles	Gravity
Speed	The speed at which the particles will move	Gravity
speedVar	The variance of that speed	Gravity
tangentialAccel	The tangential acceleration of the particles	Gravity
tangentialAccelVar	The variance of that tangential acceleration	Gravity
radialAccel	The radial acceleration of the particles	Gravity
radialAccelVar	The variance of that radial acceleration	Gravity
startRadius	The starting radius of the particles	Radius
startRadiusVar	The variance of that starting radius	Radius
endRadius	The ending radius of the particles	Radius
endRadiusVar	The variance of that ending radius	Radius
rotatePerSecond	The amount of degrees a particle rotates around the source in a second	Radius
rotatePerSecondVar	The variance of that amount of degrees	Radius

Implementing particle systems in your game using Gravity mode

We will now see how to actually implement the particle systems inside your game. However, before that, let me explain a couple of things.

Beginning from Version 0.9.3, there are two modes of particle systems. They are, Gravity Mode and Radius Mode. We will start by taking a look at particles using the Gravity mode.

Both modes behave in different ways. They have different sets of properties, thus letting you achieve different effects. Later in this chapter, we will implement both types of systems.

There is one more thing that you have to know before getting started. Cocos2d lets you choose between two different types of particle systems: `CCPointParticleSystem` and `CCQuadParticleSystem`.

CCPointParticleSystem

- It consumes little memory, using just one vertex per particle
- Its particles can't be bigger than 64px
- The system can not be scaled
- On the newest devices it performs much slower than `CCQuadParticleSystems`

CCQuadParticleSystem

- Particles can be of any size
- The system can be scaled
- Particles can be rotated
- It consumes more RAM and GPU memory than the `CCPointParticleSystems`
- It supports subrects

Which one you use just depends on your needs, but if you are using simple particle systems and you are aiming to get a good performance on slower devices, you should use the CCPointParticleSystem variant.

That being said, now let's start adding particles to our game.

Time for action – making bombs explode

We will now use our first particle system. These particles will represent the explosion caused by dropping a bomb. What we'll do first is create the logic for the bomb, and then have the game create a particle system.

The game will start with three bombs, each time the player touches the screen with two fingers, one bomb will be dropped, and this bomb will destroy every enemy on the screen. So what we have to do is detect a two finger touch on the screen, create the particle system, remove every active enemy, and update the remaining bombs label. So, let's get on with it.

1. First add a new BOOL property to the `GameLayer`, and name it `canLaunchBomb`. This will help us to prevent the player from dropping three bombs consecutively.

2. In the `init` method of the `GameLayer` class, set `canLaunchBomb` to `YES` and the property bombs (which should be there from previous chapters) to 3.

3. In the `ccTouchesBegan` method, add the following lines of code:

    ```
    if([touches count]==2 && canLaunchBomb && bombs>0)
    {
       [self explodeBomb];
    }
    ```

    This will let us know if the user touched the screen with two fingers. If he does and he has bombs remaining, then we drop one.

4. Add the `explodeBomb` method to the `GameLayer` class:

    ```
    -(void)explodeBomb
    {
      self.canLaunchBomb=NO;
      self.bombs--;

      HudLayer * hl = (HudLayer *)[self.parent
      getChildByTag:KHudLayer];
      [hl.bombs setString:[NSString stringWithFormat:@"X%d",
       self.bombs]];

      CCParticleExplosion * bomb = [CCParticleExplosion node];
      [self addChild: bomb z:4];

      bomb.texture = [[CCTextureCache sharedTextureCache] addImage:
         @"explosionParticle.png"];
      bomb.autoRemoveOnFinish = YES;
      [bomb setPosition:ccp(160,240)];
    ```

Implementing Particle Systems

```
    bomb.speed = 200;

    for(Enemy *n in enemies)
    {
      if(n.launched)
        [n destroy];
    }

    [self schedule:@selector(allowBombs) interval:2];
}

-(void)allowBombs
{
    [self unschedule:@selector(allowBombs)];
    self.canLaunchBomb=YES;
}
```

Also add the `explosionParticle.png` file included in this chapter's companion files. I created this image for you to use. Of course, you can change it to any other graphic that you like better.

5. Run the game now. When you touch the screen with two fingers you should see a nice particle system exploding up, the enemies being destroyed, and the corresponding labels updating, as shown in the following screenshot:

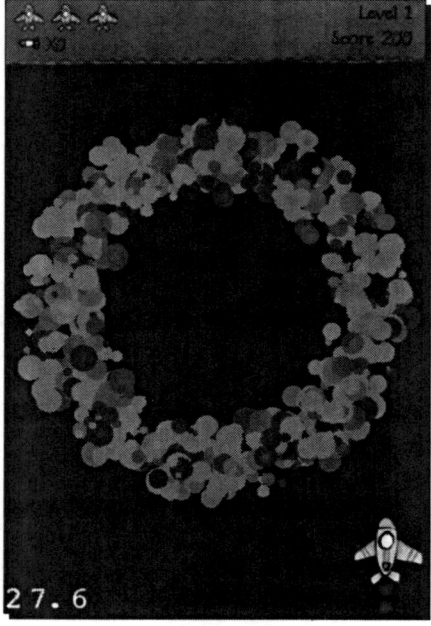

What just happened?

Let's take a look at the code involved in making the particles show up:

```
CCParticleExplosion * bomb = [CCParticleExplosion node];
[self addChild: bomb z:4];

bomb.texture = [[CCTextureCache sharedTextureCache] addImage:
@"explosionParticle.png"];
bomb.autoRemoveOnFinish = YES;
[bomb setPosition:ccp(160,240)];
bomb.speed = 200;
```

Since we used an existing particle system, we instantiated a `CCParticleExplosion` object instead of creating a particle from scratch. If you check the implementation of that class, you will see all the configurations of this system. It looks as follows:

```
-(id) initWithTotalParticles:(int)p
{
  if( (self=[super initWithTotalParticles:p]) )
  {
    // duration
    duration = 0.1f;

    self.emitterMode = kCCParticleModeGravity;

    // Gravity Mode: gravity
    self.gravity = ccp(0,0);

    // Gravity Mode: speed of particles
    self.speed = 70;
    self.speedVar = 40;

    // Gravity Mode: radial
    self.radialAccel = 0;
    self.radialAccelVar = 0;

    // Gravity Mode: tagential
    self.tangentialAccel = 0;
    self.tangentialAccelVar = 0;

    // angle
    angle = 90;
    angleVar = 360;
```

Implementing Particle Systems

```
        // emitter position
        CGSize winSize = [[CCDirector sharedDirector] winSize];
        self.position = ccp(winSize.width/2, winSize.height/2);
        posVar = CGPointZero;

        // life of particles
        life = 5.0f;
        lifeVar = 2;

        // size, in pixels
        startSize = 15.0f;
        startSizeVar = 10.0f;
        endSize = kCCParticleStartSizeEqualToEndSize;

        // emits per second
        emissionRate = totalParticles/duration;

        // color of particles
        startColor.r = 0.7f;
        startColor.g = 0.1f;
        startColor.b = 0.2f;
        startColor.a = 1.0f;
        startColorVar.r = 0.5f;
        startColorVar.g = 0.5f;
        startColorVar.b = 0.5f;
        startColorVar.a = 0.0f;
        endColor.r = 0.5f;
        endColor.g = 0.5f;
        endColor.b = 0.5f;
        endColor.a = 0.0f;
        endColorVar.r = 0.5f;
        endColorVar.g = 0.5f;
        endColorVar.b = 0.5f;
        endColorVar.a = 0.0f;

        self.texture = [[CCTextureCache sharedTextureCache] addImage:
          @"fire.png"];

        // additive
        self.blendAdditive = NO;
    }

    return self;
}
```

Chapter 7

All those values are what make the ParticleExplosion like that.

In the `explodeBomb`, I am changing some of those values at runtime to make it look more like what I wanted. Notice, I could have made those changes directly to the `CCParticleExplosion` class or I could have created a new class. Generally, you wouldn't want to change the code directly since an update in the Cocos2d source files will overwrite your changes to the examples.

Once we instantiate a `CCParticleExplosion` object, we add it to the layer, like any other `CCNode` and change a couple of parameters. What we changed was the position, the speed value to make the particles move faster, and the texture.

We are also setting the `autoRemoveOnFinish` property to `YES`; this will remove the system from its parent automatically when it has no more particles. If we didn't set this to `YES`, we would have to remove the system ourselves.

So, to sum up, in order to create some particles you just have to instantiate the desired Particle System, change its properties if desired, add it to the scene, and see it play.

Have a go hero – giving the sense of motion

As we haven't still made any background for our game, it doesn't look like our hero is moving at all. You could try to change that by using some particle and having them move fast from the top of the screen to the bottom.

A good example of this could be the `ParticleRain` sample. Try adding that particle system like we did with the `ParticleExplosion` system and then modifying some of its properties, so the rain drops move faster, giving the illusion of high speed.

Using the radius mode

As I mentioned before, there are two modes for particle systems, namely, gravity and radius. Up until now, we have been using the first type.

Radius mode supports some properties that gravity mode doesn't, which allows for other effects. However, its usage is the same. Let me show you.

Implementing Particle Systems

Time for action – hurting your enemies

In order to illustrate the usage of the radius mode, we are going to create a new class named `ExplosionParticle` which will make some fire appear and rotate around a given point of the screen. These particles will appear when an enemy is hit by a bullet. Let's take a look:

1. Begin by creating the `ExplosionParticle` class, which is going to be a subclass of `CCQuadParticleSystem`, as follows:

```
ExplosionParticle.h:
#import <Foundation/Foundation.h>
#import "cocos2d.h"

@interface ExplosionParticle : CCQuadParticleSystem {
}
@end

ExplosionParticle.m:
#import "ExplosionParticle.h"

@implementation ExplosionParticle
-(id) init
{
  return [self initWithTotalParticles:144];
}
-(id) initWithTotalParticles:(int) p
{
  if( (self=[super initWithTotalParticles:p]) )
  {

    self.texture = [[CCTextureCache sharedTextureCache] addImage:
      @"explosionParticle.png"];

    // duration
    self.duration = 0.3;

    // Set "Radius" mode (default one)
    self.emitterMode = kCCParticleModeRadius;

    self.startRadius =60;
    self.startRadiusVar =53;
    self.endRadius =0;
    self.rotatePerSecond=0;
    self.rotatePerSecondVar =360;
```

[240]

```
    // self position
    self.position = ccp(160,240);

    // angle
    self.angle = 360;
    self.angleVar = 205;

    // life of particles
    self.life = 0.55;
    self.lifeVar = 0.15;

    // spin of particles
    self.startSpin = 0;
    self.startSpinVar = 0;
    self.endSpin = 0;
    self.endSpinVar = 2000;

    // color of particles
    ccColor4F startColor = {1.0f, 0.15f, 0.65f, 1.0f};
    self.startColor = startColor;

    ccColor4F startColorVar = {1,1,1,0};
    self.startColorVar = startColorVar;

    ccColor4F endColor = {0.1f, 0.1f, 0, 0};
    self.endColor = endColor;

    ccColor4F endColorVar = {0.1f, 0.1f, 0, 0};
    self.endColorVar = endColorVar;

    // size, in pixels
    self.startSize = 12.0f;
    self.startSizeVar = 05.0f;
    self.endSize = 0;
    self.endSizeVar = 39;

    // emits per second
    self.emissionRate = self.totalParticles/self.life;

    // additive
    self.blendAdditive = NO;

    self.autoRemoveOnFinish =YES;
  }

  return self;
}
@end
```

Also add the `explosionParticle.png` image to the project which is included in the companion files.

2. Import the ExplosionParticle header inside your `Enemy.h` file:

   ```
   #import "ExplosionParticle.h"
   ```

3. Now all we have to do is instantiate one of these `ExplosionParticle` objects and add it to the layer when an enemy is hit. So, open the `Enemy.m` file and at the beginning of the `damage` method, add the following lines:

   ```
   ExplosionParticle * stars = [ExplosionParticle node];
   [self.theGame addChild:stars z:5];
   [stars setPosition:self.mySprite.position];
   [stars runAction:[CCMoveBy actionWithDuration:1
   position:ccp(0,-100)]];
   ```

4. Run the game and shoot at an enemy. You should see some explosion-like effect coming out of them, as shown in the following screenshot:

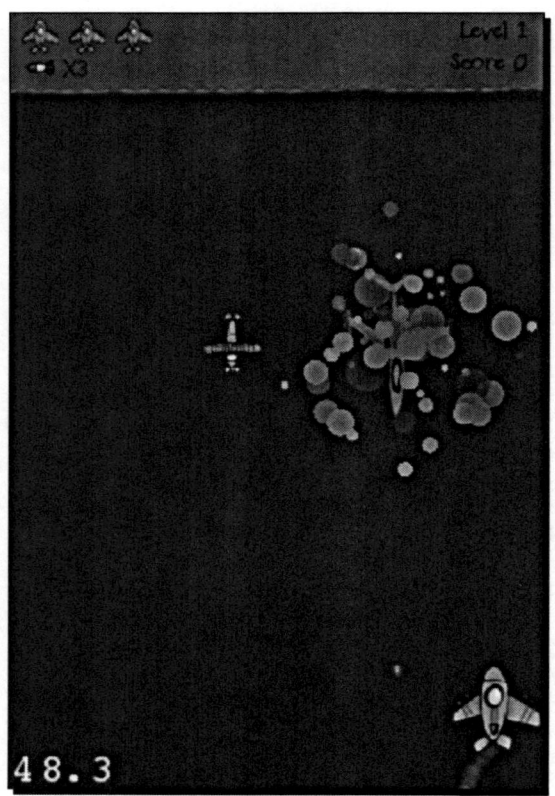

What just happened?

Using the particle system's radius mode is as simple as using the gravity mode. There are just three new properties that determine the outcome of the system. They are:

- `StartRadius`
- `EndRadius`
- `RotatePerSecond`

You can play with those values in order to change the speed with which the particles rotate around a point and the distance from the point at which they do so

In the previous example, we created a new particle system from scratch and used it just like the ones already included. Having your particles systems inside of a class allows you to change them quite easily and also to move them around other projects where you might need them.

Changing the way particle systems move

Normally, if you move your particle system around the result, you will get the emitter moving, and spawning particles would come out of that new position. For some situations this is ok, but how would you do it if you needed to move the whole system around without affecting its behavior?

The solution to this is quite simple. Particle systems have a property that allows you to set them to be either *Free* or *Grouped*.

In a *Free* system, particles will move independently from its emitter and in a *Grouped* system, they will be moved along with the emitter.

You can change this property by calling:

```
emitter.positionType = kPositionTypeFree
```

Or

```
emitter.positionType = kPositionTypeGrouped
```

Implementing Particle Systems

Using Particle Designer to create particle systems

After making a couple of particle systems and playing around with them, I am sure you must be thinking, "Isn't there a simpler way to do this?"

Searching for the correct particle effect by trial and error is very painful and time consuming; every little change you make, you have to compile the project again and see the effect on the screen.

Fortunately, there is one tool that can help you in this process. This tool is called Particle Designer and it is made and supported by the people from 71squared. Visit the following website for more information:

http://particledesigner.71squared.com/

This Mac OS X is the tool that allows you to create and configure particle systems and previsualize them right there. Once you have the right effect you can export it in a .plist format which is supported by Cocos2d and with just one line of code you get your particle system.

>  Particle Designer is not free. You can download a trial version which allows you to try all the functionalities but does not allow you to save the result. If you have some spare money and your game uses lots of particle effects, I really recommend buying it because it will save you hours and hours of trial and error.

Let's give Particle Designer a go and use it to create one last particle system for our game.

Time for action – creating a smoke trail

In the following example, we are going to use Particle Designer to create a smoke trail which will come out from our hero's rear, giving the impression that it is moving forward all the time. Here's what you have to do in order to generate a particle system with Particle Designer.

1. First of all, if you haven't done this yet, go ahead and download Particle Designer from `http://particledesigner.71squared.com/`

2. Run Particle Designer, and you should see a screen like the following:

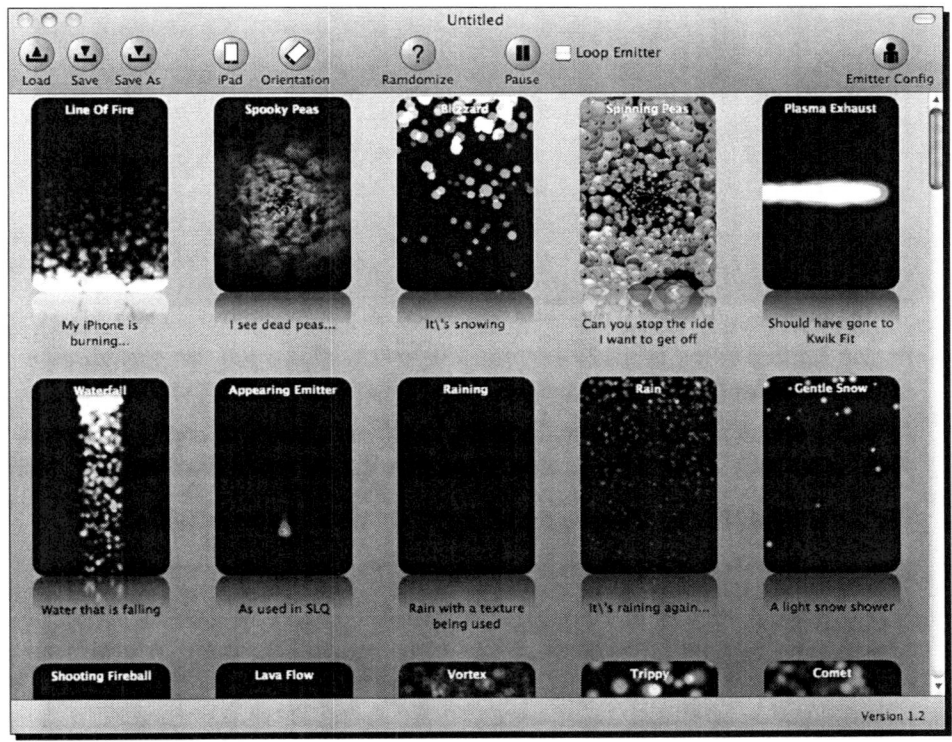

The preceding screen is your starting point for any particle system that you make. There, you can see a list of "Shared emitters" which are particle systems created by other people.

You can click on them to see how they would look in your iPhone by using the simulator included with the tool.

From the top menu you can load or save your particle system, change the orientation of the simulator, even change it to an iPad, get a random particle system generated, and enter the Emitter's configuration.

Implementing Particle Systems

3. Select any of the shared emitter and click on the **Emitter Config** button at the top right of the window. You will enter the configuration screen where you can change all the values for that given particle system, as shown in the following screenshot:

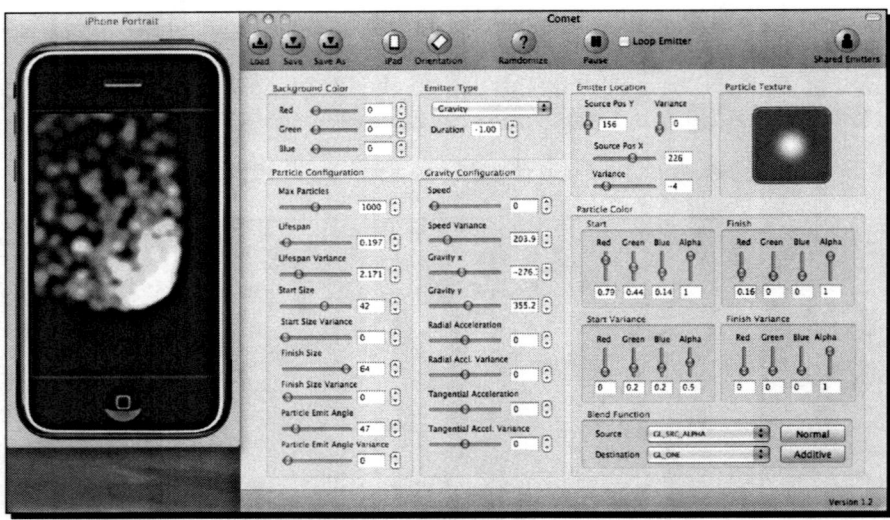

As you can see in the preceding screenshot, this is where you can configure an emitter in order to change its behavior or start a new one from scratch.

All those values are available in Cocos2d, but if you wanted to create this effect directly on code without being able to preview it, how much time would it take?

4. We'll change all those values in order to get the desired smoke trail effect.

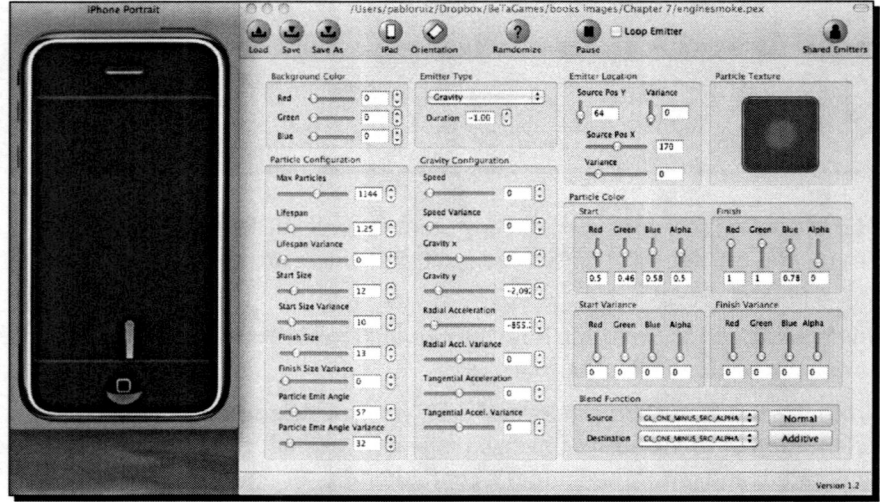

That is the result I got in a few minutes. It doesn't look that good, but you are free to make your own.

 You can change the particle texture by dragging a 64 x 64 pixel image into the upper-right corner of the config screen. When exporting your particle system, Particle Designer let's you export the texture inside the .plist file, so you don't have to be carrying the used image around.

5. Once you have the final particle system, and if you have the full version of the tool, save it as a new particle system into your hard drive as a .pex file for later editing, and also save it as a Cocos2d plist so we can read it in our game.

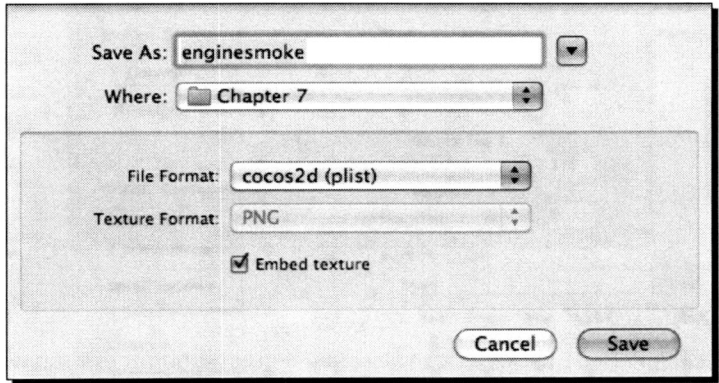

6. Open the project in Xcode and import this new enginesmoke.plist file into your resources folder.

7. Add a new property to your GameLayer class, a CCPointParticleSystem * smoke.

8. In the init method of the GameLayer class, add the following lines of code:

   ```
   smoke = [CCPointParticleSystem particleWithFile:@"enginesmoke.plist"];
   [self addChild:smoke z:1];
   ```

   That is all you need to do in order to create the new particle system and add it to the layer.

Implementing Particle Systems

9. All we have to do now is to have the emitter follow the hero all the time. So add the following line of code to the hero class's update method:

   ```
   [theGame.smoke setPosition:ccp(self.mySprite.position.x-
      2,self.mySprite.position.y-20)];
   ```

10. That is all there is to it. Run the game now and you should see something like the following:

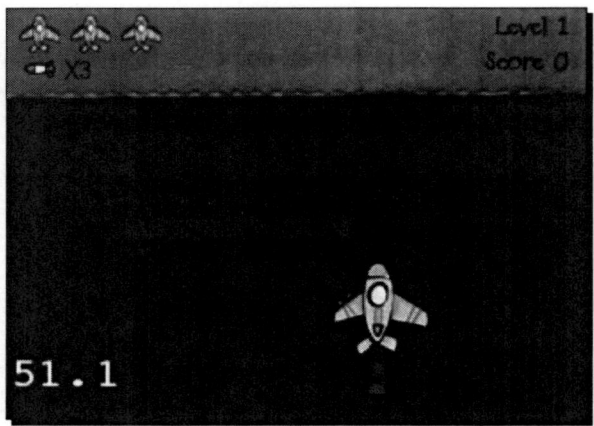

What just happened?

As you can see, using Particle Designer can save you a great amount of time with changing values, compiling, and trying the effect on the device.

Particle designer also comes with a bunch of already made effects, shared by people which you can use or edit for your projects.

Using these particle systems is very easy. We just created one by creating a particle system from the generated plist.

```
smoke = [CCPointParticleSystem particleWithFile:@"enginesmoke.plist"];
```

That was all the code required; compare that to the code we needed to write before for the other particle systems we made!

Also changing the particle system is really quick if you save the .pex file. Just load it, make some changes and export it again.

Pop quiz – particle systems

1. Which one of the following is not a valid way to create a particle system in Cocos2d?
    a. Subclassing one of the existing particles systems
    b. Using Particle Designer to create a `.plist` with the particle system properties
    c. Creating a new class from CCPointParticleSystem or CCQuadParticleSystem
    d. They are all valid options

2. Which of the following statements are not true about `CCQuadParticleSystem`?
    a. Particles can be of any size
    b. It consumes more RAM and GPU memory than the `CCPointParticleSystems`
    c. The system cannot be scaled
    d. It supports subrects

3. Which of the following is not a property of a particle system set in gravity mode?
    a. Speed
    b. Duration
    c. Radial acceleration
    d. Min radius
    e. Lifespan

Summary

We have reached the end of the particle systems chapter. In this chapter you were taught all about:

- The different types and modes of particle systems
- Creating particles from existing examples and from scratch
- Using different types of particles in your game
- Creating particle systems with Particle Designer tool

Next chapter we are going to take on Tilemaps, a very important subject in most games.

8
Familiarizing Yourself with Tilemaps

In this chapter we are going to take a quick look at tilemaps. Tilemaps are 2-dimensional arrays, with each element in the array containing information about a particular section of the map. This includes details on the image displayed in that section, the tile's collision properties, and so on.

In this chapter, we'll go through the following topics:

- What tilemaps are and how to use them
- Using **Tiled**. This is a free tool used to create tilemaps
- Loading tilemaps in Cocos2d
- Managing and modifying tiles at runtime

Let's get to it.

Using tilemaps

Tilemaps are very useful for creating big levels for your game. Let's take, for example, our game, which doesn't even need a huge map. However, suppose you wanted to make some nice, varied scrolling background for each level; you make a level where the background is 320px width and 3200px height. You would run into the following problems:

- A 320 * 3200 image is way too big; your game will never run smoothly with such an image in there. This image would exceed memory limits as well.
- You would have to make each of your backgrounds from scratch.
- You couldn't manage different parts of the map individually if you wanted to.

Familiarizing Yourself with Tilemaps

- If there are special places on the map you want to set you, will have to do it on your own.

These are some problems you could potentially find and that tilemaps can help you overcome.

Basically, what tilemaps do is allow you to divide your map into small pieces and use those pieces to build maps in a simple fashion, thus using much less memory. This is because instead of needing a gigantic image, now you just need many smaller images, which you repeat all around your map.

Take a look at the following image; there, you can see a portion of the map we'll build for the game and the tiles used to build it. As you can see, that part only uses around 10 different small images.

The first thing we'll do now is see how you can build a map, and for that, we'll use a tool called Tiled.

Chapter 8

Creating tilemaps with Tiled

Tiled is a free, general purpose tile map editor which can be used for any tiled based game, such as an RPG, platformers, and so on.

It allows you to create maps with any number of layers or tiles and set special properties to those layers, tiles, and other objects you may place.

Tiled has a Windows and OS X version although the Windows one is more up to date. In this book we'll be using Version 4.0 for OS X.

Tiled and Cocos2d support the following three types of tilemaps:

- Orthogonal (where the elements are arranged as seen from a top-down view)
- Isometric (where elements are seen in a 3D like way)
- Hexagonal (this one is not supported in Version 4.0 of Tiled)

We are going to see how to use orthogonal maps, as they are the simplest to implement, but of course, you can later take a look at the Cocos2d samples to see examples of how to use the other ones.

Time for action – creating your first map

So, continuing with our game, one thing it is missing is the background. Until now we have left a black screen behind, which looks awful, and we are going to fix that now. The idea here is to build a big map which we can scroll later to give the sense of motion.

In order to be able to build a map with Tiled, what we need first is the tileset, that is, the image which contains all the small tiles that will be used in the editor to build the whole map. This tileset uses the same concept as spritesheets; what we need is a huge image with the small images inside.

Familiarizing Yourself with Tilemaps

I have already included the tileset with all the tiles we'll use in this chapter. However, you are free to use your own. The only thing you have to have in mind is to give a 1 or 2 pixel separation between each tile, and paint those pixels with any color not used within your artwork (magenta or a pure green are two common examples) in order to avoid artifacts. This is the `tileimages.png` that we will be using:

Once we have that image ready we can begin working with Tiled to get our map done.

1. Get a copy of Tiled. You can download it from `http://www.mapeditor.org/`.
2. Once you launch Tiled, you will see a screen like the following one:

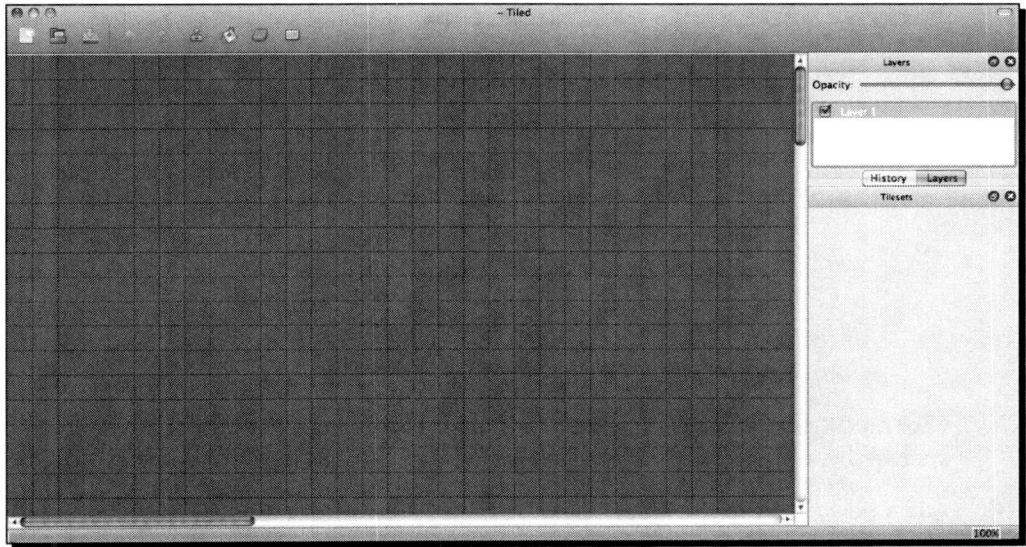

This is the screen where you will do all the work. The main screen is where you will add all the tiles to make your map. To the right you have the Layers panel and below that, the Tileset panel; we'll see how those work in a moment.

At the top, we have the toolbar where you can choose whether to create a new project, load an existing one, or save it. To the right you can choose the painting mode.

3. Create a new *map*. To do that, go to **File** | **New** (*cmd + N*).

A menu will pop up. From there you can choose:

- Orientation: Orthogonal or Isometric
- Map size: How many tiles make up the tilemap
- Tile size: The size of all the tiles

We are going to make an Orthogonal map with 32px * 32px tiles and as this is a vertical scrolling game we just need a width of 10 tiles and any height you want (that will determine the length of the levels). I am leaving it at 100.

This is how it should look:

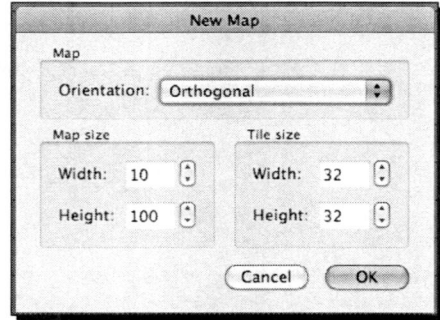

Click on **OK**, and you should have a new blank canvas with the new size you specified.

4. Add a new *tileset* to the map. Open the **Map | New tileset** menu.

From there you must browse your hard disk to find the tileset that we made at the beginning of the chapter.

Also you can choose the tiles' size and the margin spacing for them. (This depends on what separation you gave to the tiles when making the tileset. In our case we have to set both of them to 2.)

Once you do that your screen should look like the following:

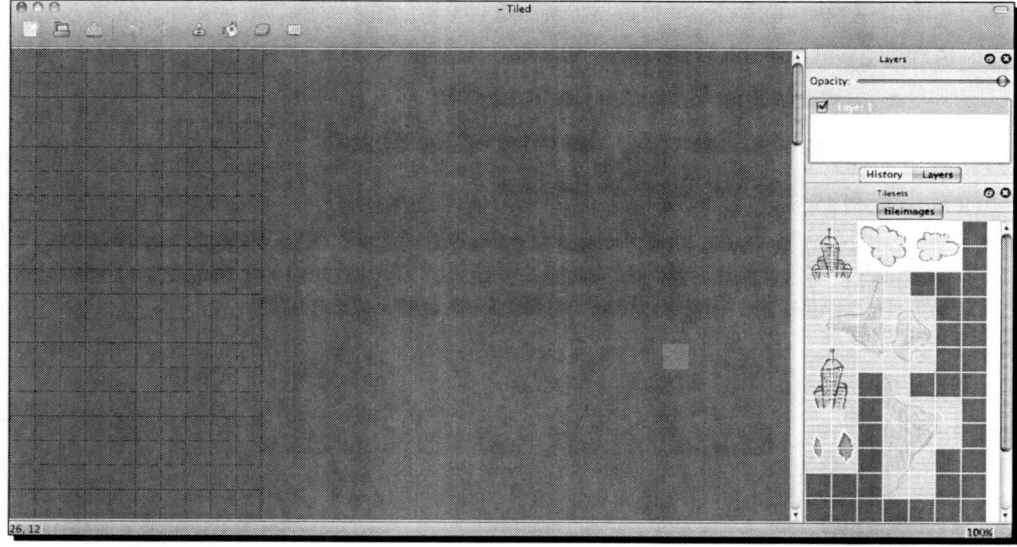

As you can see, all the tiles you made have been loaded on the right panel. From there you will be able to select one or more tiles and start painting on the canvas.

5. Before painting anything, we'll create a couple more *layers*. Select **Layer** | **Add Tile Layer**. Then specify the new layer's name. We'll name it `Clouds`.

   Add one more layer and name it `Others` (this will hold elements like the buildings and water patches).

   Also rename the existing `Layer 1` to `Background`. The Layers panel should look like the following:

   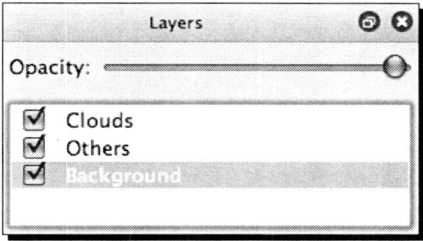

The layers should be in the order shown in the screenshot. The closest layer to the player should be on top, so if they aren't ordered like that in your screen, don't worry. Select one of them and in the Layer menu, select **Move Layer up** (*Shift + cmd + UP*) or **Move Layer Down** (*Shift + cmd + DOWN*)

Layers in Tiled serve the same purpose as in any painting program. You can use them to separate content, to place some elements on top of others, and with the added benefit of being able to retrieve them later, individually from Cocos2d.

Familiarizing Yourself with Tilemaps

6. We can start painting now. With the background layer selected, click on the ground tile and select the paint bucket from the toolbar. Then click on the map to paint all of it with that tile.

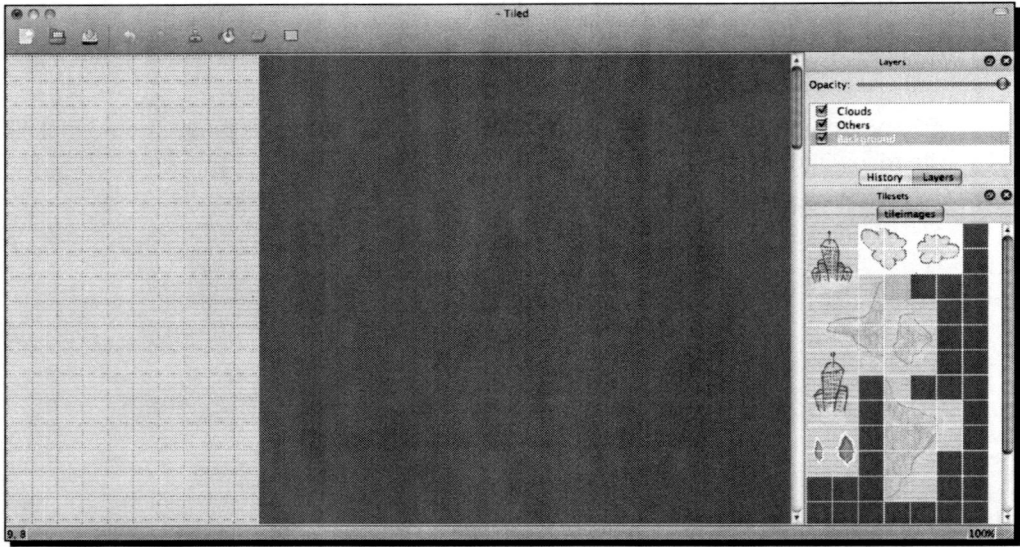

Then select the `Others` layer and select some water tiles or building tiles and paint some of them around your map. When loading a map, Tiled places you at the top of it, so scroll down the entire map first, or you won't see the results later!

 You can *CMD + click over* the tiles in the tileset panel to select multiple ones in order to paint a whole building or water patch at once.

Finally, select the clouds layer and paint some clouds. Also change the opacity of the layer so they look a little transparent, as this layer will be placed on top of all the content of the game. Cocos2d will respect the opacity you set for the layer.

7. Once you are done painting, save the map. Select **File | Save** (*cmd + S*). Name it `tilemap.tmx`.

   In a moment we'll see how to load it in Cocos2d. Meanwhile, the following is how mine looks:

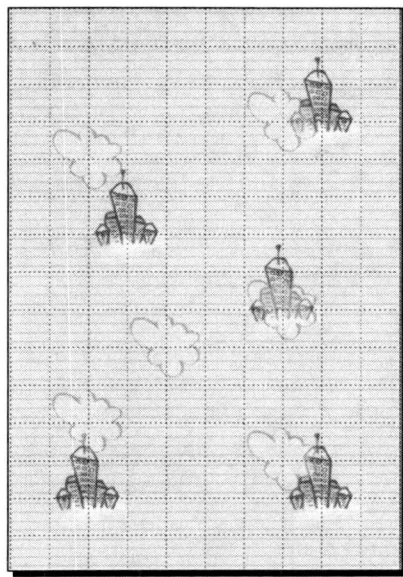

What just happened?

We just built our first tilemap with Tiled. As you can see, it is a nice tool and a very powerful one, if used right. With Tiled, you can make almost anything for a large variety of games.

We will use Tiled again later to add more content to the game, but for now this should be enough for getting started and seeing some results in-game.

Loading tilemaps in Cocos2d

In order to load the tilemaps we just created, we have to parse the tmx file. Fortunately, Cocos2d includes a class that does just that.

CCTMXTiledMap is responsible for parsing and displaying the tilemaps. It is just a container for all the layers the tilemap has. It is a subclass of CCNode and as such, it can be added to a CCLayer. When you do so, every CCTMXLayer it contains will be shown.

Each CCTMXLayer is created, one for each layer you inserted in Tiled (unless you set their visibility off), and you can retrieve them at runtime by using the CCTMXTiledMap's layerNamed method.

CCTMXLayer is a subclass of CCSpriteSheet and it contains every tile that was placed in that Layer. You can access each tile individually, those being CCSprites. That means you can move them around, rotate them, scale them, and so on.

Let's see them in action.

Familiarizing Yourself with Tilemaps

Time for action – using tilemaps in Cocos2d

Now that we have our nice tilemap, how do we use it in Cocos2d? That is very simple to do and requires little work.

1. Import both the tileimages.png and the tilemap.tmx file into your project.

2. In the `init` method of your `GameLayer` class, before the lines where you instantiate your hero, add the following code:

   ```
   CCTMXTiledMap * map = [CCTMXTiledMap
   tiledMapWithTMXFile:@"tilemap.tmx"];

   [self addChild:map];

   CCTMXLayer * clouds = [map layerNamed:@"Clouds"];

   [self reorderChild:clouds z:10];
   ```

3. Run the game. You should see the new background, and if everything is fine, clouds should appear on top of the other elements, even the hero and enemies, as shown in the following screenshot:

What just happened?

With just a couple of lines of code, we placed our tilemap inside the game. In order to do that, we created a `CCTMXTiledMap` object to which we passed our `tilemap.tmx` file.

Then we added this new object as a child of the layer in order for it to be shown.

We wanted the clouds to appear on top of every object. So what we needed to do is retrieve the layer that contains all the clouds and set its z value to be higher than all the other game elements. We achieved that by calling [map layerNamed:@"Clouds"]; to get a reference of that `CCTMXLayer`, and then we called the GameLayer's `reorderChild` method to assign `CCTMXLayer` a new, higher z value.

Now that we have our tilemap in place, all that remains is making it scroll down to give the sense of movement.

Time for action – running actions on layers

As you may know by now, as `CCTMXLayer` is a subclass of `CCSpriteSheet`, we can run actions on it. We are going to do so in order to have our background elements move down.

The code involved is quite simple; add the following lines after what we did in the previous example:

```
backLayer = [map layerNamed:@"Background"]; //backLayer is an iVar
defined in his class' interface.CCTMXLayer * others =
[map layerNamed:@"Others"];
[clouds runAction:[CCRepeatForever actionWithAction:[CCMoveBy
   actionWithDuration:0.3 position:ccp(0,-32)]]];
[backLayer runAction:[CCRepeatForever actionWithAction:[CCMoveBy
   actionWithDuration:0.6 position:ccp(0,-32)]]];
[others runAction:[CCRepeatForever actionWithAction:[CCMoveBy
   actionWithDuration:0.6 position:ccp(0,-32)]]];
```

After doing that, if you run your game, you should see the background elements moving down.

What just happened?

That is all we need to do in order to move layers around, as they are `subclasses` of `CCSpriteSheet`, we can apply any action on them like we have been doing all this time.

You may notice the following two problems arise from doing this:

- After a while of scrolling down you will run out of tiles

Familiarizing Yourself with Tilemaps

- When moving the layers down, you may notice some black gaps or glitches sometimes, which are very annoying.

Don't worry, both problems can be solved.

Time for action – reaching the end of the level

In order to avoid running out of tiles, you can do one of the following things:

1. When you detect that you have reached the end of the map, end the level, or the game
2. Each time a row of tiles goes beyond the screen bounds, move them to the top of the tilemap
3. Create two not so big tilemaps for the background and place them one on top of the other, when one of them completely goes past the screen bounds, move it on top of the other one

Any of these options are valid, depending of the needs of your game. We'll do the first option, although for the sake of simplicity, I will just reset the game when the end of the map is reached. If you wish you can later change this so a "Level finished" screen is shown and then a new map is loaded.

Add the following lines at the beginning of the `step` method:

```
float pos = -bck.position.y;
float limit = bck.mapTileSize.height * bck.layerSize.height
-[CCDirector sharedDirector].winSize.height;
if(pos > limit)
{
  MainMenuScene * g = [MainMenuScene node];
  [[CCDirector sharedDirector] replaceScene:g];
}
```

That will detect when the tilemap has ended and then go back to the MainMenuScene.

What just happened?

Doing any of the things mentioned earlier will fix the problem nicely. As mentioned, the method you use will depend on your game's particular needs.

Let's tackle the other problem.

Time for action – fixing black gaps and glitches

Now, for the other problem; there are a few things you can try in order to solve it. Try combining them until the problem gets solved; sometimes a little more work will be involved.

You can do one or more of the following things:

1. Set the director's projection to 2D. In order to do that, add the following line before the `CCDirector` is initialized in the `AppDelegate`:

   ```
   [[CCDirector sharedDirector] setProjection:kCCDirectorProjection2D];
   ```

2. Turn off anti-aliasing for the tilemap's layers. Add the following lines of code after instantiating the `CCTMXTileMap` object:

   ```
   for( CCSpriteSheet* child in [map children] )
   {
      [child texture] setAliasTexParameters];
   }
   ```

3. Run the `spritesheet-artifact-fixer.py` script. It is included in the cocos2d sources, in the tools folder. You can run it like this inside the Terminal:

   ```
   $ python spritesheet-artifact-fixer.py -f tileimages.png -x 32 -y 32 -m 2 -s 2
   ```

   It copies the borders of your tiles, into the spacing/margin pixels. Those should not be shown, but sometimes it might happen that they are. This way we at least show a similar image instead of a black border.

4. Modify the Cocos2d sources:

   This is trickier, but is sometimes needed. It is also dangerous to do this, as you could lose your changes when upgrading to a newer version of Cocos2d.

In our case, since we are moving around our tiles by using a `CCMoveBy` action, sometimes their positions may not be exact. At any given point one of them may end up being at a decimal pixel position, which causes the tiles not to be rendered correctly. What we have to do is fix the `CCMoveBy` action so this does not happen.

Open the `CCIntervalAction.m` file, and search for the `CCMoveBy` class which inherits from `CCMoveTo`. We have to modify CCMoveBy's `update` method:

```
-(void) update: (ccTime) t
{
   [target setPosition: ccp( round(startPosition.x + delta.x * t ),
     round(startPosition.y + delta.y * t ) )];
}
```

That should fix our nasty problem.

What just happened?

Doing any of the tricks described earlier should fix the black gaps problem. Their effectiveness depends on what you are doing, the Cocos2d version, and so on. So, if none of those tricks work, don't hesitate to take a look at the posts in the cocos2d forum or ask around there if you still can't find an answer.

Pop quiz

1. Which kind of tilemaps can you create and load in Cocos2d?
    a. Orthogonal
    b. Isometric
    c. Hexagonal
    d. All of them
    e. None of them

2. Are there any limitations to the size of the tilemaps you use?
    a. No, you can make them of any size
    b. Yes, they have to have the same width and height
    c. No, but since the iPhone has limited memory resources, you should break them into multiple chunks if they are very big

3. Which of the following statements is false?
    a. You can retrieve a `CCTMXLayer` from a map by calling its `layerNamed` method and passing the name of the layer to it
    b. You can run actions on `CCTMXLayers` and each of its individual tiles
    c. There is no way to retrieve an individual tile from a layer, even if I know its position in the tilemap

Using layers to hold objects

There are many more things you can do with Tiled that we haven't seen so far.

Tiles supports two kinds of layers, namely, tile layers and object layers.

These object layers are used to mark places in the map where you want something to happen. You can add markers in these kind of layers of any size and at any position, even setting properties to them. All this data can then be retrieved in Cocos2d to do whatever you want. For example in a top-down RPG you could mark special locations where events could happen, spawn points of enemies, and so on.

Let's see an example of object layers in our game.

Time for action – adding object layers in tiled

We are going to add an extra "Enemy" to our game. As it is a doodle style game, you know the action happens on a piece of sheet. We are going to create some obstacles that look like the background has been torn out. These obstacles will destroy the player's airship if a collision occurs between them.

We are going to add zones, where if the hero touches them he loses a life, and for that we are going to use an object layer.

1. Open the Tiled project we were working on before.
2. Select the Others layer and add some ripped tiles to the map.
3. Select **Layer | Add Object Layer** from the Tile menu and name the new layer `RippedZones`.
4. Select this new layer (which should have appeared in the Layers panel).
5. Now if you click on the map, instead of placing tiles, you will be adding some grey markers. You can place them anywhere and if you click and drag you can make them bigger. Place these markers in such as way that they cover each ripped tile in your map.
6. Right click on each marker and name them ripped.
7. Save the map, replacing the one we had before.

Familiarizing Yourself with Tilemaps

8. The following screenshot shows how it should look in Tiled:

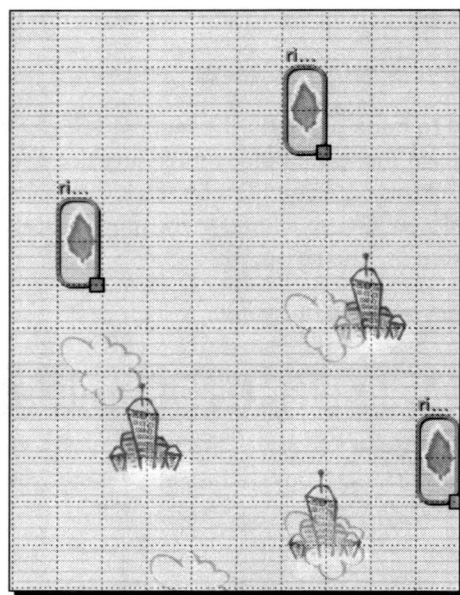

What just happened?

We just added an object layer. This kind of layer gives you the ability to mark special places within your map. You can make those areas the size you want, give each one a name (so you can later identify them in code), and even add properties to them. In our case, we just gave them a name, which will let us know each one's position and size later. That is all we need to know.

Now we'll take a look at how to load these objects and handle them in Cocos2d.

Time for action – retrieving objects in Cocos2d

Retrieving these objects we added to the tilemap is as easy as retrieving the tile layers.

Instead of creating a `CCTMXLayer`, we have to get the `CCTMXObjectGroup` object from the map. Let's do it now:

1. Replace the `tilemap.tmx` file in our project for the one we created in the previous example.

2. In the `init` method of the `GameLayer` class, just below our backgrounds and cloud add the following lines:

```
ripped = [[NSMutableArray alloc]init];

CCTMXObjectGroup * rippedZones = [map objectGroupNamed:@"RippedZon
es"];
for(NSMutableDictionary * d in [rippedZones objects])
{
  CGRect rect = CGRectMake([[d valueForKey:@"x"]floatValue], [[d
    valueForKey:@"y"]floatValue], [[d valueForKey:@"width"]
    floatValue], [[d valueForKey:@"height"]floatValue]);
  RippedHolder * holder = [[RippedHolder alloc]initWithRect:rect];
  [ripped addObject:holder];
  [holder release];
}
```

The ripped `NSMutableArray` is an ivar, so add it to the interface of the class.

3. Create a `RippedHolde` class that will act just as a wrapper for a CGRect, so we can add those to the `NSMutableArray`:

```
RippedHolder.h
#import <Foundation/Foundation.h>

@interface RippedHolder : NSObject
{
  CGRect rippedRect;
  float originalY;
}
@property (nonatomic, readwrite)CGRect rippedRect;
@property (nonatomic, readwrite)float originalY;

@end
RippedHolder.m
#import "RippedHolder.h"

@implementation RippedHolder
@synthesize rippedRect,originalY;

- (id) initWithRect:(CGRect)rect
{
  if ((self = [super init]))
  {

    self.rippedRect = rect;
    self.originalY = rect.origin.y;

  }
```

```
    return self;
}

-(void)dealloc
{
  [super dealloc];
}
    @end
```

4. Add the following lines in the `step` method of the `GameLayer` class:

   ```
   for(RippedHolder * holder in ripped)
   {
     holder.rippedRect = CGRectMake(holder.rippedRect.origin.x,
       holder.originalY+backLayer.position.y,
       holder.rippedRect.size.width,holder.rippedRect.size.height);
   }
   ```

5. Finally, add the following lines to the `update` method of the `Hero` class:

   ```
   for(RippedHolder * holder in theGame.ripped)
   {
   
     if(ccpDistance(self.mySprite.position,ccp(holder.rippedRect.
     origin.x+
       holder.rippedRect.size.width/2,holder.rippedRect.origin.y+
       holder.rippedRect.size.height/2)) <30)
     {
       if([self checkCollisions:holder.rippedRect])
       {
         [self destroy];
       }
     }
     
   }
   ```

6. Run the game and try passing over some ripped places. Your hero should lose a life just as when he passes over a bullet.

What just happened?

Let's go over everything we did here.

First, we created an instance of the `CCTMXObjectGroup` class; we did so by calling the `objectGroupName` method from the `CCTMXMap` class. This method gets the content of the object layer you have in the tmx map with the name you pass to it.

Once we have this group of objects, we iterate through them to get their properties. Since we didn't add any custom property in Tiled, we just have each marker's *x* and *y* components and their width and height, which is all we need to have in order to define the parts of the map that will destroy the hero upon collision.

For each `CGRect` we make, we create an instance of the `RippedHolder` class and add them to our ripped `NSMutableArray`.

Since we have a scrolling map, which has elements that are constantly moving, we have to "move" our CGRects so they get updated along with the moving background. We do that in the `step` method.

Finally, in the `hero` class, we check the collision of the hero and these CGRects in order to determine that they are touching and react to that overlapping by destroying the hero.

As you can imagine, these object layers give you a lot of power and freedom to do whatever you want.

Have a go hero – creating enemies spawn points

In our game we are making enemies appear at random times and positions. However, what if you wanted to have them appear in predetermined positions? Well, you can apply what you just learned in order to do that. Try the following:

- Add an object layer named "enemies" in Tiled
- Add some markers to the layer you just created
- Add a custom property to them called type, this will be either 1, 2, 3, or 4 and will determine the type of enemy you want to spawn from there
- Retrieve all this data in Cocos2d
- What you would have to do is check if the hero is close to reaching one of these spawn points, and if he is, launch an enemy from there with the type specified by the marker you set in Tiled

Summary

This is the end of the tilemaps chapter. By now you should have an idea of how to put together a game that uses tiles not only for displaying large backgrounds, but also for placing objects.

In this chapter, you learned:

- How to create tilemaps in Tiled
- How to fix artifacts on the images used for the tilemaps
- How to load tilemaps, layers and objects within Cocos2d

In the next chapter, we are going to add some music and sound effects to the game.

9
Playing Sounds with CocosDenshion

Sounds are an important aspect in any game. Having immersive, good quality sound effects and music can make the difference between a good and an excellent game. In this chapter, we are going to go over the steps needed to play music in your games.

We'll cover the following in this chapter:

- The different sound engines included with Cocos2d
- Initializing CocosDenshion
- Playing background music
- Playing background effects
- Managing the music playback
- Preloading sounds

What is CocosDenshion?

CocosDenshion is an audio library for iOS which is included in Cocos2d, although you can use it in any other project, if you wish to.

You can use it in the following three different ways depending on your needs. Each one has its complexities, but offers different features that you might want to use:

- SimpleAudioEngine: This is the most basic form and is suitable for simple sound needs, and most people don't need more than this.

- **CDSoundEngine**: This is built upon OpenAL, being able to play up to 32 simultaneous sounds; you can control each sound's pitch, pan, and gain. CDSoundEngine can control audio session interruption automatically.
- **CDAudioManager**: This is a wrapper for an AVAudioPlayer object and uses CDSoundEngine to play sounds. It handles audio session interruption and it is of a very low level, so in order to use it, you should have some experience with AVAudioPlayer.

In our game, we don't have any complex needs that would make using CDAudioManager a must; using SimpleAudioEngine would suffice, but anyways we are going to go over it later in this chapter.

Let's begin working with the audio by using SimpleAudioEngine.

Getting started with sounds

Let's begin filling our game with sounds. First, we'll add some sound effects to it with SimpleAudioEngine.

Time for action – using SimpleAudioEngine

The first thing we'll do for you to get accustomed to working with sounds is add a sound effect to our menu items. Each time you touch a menu item, a short sound will play. Carry out the following steps:

1. If they are not already included in your project, you must include the OpenAL, AudioToolbox, and AVFoundation frameworks.

2. Add the sound that you wish to play to your `resources` group folder.

3. We are going to play a simple sound in our main menu, so open the `MainMenuScene.h` file, and add the following line:

   ```
   #import "SimpleAudioEngine.h"
   ```

4. Playing the actual sound file is quite easy. Just put the following line wherever you wish the sound to be played. I will add it at the beginning of the `newGame` method:

   ```
   [[SimpleAudioEngine sharedEngine] playEffect:@"click.caf"];
   ```

5. Run the game and select `New game`. You should hear your sound getting played.

That is all you need to do in order to play a sound with SimpleAudioEngine. Now play the game again; do you notice a lag when playing the sound? If you do, it is because this is the first time that we used SimpleAudioEngine in the application. It has to initialize itself, so in order to solve that, let's use it before that moment. We'll set its volume in the `AppDelegate` just to get the SimpleAudioEngine started. In the `AerialGunAppDelegate` add the following line to the `applicationDidFinishLaunching` method:

```
[[SimpleAudioEngine sharedEngine] setEffectVolume:0.5];
```

If you run the game now, you should hear the sound playing almost instantly after touching the corresponding button.

What just happened?

As its name implies, SimpleAudioEngine is very simple to use. You tell it to play a sound whenever you want just by calling its `playEffect` method and passing the name of the sound effect to be played to it.

Methods for handling sound effects

With SimpleAudioEngine, you can do a couple more things other than just playing the sound. You can also use the following methods:

- `stopEffect`: Stops the sound. You must pass the sound ID to it. That sound ID is assigned when you call `playEffect`, so you must assign that value to a variable and store it for later use.

- `playEffect(NSString*) pitch:(float) pan:(float) gain:(float)`: By calling this method, you can play an effect and set its pitch, pan, and gain values for it.

- `preloadEffect(NSString *) filepath`: You can also preload an effect so if it is a large sound file and you don't want a noticeable delay when playing it for the first time you just call the `preloadEffect` method.

- `unloadEffect`: You can unload an effect from memory if you are not going to use it anymore.

SimpleAudioEngine allows you to play background music too, so that is what we'll do next.

Time for action – playing background music with SimpleAudioEngine

Playing background music with SimpleAudioEngine is as easy as playing sound effects. Once you find a suitable, loopable sound file, carry out the following steps:

1. If they are not included in your project, you must include the OpenAL, AudioToolbox, and AVFoundation frameworks.

2. Add the music file that you wish to play to your `resources` group folder.

3. We are going to play a simple music soundtrack in our main menu, so open the `MainMenuScene.h` file and add the following line:

   ```
   #import "SimpleAudioEngine.h"
   ```

4. In the `init` method of the `MainMenuLayer` class, add the following line:

   ```
   [[SimpleAudioEngine sharedEngine]
     playBackgroundMusic:@"menu_music.mp3" loop:YES];
   ```

5. We now have to stop the background music from playing when we leave this scene, so at the beginning of the `selectMode` method, add the following line:

   ```
   [[SimpleAudioEngine sharedEngine] stopBackgroundMusic];
   ```

6. Run the game and you should hear your background music playing over and over, then get into the game and it should stop.

What just happened?

SimpleAudioEngine includes several methods to manage your background music. We just used two of them, namely, `playBackgroundMusic` with the loop parameter to which you pass the name of the file that you wish to play and whether to have it loop or not, and the `stopBackgroundMusic` method that just stops the current music.

Methods for handling background music

There are other methods which you may find useful. They are as follows:

- `pauseBackgroundMusic`: This method pauses the background music playback
- `resumeBackgroundMusic`: This method resumes the paused background music
- `rewindBackgroundMusic`: This method starts playing the background music from the beginning

- `stopBackgroundMusic`: This method stops the background music from playing
- `preloadBackgroundMusic`: Just as with sound files, you can also preload the background music by calling the `preloadBackgroundMusic` method and passing the filename to it
- `isBackgroundMusicPlaying`: This method lets you know whether the background music is playing or not

That is all there is to the SimpleAudioEngine, which for your basic needs is quite enough and very easy to use. Next we'll take a look at CDSoundEngine, which is a little more complex to setup and use, but offers a few more functionalities which might be useful in your games.

Have a go hero – turning the music down

In Chapter 6, we added an options menu which should allow the player to turn the music off if he wants so. It is time for you to get that part working. The following is a simple way to do that:

- When you set the sounds to OFF, set some property of the AppDelegate to NO
- Each time a sound is about to be played, ask the delegate if it should play it or not (by checking the variable that we set through the menu)
- If that variable is set to YES, play the sound, else do nothing

Using CDSoundEngine

As noted earlier in this chapter, SimpleAudioEngine can cover your most basic needs, but there are times when you'll need more. So in such cases, we can use CDSoundEngine.

CDSoundEngine allows you to play lots of sounds at the same time (as much of them as the iPhone can handle) to organize them into groups, to modify their pitch, gain, and pan at runtime, and to handle audio session interruption.

All these things are very useful in lots of situations, so in further examples we are going to see how to initialize CDSoundEngine and how to use it to play sounds, then we'll use CDAudioManager to play a background music instead of SimpleAudioEngine.

Playing Sounds with CocosDenshion

Time for action – setting it up

Unlike SimpleAudioEngine, playing sounds with CDSoundEngine requires some setting up first. We'll begin by doing that.

Generally, you will want to play sounds at the very first scene of your game and keep those sounds loaded for later use. Maybe if memory is a concern in your game, you won't want to have 30 sound files loaded into memory. For our simple game, we'll initialize CDSoundEngine in the `AppDelegate` and load all the sounds in there. This is not optimal in many cases and you are free to change it, maybe loading some sounds at the beginning and many others just in scenes where you'll use them.

The first thing you want to do is to remove all the SimpleAudioEngine code that we wrote a little earlier. This will ensure that the new audio is played correctly and the audio session interruption will be handled properly.

So, we'll do all the initialization in our `AerialGunAppDelegate` class as follows:

1. First, CDSoundEngine requires the OpenAL and AudioToolbox frameworks, so include them in your project.

2. Then in the `AerialGunAppDelegate.h` file, import the `CocosDenshion.h` file.

3. Add the following constants just below the import statements:

   ```
   #define SND_ID_EXPLOSION 0
   #define SND_ID_BULLET 1
   #define SND_ID_CLICK 2
   #define CGROUP_ALL 0
   ```

4. Add a new ivar to the `AerialGunAppDelegate` interface and then make it a property:

   ```
   CDSoundEngine * soundEngine
   ```

5. Move to the `AerialGunAppDelegate.m` file and synthesize the soundEngine property.

6. In the `applicationDidFinishLaunching` method, add the following lines of code:

   ```
   //SOUND ENGINE INIT
   self.soundEngine = [[[CDSoundEngine alloc]
   init:kAudioSessionCategory_AmbientSound]autorelease];
   
       NSArray *defs = [NSArray arrayWithObjects:
   ```

```
            [NSNumber numberWithInt:2],nil];
    [self.soundEngine   defineSourceGroups:defs];

    [self.soundEngine   loadBuffer:SND_ID_BULLET
        filePath:@"bullet.mp3"];
    [self.soundEngine   loadBuffer:SND_ID_EXPLOSION
        filePath:@"explosion.mp3"];
    [self.soundEngine   loadBuffer:SND_ID_CLICK
        filePath:@"click.mp3"];
```

7. Ok, that is all we need to do in order to initialize the CDSoundEngine. Now we are ready to start playing sounds with it.

What just happened?

We didn't do much here, but let's go over the details.

After including the necessary frameworks and files, we added a couple of constants. We'll use those, so each time we need to play a sound you know what you are doing.

So, the first thing to do in order to initialize the sound engine is to instantiate by also passing to it the audio session category that it will use. You can find each category's description in the `AudioService.h` file, but I will list them here for you:

- `kAudioSessionCategory_AmbientSound`: Use this category for background sounds. It mixes with other music.
- `kAudioSessionCategory_SoloAmbientSound`: Use this category for background sounds, but other music will stop.
- `kAudioSessionCategory_MediaPlayback`: Use this category for music tracks.
- `kAudioSessionCategory_RecordAudio`: Use this category when you are recording audio.
- `kAudioSessionCategory_PlayAndRecord`: Use this category when recording and playing audio.
- `kAudioSessionCategory_AudioProcessing`: Use this category when using hardware codec or signal processor while not playing or recording audio.

After doing that, we need to define different source groups and the number of sounds each can play at a given time:

```
NSArray *defs = [NSArray arrayWithObjects:
            [NSNumber numberWithInt:2],nil];
[self.soundEngine   defineSourceGroups:defs];
```

In our case, we just have one group that can play two sounds at a time.

Playing Sounds with CocosDenshion

Groups are useful for working with several sounds at the same time, for example, if you want to stop all the sounds from that group.

Then we tell the sound engine to load the buffers with our sounds just by calling the `loadBuffer` method and passing the ID we intend to give to that particular sound and its path.

```
[self.soundEngine  loadBuffer:SND_ID_BULLET filePath:@"bullet.mp3"];
```

Loading the sound into a buffer will ensure that it is loaded into memory and ready for playing when we need it.

That's pretty much all we need to do, now let's see how to actually play those sounds that we have loaded.

Time for action – playing sound effects for explosions

Now that we have the sound engine initialized and some sounds loaded we can play them.

We are going to play the bullet sound when a bullet is fired and the explosion sound when an enemy is hit. In order to do that, add the following line of code in the `Bullet` class's `fire` method:

```
[[AerialGunAppDelegate get].soundEngine playSound:SND_ID_BULLET
    sourceGroupId:CGROUP_ALL pitch:who pan:0.0f gain:1.0f loop:NO];
```

And in the `Enemy` class's `destroy` method add the following line of code:

```
[[AerialGunAppDelegate get].soundEngine playSound:SND_ID_EXPLOSION
    sourceGroupId:CGROUP_ALL pitch:1 pan:0.0f gain:1.0f loop:NO];
```

That's all you need to do.

What just happened?

Playing a loaded sound with CDSoundEngine is very simple. Just call the `playSound` method that takes the following parameters:

- `sound`: The ID you assigned to a particular sound when you loaded the buffer
- `sourceGroupId`: The source group you created at initialization
- `Pitch`: Takes values from 0 to 1 (changing the pitch affects how the effect sounds, and its duration)
- `Pan`: Takes values from 0 to 1 (pan affects the speakers from which the sound comes from. A pan value of 0 would make all the sound come from the left speaker)
- `Gain`: Takes values from 0 to 1 (the volume of the sound)

- Loop: Whether the sound should loop or not

Let's see how we can use CDAudioManager to play some background music now.

Time for action – loading effects asynchronously with CDSoundEngine

CDSoundEngine allows you to load your effects asynchronously. That means that while your sounds are being processed, execution of the rest of the application is not halted. This behavior allows you to have, for example, a loading screen where you can display some loading bar or whatever you want.

In order to have our sounds loaded in that way, we need to change the code that we used before to load the buffers.

1. Open the `AerialGunAppDelegate.m` file.

2. In the `applicationDidFinishLaunching`, search for the following lines:

    ```
    [self.soundEngine    loadBuffer:SND_ID_BULLET
       filePath:@"bullet.mp3"];
    [self.soundEngine    loadBuffer:SND_ID_EXPLOSION
       filePath:@"explosion.mp3"];
    [self.soundEngine    loadBuffer:SND_ID_CLICK
       filePath:@"click.mp3"];
    ```

3. Replace the preceding lines with the following:

    ```
    NSMutableArray *loadRequests = [[[NSMutableArray alloc] init]
       autorelease];
    [loadRequests addObject:[[[CDBufferLoadRequest alloc]
       init:SND_ID_BULLET filePath:@"bullet.mp3"] autorelease]];
    [loadRequests addObject:[[[CDBufferLoadRequest alloc]
       init:SND_ID_EXPLOSION filePath:@"explosion.mp3"] autorelease]];
    [loadRequests addObject:[[[CDBufferLoadRequest alloc]
       init:SND_ID_CLICK filePath:@"click.mp3"] autorelease]];
    [soundEngine loadBuffersAsynchronously:loadRequests];
    ```

What just happened?

We just made our game load the sounds in an asynchronous fashion.

Remember this won't speed anything up or make your app run faster, it will just allow you to do something while the sounds are being loaded.

Playing Sounds with CocosDenshion

Time for action – playing background music with CDAudioManager

CDAudioManager provides access to two `CDLongAudioSource` objects (one for each channel). These `CDLongAudioSource` objects represent an audio source which is long and thus very costly to load using CDSoundEngine. Bear in mind that the current devices can only decode one compressed audio file at a time, so playing multiple compressed files will reduce the performance.

CDAudioManager is ideal for playing background music or narration tracks and it also manages audio session interruption and interaction of other applications with audio.

Let's see how to use it:

1. Include the OpenAL, AudioToolbox, and AVFoundation frameworks in your project.
2. In your `AerialGunAppDelegate`, import the `CDAudioManager.h` file.
3. The first thing to do in order to use the engine is to configure it. In the `applicationDidFinishLaunching` method, add the following line:

   ```
   [CDAudioManager configure:kAMM_FxPlusMusicIfNoOtherAudio];
   ```

   The available modes for passing to the `configure` method are as follows:
   - kAMM_FxOnly: Other apps will be able to play audio.
   - kAMM_FxPlusMusic: Only this application will play audio.
   - kAMM_FxPlusMusicIfNoOtherAudio: If there is music playing, when the application starts, it will continue and the application won't play music.
   - kAMM_MediaPlayback: This application will take over audio.
   - kAMM_PlayAndRecord: This application will take over audio and has input and output.

4. We are going to play the music when a new game starts, so we need to import the `CDAudioManager.h` file in the `GameScene.h` file.
5. Now, in the `initWithDifficulty` method of the `GameLayer` class, add the following line:

   ```
   [[CDAudioManager sharedManager]playBackgroundMusic:@"game_music.mp3" loop:YES];
   ```

6. That's all. Run the application and you should hear your background music playing.

Try playing some music from your iPod library and then running the application to see what happens under different configurations.

What just happened?

With just a couple of lines we played our background music. For your simple needs there are just two steps involved in playing the music, which are as follows:

- Configuring the CDAudioManager
- Calling the `playBackgroundMusic` method with the audio file path and whether it should loop or not.

Pop quiz – playing with CDAudioManager

1. Which of the following is not an audio engine included in Cocos2d?
    a. CDAudioManager
    b. SimpleAudioEngine
    c. CDSoundEngine
    d. CocosSoundMnager

2. Which of the following properties can you set when you play a sound with CDAudioManager?
    a. Pitch
    b. Pan
    c. Gain
    d. Loop
    e. All of the above

3. What is the default number of maximum sources that you can load with CDAudioManager?
    a. 8
    b. 16
    c. 32
    d. 64
    e. There is no default limit

4. Which of the following audio session categories should you use when playing and recording sound?

    a. kAudioSessionCategory_MediaPlayback

    b. kAudioSessionCategory_RecordAudio

    c. kAudioSessionCategory_PlayAndRecord

    d. kAudioSessionCategory_AudioProcessing

Summary

We have reached the end of the audio chapter. After reading this chapter, you should have some basic knowledge of how to play sound effects and music in your game, and know a little of each audio engine included with Cocos2d.

- We saw how to use SimpleAudioEngine for playing audio in a quick and simple way
- Then we used the CDSoundEngine to load sounds and then played them
- Finally, we saw how to load long audio files for background music using CDAudioManager

In the next chapter, we'll start with a new game. We'll use this new game to illustrate the usage of one of the physics engines included in the Cocos2d sources. The next chapter will be very interesting, so keep reading!

10
Using Physics Engines

In this chapter, we will try one of the physics engines included in Cocos2d. Physics engines are used in lots of situations when you want a more realistic simulation in your game. These engines allow you to apply gravity, forces, impulses, check for accurate collisions, to create joints between many objects, and so on.

Even if your game doesn't need to be physically accurate, you can still use these engines for just the collision detection part, which is very difficult and time consuming to get right on your own.

In this chapter, we will:

- Talk about the characteristics of the physics engines included, and why you should use one or another
- Create a new game named Totem Balance which relies a lot on physics
- Learn how to set up a simulation with Chipmunk, add shapes, and bodies
- Learn how to react to collisions between objects

Let's begin.

A word about physics engines

Physics engines are a very powerful thing. They let you simulate real world behavior with a lot of ease. That is why we find ourselves using them a lot, sometimes unnecessarily. When starting your new game, you should consider whether using a physics engine is going to help you, or you are going to make lots of tweaks to make it behave like you need it to.

If your game is a typical board game and you don't need physics, you should avoid using a physics engine just for the collision stuff. These kinds of games use very simple collision detection methods, and you can surely avoid the overhead of having the engine make lots of calculations.

I will give you a brief introduction to both of the available physics engines that you can use with Cocos2d; they are **Chipmunk** and **Box2D**. In the rest of the chapter, we'll be using Chipmunk only because it is easier to learn. Once you are a little more seasoned you should try them both and see which one suits you better.

Both engines are very mature by now and support almost the same features.

Box2d

Box2d was developed by Erin Catto back in 2006. It is an open source, 2D rigid body simulation library for games, and it is written in portable C++.

You can find its documentation at the following URL:

`http://box2d.org/manual.html`

If you need to check their forum, visit the following URL:

`http://box2d.org/forum/`

Chipmunk

Chipmunk was developed by Scott Lembcke. It is an open source, 2D rigid body simulation library, written in C.

You can find its documentation at the following URL:

`http://code.google.com/p/chipmunk-physics/wiki/Documentation`

If you need to check their forum, visit the following URL:

`http://www.slembcke.net/forums/`

So, which one should I use?

If it is the first time that you are using a physics engine, it is really up to you. They are equally excellent engines, both are constantly supported, both forums are always populated with users with lots of questions and answers. So, the deciding factor could be whether you are more comfortable writing code in C or C++.

As you may know, you can compile C or C++ code in your iPhone project. Don't worry it doesn't require a lot of knowledge of these languages (at least for what we are going to do in this book).

Chipmunk also offers an Objective-C wrapper if you don't want to mix C and Objective-C code. You can find it in the source code at the following URL:

http://code.google.com/p/chipmunk-physics/source/checkout

In this chapter, we are going to use Chipmunk for our game and we won't use any Objective-C wrapper. Since most of the examples you will find around the Internet and in the documentation are written in C; you will be better that way.

Totem balance, a physical game

This is the final game we'll be building. It is a physics-based game where you've got blocks of different sizes and shapes piled up, and a totem on top. The objective of the game is removing some of these blocks while keeping the totem from falling to the floor.

The game will feature just a few different types of blocks and no menus or anything else other than the physics part. So we can focus on that.

We'll start by taking a look at the template included in Cocos2d, which is a very good starting point.

Time for action – taking a look at the Chipmunk template

As we saw, back in the first chapter, Cocos2d includes three templates for you to start a project. The regular template that creates a layer and includes the Cocos2d files for you, and two other templates; one includes the necessary files to use Box2D and the other one includes the necessary files to use Chipmunk within your game.

Let's create a new project from the Chipmunk template to see what happens, as follows:

1. Go to **File | New Project** and search for the Cocos2d Chipmunk application template.

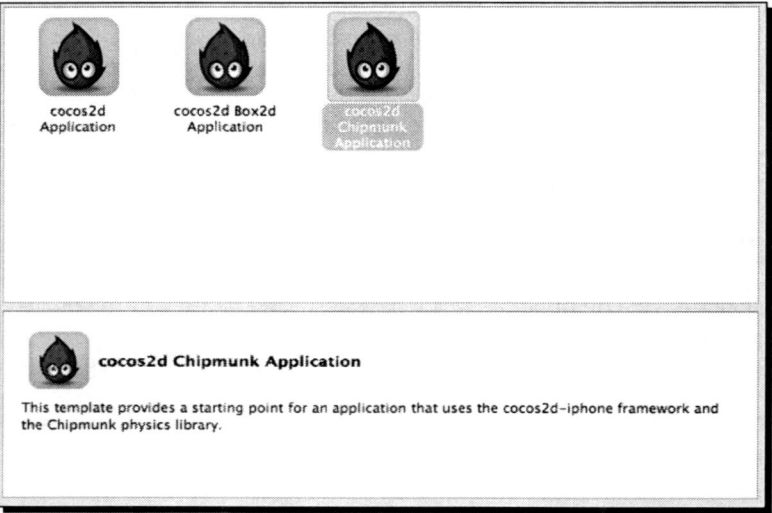

2. Name the new project TotemBalance.
3. Once the project is created, run it. Play a little with it. As you can see, the sprite onscreen will fall depending on how you tilt your device. Also by tapping on the screen, you can add more sprites and see how they behave when they collide.

Chapter 10

What just happened?

We have just tried the Cocos2d + Chipmunk template. Let's take a look at what it does now.

There are a few steps you have to go over in order to be able to use Chipmunk in your game. If you check the init method of the recently created HelloWorld class, you can find the following required lines of code:

```
cpInitChipmunk();

space = cpSpaceNew();
cpSpaceResizeStaticHash(space, 400.0f, 40);
cpSpaceResizeActiveHash(space, 100, 600);

space->gravity = ccp(0, 0);
space->elasticIterations = space->iterations;
```

As you can see, Chipmunk code is written in C language.

The first function call, as its name implies, takes care of initializing Chipmunk.

Then, it creates a cpSpace structure. This space is where all the Chipmunk objects live. Later, we'll add our bodies, shapes, constraints, and so on to the space and make them run, so in each step of the simulation, all the objects contained in it are moved accordingly.

You can set a few properties of the space, which are as follows:

- iterations
- elasticIterations
- gravity

Using Physics Engines

Iterations are the number of passes that Chipmunk does on each body, joint, and other constraints to figure out the forces between the objects in the space. The more iteration, the more accurate the simulation is, but that accuracy has a price, CPU usage. If you set the iterations to a high number, the simulation will consume lot of resources, making the game slower. You should try to find a balance between the accuracy and CPU usage.

Elastic Iterations enhance the simulation of elastic shapes allowing bodies with elasticity higher than 0 to stack nicely.

Gravity is a force applied to all the bodies that are added to the space.

Once we have the space properly set, then we start adding objects to it. In order to do that, you need to do a couple of things. Check the `addNewSpriteX` method in the `HelloWorld` class. This is the method that get's called every time you touch the screen, adding a new sprite to it:

```
-(void) addNewSpriteX: (float)x y:(float)y
{
  int posx, posy;

  CCSpriteSheet *sheet = (CCSpriteSheet*)
  [self getChildByTag:kTagAtlasSpriteSheet];

  posx = (CCRANDOM_0_1() * 200);
  posy = (CCRANDOM_0_1() * 200);

  posx = (posx % 4) * 85;
  posy = (posy % 3) * 121;

  CCSprite *sprite = [CCSprite spriteWithSpriteSheet:sheet
     rect:CGRectMake(posx, posy, 85, 121)];
  [sheet addChild: sprite];

  sprite.position = ccp(x,y);

  int num = 4;
  CGPoint verts[] =
  {
    ccp(-24,-54),
    ccp(-24, 54),
    ccp( 24, 54),
    ccp( 24,-54),
  };

  cpBody *body = cpBodyNew(1.0f, cpMomentForPoly(1.0f, num, verts,
     CGPointZero));
```

```
    // TIP:
    // since v0.7.1 you can assign CGPoint to chipmunk instead of
       cpVect.
    // cpVect == CGPoint
    body->p = ccp(x, y);
    cpSpaceAddBody(space, body);
    
    cpShape* shape = cpPolyShapeNew(body, num, verts, CGPointZero);
    shape->e = 0.5f; shape->u = 0.5f;
    shape->data = sprite;
    cpSpaceAddShape(space, shape);

}
```

Don't worry if you don't understand the preceding code. We'll go over it in more detail in this chapter.

When touching the screen, a new sprite is created at random from a spritesheet and added to the layer. So far so good. We have been doing that for a while. The other half of the method is the new stuff.

Understanding cpBodies and cpShapes

We have to create two things for this sprite in order to have it simulated, namely, a `cpBody` and a `cpShape`.

A `cpBody` is a structure that handles the position of the entity among other things. You can apply forces and impulse to it, and rotate it.

A `cpShape` is what gives the entity the ability to collide with its environment correctly. You can create a line shape, a circle shape, or a poly shape for a given object and then manage which shapes collide with other shapes.

First, we create a `cpBody` structure and pass a few parameters to it. Don't worry about them for the time being, just pay attention to the `verts` array that defines the boundaries of the said object. In this case, it is a rectangle of the sprite size. It could be any polygon, as long as it is convex.

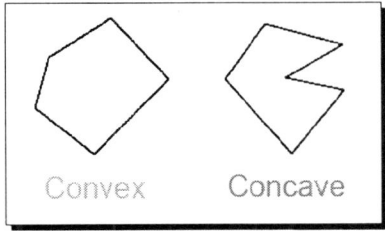

Using Physics Engines

Once this body is created, we set its position to be the point we touched. Then we call the `cpSpaceAddBody` function (passing the space and the newly created body to it) to add this body to the space.

Next, we have to create this object's shape. We do so by calling `cpPolyShapeNew` and passing a few parameters to it, including the verts array that we used before. This will define the collision boundaries of the shape. Then we set the elasticity and friction of the shape. This will change how the shape reacts to collision with other shapes.

Shapes have a user defined property that you can set to anything you want; in this case, we are using it to hold a reference to the object's sprite.

Finally, the shape is added to the space.

Now that we have a new object on the screen, we have to update its position in every frame. Chipmunk takes care of calculating all of that in the `step` method. This method is scheduled to run as fast as the device can handle, thus updating the changes in the simulation at a high rate.

Let's take a look at it:

```
-(void) step: (ccTime) delta
{
  int steps = 2;
  CGFloat dt = delta/(CGFloat)steps;

  for(int i=0; i<steps; i++)
  {
    cpSpaceStep(space, dt);
  }
  cpSpaceHashEach(space->activeShapes, &eachShape, nil);
  cpSpaceHashEach(space->staticShapes, &eachShape, nil);
}
```

Here, the `cpSpaceStep` method is called, thus advancing the simulation.

You can change the amount of steps for a more accurate simulation, of course with a performance penalty.

The `eachShape` parameter that is passed to the `cpSpaceHashEach` function is another function that actually takes care of adjusting the sprite's position and rotation to the body's position and rotation.

In this particular example, when the device is tilted, the gravity is changed to make all the objects on the screen move around.

```
- (void)accelerometer:(UIAccelerometer*)accelerometer
didAccelerate:(UIAcceleration*)acceleration
{
    static float prevX=0, prevY=0;

    #define kFilterFactor 0.05f

    float accelX = (float) acceleration.x * kFilterFactor + (1-
      kFilterFactor)*prevX;
    float accelY = (float) acceleration.y * kFilterFactor + (1-
      kFilterFactor)*prevY;

    prevX = accelX;
    prevY = accelY;

    CGPoint v = ccp( -accelY, accelX);

    space->gravity = ccpMult(v, 200);
}
```

Normally, you may want to move your objects by applying forces and impulses to them instead. We'll see how to do that.

So, that is pretty much what is going on in the template. Now it is our turn to write some code.

Preparing the game

We'll begin by creating our physics-enabled Totem, which just happens to be a rectangle. However, first, we have to make the same modifications that we have made before to the template.

1. Rename the `HelloWorldScene` file to `GameScene`.
2. Rename the `HelloWorld` class to `GameLayer`.
3. Remove the code that makes the sprite appear.
4. Remove the accelerometer code so the gravity doesn't change like in the original template.
5. In the `init` method of the `GameLayer` class, change the space's gravity to (0,-200) so our objects fall down.
6. After that, you can see that four shapes are created, labelled `BOTTOM`, `TOP`, `LEFT`, and `RIGHT`. These are lines that define the boundaries of the game, so elements don't go off the screen. Remove all of them except for the bottom one.

Using Physics Engines

7. Change the device's orientation in the `TotemBalanceAppDelegate` to `kCCDeviceOrientationPortrait`.

Once you do all those changes, check whether the game still runs fine and whether you have a completely blank screen. If everything is running correctly, you can proceed to the next section.

Bringing objects to life

Let's work on the actual game's elements now. We'll create a class for each one which will handle how these objects look and behave.

The Totem

This piece is supposed to be the main one. If it touches the floor, it will break and it's game over. For now, we'll just add it to the scene and have it fall due to gravity.

Time for action – creating a poly-shaped object

1. Create a new class and name it `Totem`.

2. Replace the `Totem.h` file's content with the following lines:

   ```
   #import <Foundation/Foundation.h>
   #import "cocos2d.h"
   #import "chipmunk.h"
   
   @class GameLayer;
   
   @interface Totem : CCNode {
     CCSprite * mySprite;
     cpBody * myBody;
     cpShape * myShape;
     GameLayer * theGame;
   }
   
   @property (nonatomic,retain) CCSprite * mySprite;
   @property (nonatomic,retain) GameLayer * theGame;
   @property (nonatomic,readwrite) cpBody * myBody;
   @property (nonatomic,readwrite) cpShape * myShape;
   
   @end
   ```

Chapter 10

3. Then change the `Totem.m` file's content to look like the following:

```
#import "Totem.h"
#import "GameScene.h"

@implementation Totem

@synthesize mySprite,myBody,myShape,theGame;

-(id) initWithPosition:(CGPoint)pos theGame:(GameLayer*) game
{
  if ((self = [super init]))
  {
    self.theGame = game;
    [game addChild:self z:1];

    mySprite = [CCSprite spriteWithFile:@"totem.png"];
    [game addChild:mySprite z:1];
    [mySprite setPosition:pos];

    int num = 4;
    CGPoint verts[] =
    {
      ccp(-12.5,-24),
      ccp(-12.5, 24),
      ccp( 12.5, 24),
      ccp( 12.5,-24),
    };
```

/*The points above represent the vertices of the polygonal shape that will surround our object. These verts are accounted from the center of the object, that is why we are using points relative to that object. Since the sprite is 25px * 50px, the above points will create a bounding box with vertices at its corners.*/

```
    myBody = cpBodyNew(1.0f, cpMomentForPoly(1.0f, num, verts,
      CGPointZero));

    myBody->p = pos;
    myBody->data = self;
    cpSpaceAddBody(game.space,myBody);
    myShape =  cpPolyShapeNew(myBody, num, verts, CGPointZero);

    myShape->e = 0.5; myShape->u = 0.5;
    myShape->data = mySprite;
    myShape->group =1;
    myShape->collision_type =1;
```

[293]

Using Physics Engines

```
            cpSpaceAddShape(game.space, myShape);
      }

      return (self);
}
@end
```

4. Also, include the `totem.png` file in the `resources` folder.

5. Finally, add the following line to the `init` method of the `GameLayer` class:

   ```
   totem = [[Totem alloc]initWithPosition:ccp(160,340)
   theGame:self];
   ```

6. Run the game now. You should see the Totem appearing at the top of the screen and falling down, as shown in the following screenshot:

What just happened?

What you see there is your first physically simulated object. Let's take a look at the steps involved in its creation.

The first part of the code for the Totem is standard Cocos2d stuff. We add the Totem to the `GameLayer` and create a CCSprite assigning the position passed to the `init` method.

Next, we define the number of `verts` of the the body/shape and create an array specifying them. Those are necessary for poly-shaped objects; as we'll see later, circles don't require that for obvious reasons.

The coordinates for the verts may look weird at first, let me explain that. Chipmunk takes the co-ordinates from the center of the object, so in this case we have a 25 * 48 pixels rectangle. So, from the center (0, 0) we have the first point to the lower-left corner (-12.5,-24).

It doesn't matter which point you choose as the first point, but you always have to move in a clockwise fashion and always describing a convex polygon.

With that information, we proceed with the creation of the body for this object by calling the `cpBodyNew` function which takes the mass and the moment of inertia you want to give to that object. You can assign any value for the moment or let Chipmunk calculate it for you by calling the `cpMomentForPoly` function, like we are doing in our example.

Next, we assign some data to the newly created body. In this case, we set the position and the data pointer to be the Totem object itself.

You can change the body's properties later if you need to; just remember to call the corresponding functions. For example, if you need to change the body's mass, don't do myBody->m = 10. Call the `cpBodySetMass` function. When changing, for example, an object's mass, Chipmunk changes other properties too. If you set it directly, the simulation might break

After creating the body and setting its properties, we have to add it to the space; we do this by calling the `cpSpaceAddBody` function.

Finally, we have to create the object's shape. We do that by calling the `cpPolyShapeNew` function. Then we set some of its properties, such as elasticity and friction. With an elasticity of 1, if objects collide an equal force will be applied and the objects will bounce away. If the elasticity is higher, the objects will bounce away with a higher impulse than they had before colliding. This is useful, for example, in a pinball game for creating bumpers. You can play by changing those and see how the Totem behaves.

Using Physics Engines

There are two interesting properties of the shape that we are changing there, namely, `group` and `collision_type`.

Shapes with equal groups won't generate collisions between themselves. That is useful, for example. If you have to create an object whose shape is pretty irregular, you can add several different shapes to a single object and have them overlap without generating extra overhead from collision computation.

You can set the group of a shape by doing `theShape | group = x`, where x is any positive integer number.

The `collision_type` is what will allow us later to add collisions between two objects. We'll see in a moment how to tell Chipmunk what to do when a shape of type 1 collides with a shape of type 2.

You can set the collision type of a shape by doing `Shape | collision_type = y`, where y is any positive integer number.

After all that is set, we just add the shape to the space by calling the `cpSpaceAddShape` function.

Time for action – creating the goal platform

Just as we created the Totem, we now have to create the goal platform. This is just another block which we'll use later to check if the player won the level by making the Totem stand over it.

The code is almost the same as the Totem's, so not much explanation is required:

1. Create a new class named `Goal`.
2. The following is the `Goal.h` file's content:

   ```
   #import <Foundation/Foundation.h>
   #import "cocos2d.h"
   #import "chipmunk.h"
   
   @class GameLayer;
   
   @interface Goal : CCNode
   {
       CCSprite * mySprite;
       cpBody * myBody;
       cpShape * myShape;
       GameLayer * theGame;
   }
   ```

```
@property (nonatomic,retain) CCSprite * mySprite;
@property (nonatomic,retain) GameLayer * theGame;
@property (nonatomic,readwrite) cpBody * myBody;
@property (nonatomic,readwrite) cpShape * myShape;

@end
```

3. The following is the `Goal.m` file's contents:

```
#import "Goal.h"
#import "GameScene.h"
@implementation Goal
@synthesize mySprite,myBody,myShape,theGame;
-(id) initWithPosition:(CGPoint)pos theGame:(GameLayer*) game
{
  if ((self = [super init]))
  {
    self.theGame = game;
    [game addChild:self z:1];

    mySprite = [CCSprite spriteWithFile:@"goal.png"];
    [game addChild:mySprite z:1];
    [mySprite setPosition:pos];

    int num = 4;
    CGPoint verts[] =
    {
      ccp(-55.5,-13.5),
      ccp(-55.5, 13.5),
      ccp( 55.5, 13.5),
      ccp( 55.5,-13.5),
    };

    myBody = cpBodyNew(1.0f, cpMomentForPoly(1.0f, num, verts,
      CGPointZero));

    myBody->p = pos;
    myBody->data = self;
    cpSpaceAddBody(game.space,myBody);
    myShape =  cpPolyShapeNew(myBody, num, verts, CGPointZero);

    myShape->e = 0.5; myShape->u = 0.5;
    myShape->data = mySprite;
    myShape->group =4;
```

Using Physics Engines

```
        myShape->collision_type =4;
        cpSpaceAddShape(game.space, myShape);
    }

    return (self);
}


@end
```

4. Add a new ivar to the GameLayer Goal * goal, and import the corresponding Goal.h file.

5. Now, add the following line to the GameLayer's init method:

   `goal = [[Goal alloc]initWithPosition:ccp(160,25) theGame:self];`

6. Run the game and you should see a platform at the bottom of the screen, as shown in the following screenshot:

What just happened?

There isn't anything new in here. At the moment this new block behaves just like the Totem. In further examples, we'll handle the interaction of the Goal with the Totem.

Removable blocks

Let's continue with the creation of the other blocks. We'll create three types of blocks: a rectangle, a triangle, and a circle. These blocks will have the ability to disappear on touch, forcing the player to choose carefully which blocks to remove so the Totem doesn't fall to the floor.

Time for action – building blocks

We'll create a new class named `TouchableBlock`, which will hold the logic for making the blocks disappear. Then we will create three classes that will be subclasses of this `TouchableBlock` class. Each of these will represent the geometric figures that I just mentioned.

1. Create a new class named `TouchableBlock`.
2. Replace the `TouchableBlock.h` contents with the following lines:

   ```
   #import <Foundation/Foundation.h>
   #import "cocos2d.h"
   #import "chipmunk.h"

   typedef enum tagState
   {
     kStateGrabbed,
     kStateUngrabbed
   } touchState;

   @class GameLayer;

   @interface TouchableBlock : CCNode <CCTargetedTouchDelegate>
   {

     CCSprite * mySprite;
     cpBody * myBody;
     cpShape * myShape;
     GameLayer * theGame;
     touchState state;
   }
   ```

Using Physics Engines

```objc
@property (nonatomic,retain) CCSprite * mySprite;
@property (nonatomic,retain) GameLayer * theGame;
@property (nonatomic,readwrite) cpBody * myBody;
@property (nonatomic,readwrite) cpShape * myShape;
@property (readwrite,nonatomic) touchState state;

@end
```

3. Replace the `TouchableBlock.m` contents with the following lines:

```objc
#import "TouchableBlock.h"
#import "GameScene.h"

@implementation TouchableBlock
@synthesize mySprite,myBody,myShape,theGame,state;
-(id) init
{
  if ((self = [super init]))
  {
    self.state = kStateUngrabbed;
  }

  return (self);
}
-(void)dealloc
{
  [super dealloc];
}
@end
```

4. Now, create one of the subclasses; create three new classes and name them `BlockRectangle`, `BlockTriangle`, and `BlockCircle`.

5. The following is the content of `BlockRectangle.h`:

```objc
#import <Foundation/Foundation.h>
#import "cocos2d.h"
#import "chipmunk.h"
#import "TouchableBlock.h"

@class TouchableBlock;

@interface BlockRectangle : TouchableBlock {

}

@end
```

Chapter 10

The other two classes have the same content except for the class's name. Just copy the preceding code.

6. Now, let's create the `init` method of each class, so when an object of that class is instantiated, we get either a rectangle, a triangle, or a circle created and positioned on the screen.

   The following is the BlockRectangle's content:

   ```
   #import "BlockRectangle.h"
   #import "GameScene.h"

   @implementation BlockRectangle
   -(id) initWithPosition:(CGPoint)pos theGame:(GameLayer*) game
   {
     if ((self = [super init]))
     {
       self.theGame = game;
       [game addChild:self z:1];

       mySprite = [CCSprite spriteWithFile:@"block_rect.png"];
       [game addChild:mySprite z:1];
       [mySprite setPosition:pos];

       int num = 4;
       CGPoint verts[] =
       {
         ccp(-33,-12),
         ccp(-33, 12),
         ccp( 33, 12),
         ccp( 33,-12),
       };
   //As we did before we set the polygonal bounding which will serve as a //collision shape.

   //We create a cpBody for this object and then add it to the space
       myBody = cpBodyNew(1.0f, cpMomentForPoly(1.0f, num, verts,
         CGPointZero));

       myBody->p = pos;
       myBody->data = self;
       cpSpaceAddBody(game.space,myBody);
   //Then, we create a cpShape for this object and then add it to the space
   ```

[301]

Using Physics Engines

```objc
        myShape =   cpPolyShapeNew(myBody, num, verts, CGPointZero);

        myShape->e = 0.5; myShape->u = 0.5;
        myShape->data = mySprite;
        myShape->collision_type =3;
        cpSpaceAddShape(game.space, myShape);

    }

    return (self);
}
-(void)dealloc
{
    [super dealloc];
}
@end
```

BlockTriangle's code:

```objc
#import "BlockTriangle.h"
#import "GameScene.h"

@implementation BlockTriangle
-(id) initWithPosition:(CGPoint)pos theGame:(GameLayer*) game
{
    if ((self = [super init]))
    {
        self.theGame = game;
        [game addChild:self z:1];

        mySprite = [CCSprite spriteWithFile:@"block_tri.png"];
        [game addChild:mySprite z:1];
        [mySprite setPosition:pos];

        int num = 3;
        CGPoint verts[] =
        {
            ccp(0,15),
            ccp(16,-15),
            ccp( -16, -15),
        };

        myBody = cpBodyNew(1.0f, cpMomentForPoly(1.0f, num, verts,
            CGPointZero));

        myBody->p = pos;
```

```objc
      myBody->data = self;
      cpSpaceAddBody(game.space,myBody);
      myShape =  cpPolyShapeNew(myBody, num, verts, CGPointZero);

      myShape->e = 0.5; myShape->u = 0.5;
      myShape->data = mySprite;
      myShape->collision_type =3;
      cpSpaceAddShape(game.space, myShape);

   }

   return (self);
}
-(void)dealloc
{
   [super dealloc];
}
@end
```
BlockCircle's code:
```objc
#import "BlockCircle.h"
#import "GameScene.h"
@implementation BlockCircle
-(id) initWithPosition:(CGPoint)pos theGame:(GameLayer*) game
{
   if ((self = [super init]))
   {
      self.theGame = game;
      [game addChild:self z:1];

      mySprite = [CCSprite spriteWithFile:@"block_circ.png"];
      [game addChild:mySprite z:1];
      [mySprite setPosition:pos];


      myBody = cpBodyNew(1.0f, cpMomentForCircle(1,16,16,
              CGPointZero));

      myBody->p = pos;
      myBody->data = self;
      cpSpaceAddBody(game.space,myBody);
      myShape =  cpCircleShapeNew(myBody,16,CGPointZero);

      myShape->e = 0.5; myShape->u = 0.5;
```

Using Physics Engines

```
        myShape->data = mySprite;
        myShape->collision_type =3;
        cpSpaceAddShape(game.space, myShape);

    }

    return (self);
}
-(void)dealloc
{
    [super dealloc];
}
@end
```

As you can see, the code is very similar except for the images used and the body/shape created.

7. Now that we have our new classes, we can add some objects to the scene. Let's toss some blocks at any position for now. In the `GameScene` interface, add a new property: an `NSMutableArray * touchableBlocks`, which will hold our blocks.

8. In the `GameScene`, we have to import the three new classes' header files and then in the `init` method, populate the array that we just created with our new blocks. Add the following lines:

```
touchableBlocks = [[NSMutableArray alloc]init];
for(int i =0;i<5;i++)
{
  BlockRectangle * b = [[BlockRectangle
    alloc]initWithPosition:ccp(160,50+50*i) theGame:self];
  [touchableBlocks addObject:b];
  [b release];
}

for(int i =0;i<5;i++)
{
  BlockTriangle * b = [[BlockTriangle
    alloc]initWithPosition:ccp(80,50+50*i) theGame:self];
  [touchableBlocks addObject:b];
  [b release];
}

for(int i =0;i<5;i++)
{
```

```
        BlockCircle * b = [[BlockCircle
           alloc]initWithPosition:ccp(240+10*i,50+50*i) theGame:self];
        [touchableBlocks addObject:b];
        [b release];
   }
```

Remember to release the `touchableBlocks` array in the `dealloc` method of the `GameScene` class.

9. Run the game now. You should see three piles of different shaped objects falling due to the gravity force and colliding with each other nicely, as shown in the following screenshot:

What just happened?

We just created the base for our touchable blocks. The code involved is not very different from what we did with the Totem at the beginning of the chapter. We created three classes to hold different kind of shapes, added a sprite to each of them, and set the properties for their bodies and shapes.

Have a go hero – creating other complex shapes

What if you want to use some other shape? That's pretty simple! Just remember that Chipmunk only allows you to use convex poly shapes. Is that a problem? Not at all; Chipmunk does allow you to add multiple shapes to a single body and that's all you need to create more complex shapes. Just create a body like we have been doing all this time, and then create and add as many shapes as you want to the space. You just have to keep the following two things in mind:

- The collision group: All the shapes must share the same group or you'll be generating collision checkings all the time.
- The position of each shape relative to the object: When creating a shape the last parameter is always a CGPoint which is the offset of the shape. We have been setting it at 0,0 all this time, but you'll need to change it in order to arrange the shapes of an object. For example, if you want to have a rectangle with a triangle on top, you could set the first shape's offset to 0,0 and the other one to 0,30 to have it 30 px above the first one.

Time for action – destroying shapes with touch

Let's do some work on our `TouchableBlock` class now. What we want to do is remove any of these blocks on touch. For that, we are going to use the `targetedTouchDelegate` again.

1. Open the `TouchDelegate.m` file and add the following lines:

```
- (CGRect)rect
{
  //CGSize s = [self.texture contentSize];
  CGRect c = CGRectMake(mySprite.position.x-(self.mySprite.textureRect.size.width/2) * self.mySprite.scaleX ,
   mySprite.position.y-(self.mySprite.textureRect.size.height/2)*
   self.mySprite.scaleY,self.mySprite.textureRect.size.width*
   self.mySprite.scaleX,self.mySprite.textureRect.size.height *
   self.mySprite.scaleY);
   return c;
}

- (void)onEnter
{
  [[CCTouchDispatcher sharedDispatcher] addTargetedDelegate:self
    priority:0 swallowsTouches:YES];
  [super onEnter];
}
```

```objc
- (void)onExit
{
  [[CCTouchDispatcher sharedDispatcher] removeDelegate:self];
  [super onExit];
}

- (BOOL)containsTouchLocation:(UITouch *)touch
{
   return CGRectContainsPoint(self.rect, [self
      convertTouchToNodeSpaceAR:touch]);
}
```

2. Now, add the methods to handle the actual touching:

```objc
- (BOOL)ccTouchBegan:(UITouch *)touch withEvent:(UIEvent *)event
{
  if (state != kStateUngrabbed) return NO;
  if ( ![self containsTouchLocation:touch]) return NO;

  CGPoint location = [touch locationInView: [touch view]];
  location = [[CCDirector sharedDirector] convertToGL: location];

  state = kStateGrabbed;
  return YES;
}

- (void)ccTouchEnded:(UITouch *)touch withEvent:(UIEvent *)event
{
  NSAssert(state == kStateGrabbed, @"Unexpected state!");

  CGPoint location = [touch locationInView: [touch view]];

  location = [[CCDirector sharedDirector] convertToGL: location];

  cpSpaceRemoveBody(theGame.space, myBody);
  cpSpaceRemoveShape(theGame.space, myShape);
  cpBodyFree(myBody);
  cpShapeFree(myShape);

  [theGame removeChild:mySprite cleanup:YES];
  [theGame removeChild:self cleanup:YES];

  [theGame.touchableBlocks removeObject:self];

  state = kStateUngrabbed;
}
```

3. Run the game now, and touch one of those brown blocks; they should be removed on touch, as shown in the following screenshot:

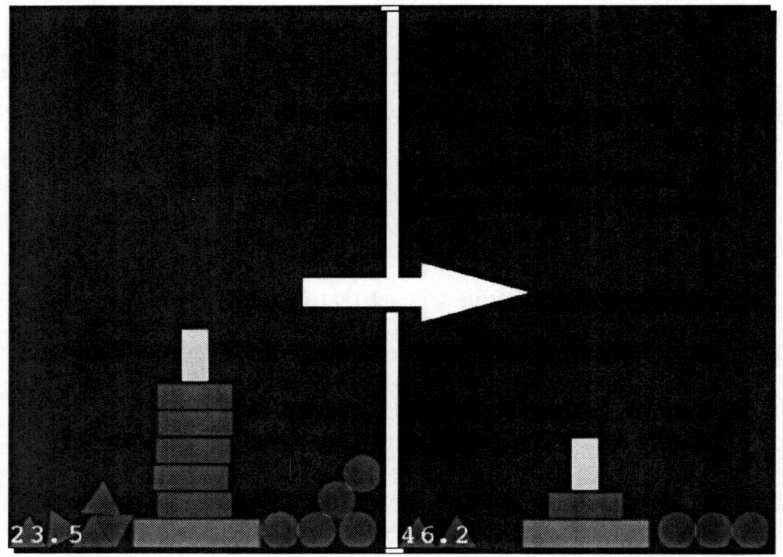

What just happened?

The code we used to detect touches on a block is the same that we used in previous chapters; let's take a look at what actually happens when a block is touched.

When a block gets touched (actually, when the finger is lifted), we call a few Chipmunk functions.

`cpSpaceRemoveBody` and `cpSpaceRemoveShape` take care of removing the body and shape you pass to them from the space.

Then we remove them from memory by calling `cpBodyFree` and `cpShapeFree`.

Finally, we remove the `TouchableBlock` node and its CCSprite from its parent, so the sprite goes away. We are also removing the object from the `NSMutableArray` containing it.

Chapter 10

Collision callbacks

Chipmunk allows you to detect the collision of two shapes with each other and allows you to define functions that get called when that happens. This is one of the most important features and it is used in every type of game in lots of situations. For example, in a shooter game you may want to check collisions between the main character and enemy bullets, between the character and powerups, between the enemies and your bullets, and so on.

As mentioned before, one pre-requisite to be able to detect collisions between two elements is that they both must have a CpShape and that CpShape must have its group attribute set to a different value. The CpShape must also have a collision_type set to any number; this number will be used to register the collision pair function. You can check the collision between objects with different collision_type numbers (for example, when character and powerups collide, collect power up) or with the same number (for example, when two enemies collide, destroy them).

Once you define the collision_type for the shapes you created all you have to do is tell chipmunk to check for collisions between those two shapes and implement the collision callback functions.

In order to register a collision callback, so Chipmunk can check when two shapes are colliding, you have to call the following function somewhere in your code:

```
void cpSpaceAddCollisionHandler(
    cpSpace *space,
    cpCollisionType a, cpCollisionType b,
    cpCollisionBeginFunc begin,
    cpCollisionPreSolveFunc preSolve,
    cpCollisionPostSolveFunc postSolve,
    cpCollisionSeparateFunc separate,
    void *data
)
```

This cpSpaceAddCollisionHandler function takes eight parameters, which are as follows:

- Space: This is the space the shapes belong to.
- Two collision_type: These are the numbers which you assigned to the two shapes that you want to check the collisions for.
- Four collision functions: These will get called in a particular order under different circumstances. I will explain them in a moment.
- Any other data you might need: Generally, this is the layer where the action occurs.

Using Physics Engines

There are four different events that you can have Chipmunk to register during a given collision between two shapes:

- `Begin`: This is called when two shapes have started touching for the first time in the current step. You can return false to ignore the collisions between them. If you do that, the `preSolve()` and `postSolve()` functions will not be called and collision forces will not be calculated. The `separate()` function will still be called.

- `preSolve`: This is called when two shapes are touching. You can return false to ignore the collision for the current step or return true to process it normally.

- `postSolve`: This is called when two shapes are touching and the collision has already been processed. You can use this function to calculate collision forces. For example, if you want to know how hard two objects hit, to play different sounds accordingly.

- `Separate`: This is called when two shapes have stopped touching for the first time in the current step.

You don't need to define the four functions for each collision you want to handle; most times just defining the `preSolve` function is more than enough.

Let's put this knowledge into practice with an example.

Time for action – losing the game

So, we said that if the Totem touches the floor, it will break and the game will be lost. Let's do that. We'll define a collision callback for the Totem's shape and the line shape that is the floor, then, when we detect a collision, we will restart the game.

1. Check whether you have defined a `collision_type` for the Totem's shape. If you haven't, set it to 1 by calling inside the Totem's `init` method as follows:

   ```
   myShape->collision_type = 1;
   ```

2. Do the same for the floor shape, setting its `collision_type` to another value, for example 2. This is situated at the `init` method of the `GameLayer` class:

   ```
   cpShape *shape;
   
   // bottom
   shape = cpSegmentShapeNew(staticBody, ccp(0,0), ccp(wins.width,0), 0.0f);
   shape->e = 1.0f; shape->u = 1.0f;
   shape->collision_type = 2;
   cpSpaceAddStaticShape(space, shape);
   ```

3. Now, at the end of the `init` method, add the following line:

   ```
   cpSpaceAddCollisionHandler(space, 1, 2, NULL,loseGame, NULL, NULL,
   self);
   ```

   As you can see, we have only defined the `preSolve` function for this callback; the three others are set to `NULL` because we don't need to do anything in there.

4. Now, let's implement the `loseGame` function. Move to the top of the `GameScene.m` file, outside of the @implementation of the class, since this is a C function. Add the following lines in there:

   ```
   static int loseGame(cpArbiter *arb, cpSpace *space, void *data)
   {
     CP_ARBITER_GET_SHAPES(arb, a, b);

     Totem * t = (Totem *) a->body->data;

     GameLayer *game = (GameLayer *) data;

     CCScene * gs = [GameLayer scene];
     [[CCDirector sharedDirector] replaceScene:gs];

     return 0;
   }

   @implementation GameLayer
   // ... Rest of the code ...
   ```

5. Run the game now and have the Totem fall to the floor. You will see how the game gets restarted as soon as the Totem touches the line shape at the bottom.

What just happened?

Those are the steps involved in creating a collision response for two shapes. As you can see, it is pretty straightforward. Just set the `collision_type` for the shapes, tell chipmunk which functions to call when the collision occurs, and then implement them.

Let's take a closer look to the implementation of the `loseGame` function (the one called in the preSolve instance).

When the `loseGame` function is called, you can retrieve three pieces of data from the collision: the cpArbiter, the space, and the custom data that you passed when you defined the collision callback (in our case we passed the `GameLayer` instance).

Using Physics Engines

The cpArbiter is the name given to the collision pair. We can get a bunch of useful things from there, such as the actual objects that generated the collision. In order to do that, we call the `CP_ARBITER_GET_SHAPES(arb, a, b);` macro to retrieve the shapes involved from the cpArbiter, then we can get the `cpBody` from that shape and the actual object from the `cpBody`, since we set them to hold that data before. We do that by calling:

```
Totem * t = (Totem *) a->body->data;
```

We can also retrieve the custom data that we sent by casting it:

```
GameLayer *game = (GameLayer *) data;
```

We are not using any of those two pieces of data here since we just replace the scene for which we didn't need any of those; I just put that in there so you know how to retrieve them if needed.

Time for action –winning the game

Now let's focus on how to have the player win the game. The game is won when the player manages to have the Totem fall over the Goal block and it remains touching it for some amount of seconds.

1. Check that you have defined a `collision_type` for the Goal's shape. If you haven't set it to 4 by calling inside the Goal's `init` method:

   ```
   myShape->collision_type = 4;
   ```

2. Add a property to the `GameLayer` class: an int `secondsForGoal` which will handle the countdown.

3. Add a new collision callback for the Totem and the Goal in the GameLayer's `init` method:

   ```
   cpSpaceAddCollisionHandler(space, 1, 4, startCounting,NULL, NULL, stopCounting, self);
   ```

4. Add the two collision functions that get called:

   ```
   static int startCounting(cpArbiter *arb, cpSpace *space, void *data)
   {
     CP_ARBITER_GET_SHAPES(arb, a, b);

     //The above macro "generates" 2 structs for us (a and b) which are the 2 shapes that collided. We can retrieve their bodies from them and then their "data"  property which we set to be the actual instance of the class.
   ```

```
   Totem * t = (Totem *) a->body->data;
   Goal * g = (Goal *) b->body->data;

//We know the "a" struct will always represent the Totem
and the struct "b" will always represent the Goal because
that is the order we pass those 2 object's groups in the
cpSpaceCollisionHandler function.

   GameLayer *game = (GameLayer *) data;

   [game schedule:@selector(winCount) interval:1];

   return 1;
}

static void stopCounting(cpArbiter *arb, cpSpace *space, void
*data)
{
   CP_ARBITER_GET_SHAPES(arb, a, b);

   Totem * t = (Totem *) a->body->data;
   Goal * g = (Goal *) b->body->data;

   GameLayer *game = (GameLayer *) data;

   [game unschedule:@selector(winCount)];
   game.secondsForGoal =0;
   NSLog(@"SEPARATED");

}
```

5. Finally, add the `winCount` method to the `GameLayer` class:

```
-(void)winCount
{
  secondsForGoal++;
  NSLog(@"Seconds passed: %d",secondsForGoal);
  if(secondsForGoal >=5)
  {
    NSLog(@"WON!!!");
    [self unschedule:@selector(winCount)];
    secondsForGoal =0;
  }
}
```

Using Physics Engines

6. Run the game now, and check the console for the messages. When the Totem is touching the Goal, you should see the number of seconds that passed since the contact began. When it reaches 5, you should see a "WON!!!" message. If the blocks get separated, you should see a "SEPARATED" message.

What just happened?

We have just seen other ways of using the collision callback functions.

First, we created a new collision handler, but this time we defined begin and separate functions, naming them `startCounting` and `endCounting` respectively.

The `startCounting` function just schedules the `winCount` method to be called every second, and it returns 1 to tell chipmunk not to ignore the collision.

The `winCount` method will increment the `secondsForGoal` ivar and will check if it reached 5; if it does, it lets us know the game has been won.

If for some reason the Totem and the Goal stop touching, the `stopCounting` function gets called. this function resets the countdown and unschedules the `winCount` method.

Placing static shapes

Chipmunk allows you to create these so-called static shapes. Static shapes are objects that don't move. Their positions are not affected by other objects and gravity is not applied to them and also, Chipmunk optimizes calculations for them.

In order to create a static shape, you must create a `cpBody` with infinite mass and moment of inertia, which must not be added to the space, so it doesn't gain velocity from the gravity force.

Then you must create a static shape by calling `cpSpaceAddStaticShape`. The rest of the code remains the same.

We have been using static shapes for our floor. Let's take a look at the code:

```
cpBody *staticBody = cpBodyNew(INFINITY, INFINITY);
cpShape *shape;

// bottom
shape = cpSegmentShapeNew(staticBody, ccp(0,0), ccp(wins.width,0),
0.0f);
shape->e = 1.0f; shape->u = 1.0f;
shape->collision_type = 2;
cpSpaceAddStaticShape(space, shape);
```

As you can see from the preceding code taken from the GameLayer's `init` method, we create a `cpBody` with infinite mass and moment of inertia, then we create a segment shape that gets added to the space by calling `cpSpaceAddStaticShape`.

 If you need to move this static shape around, you must call `cpSpaceRehashStatic()` so Chipmunk gets notified about the movement of the shape. If you don't, the precalculated cache data for the collision will be used and collisions will be missed. This is expensive to do, so do it only if the static shapes are moved from their original position.

Pop quiz – physics engines

1. How can you create a physics simulation in Cocos2d?
    a. Using Box2D, which is included in Cocos2d
    b. Using Chipmunk, which is included in Cocos2d
    c. Rolling your own solution
    d. Porting some other physics engine
    e. All of the answers above are valid

2. How can you create a static shape using chipmunk?
    a. You can't do that
    b. By setting the body's mass and moment to INFINITY, not adding the body to the space, and adding the shape with the `cpSpaceAddStaticShape` function
    c. By setting the cpShape's `isStatic` property to TRUE

3. Which of the following is a limitation imposed by chipmunk?
    a. You can't have more than 50 bodies in your simulation
    b. A body must always have one and only one shape associated with it
    c. Once a shape has been added to the space it can't be removed
    d. None of the above is a limitation imposed by chipmunk

Summary

We have gone over the basics of using Chipmunk physics engine in our game. With everything we did in the chapter, you must already have a feeling of how useful and time saving it is to use a physics engine to model objects, movements, and collisions.

In this chapter, we learned:

- How to set up Chipmunk physics engine
- How to create objects and place them into the simulation
- How to react to collisions between objects

In the next chapter, we will take a look at OpenFeint and how to set it up.

11
Integrating OpenFeint

Most games offer the player the possibility of uploading their high scores and adding friends, so they can compare their scores with them, unlock achievements, and lots of other social activities which add more interaction and enhance the gaming experience. This is a trend that started some time ago in console games and it has moved to all platforms.

What if you want your players to be able to do those things? How much time would it take you to roll out your own solution? Here is where Social Networks come to the rescue.

There are many of these Social Networks available for you to integrate within your game, to name a few: Openfeint, Scoreloop, Agon, Crystal, Plus+, Game Center, and so on.

I chose to talk about OpenFeint, as it has the following advantages:

- It is totally free for the developers and players
- It is one of the most popular ones
- You don't require an invitation to use it
- It offers lots of features such as leaderboards, achievements, challenges, forums, and so on

Integrating OpenFeint

In this chapter, we are going to learn the basics of OpenFeint:

- How to register and download the SDK
- How to integrate it into your game to display the dashboard
- How to load high scores to a leaderboard
- How to create achievements

Let's begin.

Signing up and downloading the SDK

We'll start by downloading the latest OpenFeint SDK, which at the time of this writing is 2.6.1.

The sign up process is quite fast and doesn't require you to enter lots of information. Let's go through it.

Time for action – signing up and downloading the SDK

1. Visit the OpenFeint's developer page at `http://openfeint.com/developers` and click on the **GET THE SDK** button. You'll be prompted with a sign up box where you have to enter some basic information, as shown in the following screenshot:

2. Once you have registered, you can log in at the top of the page to enter the OpenFeint's developer dashboard.

3. At the top bar in the dashboard, you can click on the **Download SDK** link to start downloading it, as shown in the following screenshot:

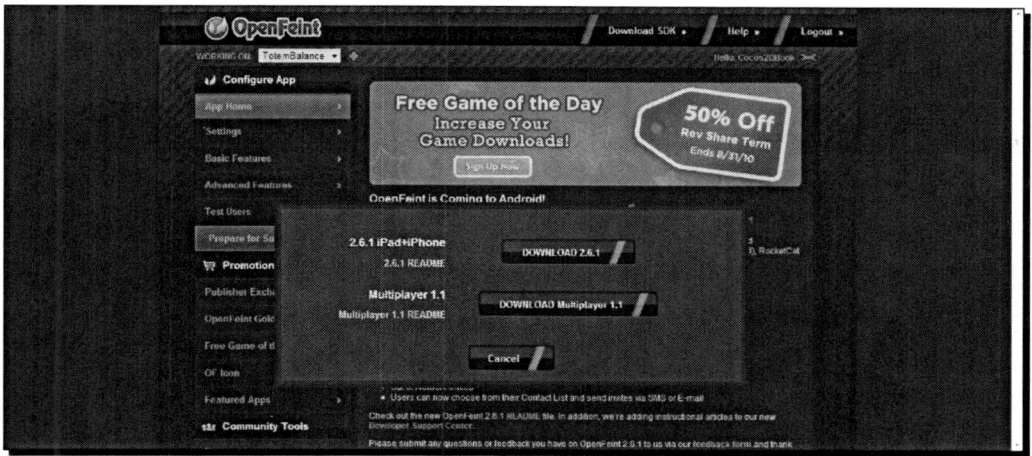

What just happened?

That's all the work that is required to download OpenFeint's SDK. In the following sections, we are going to use it in our game to be able to use all the features we want.

Before moving on, have a look around the dashboard. When we signed up, we were required to provide your game's name. With that information, OpenFeint automatically creates a game for you to start using. You can find information about the game on the main page (we'll use this soon).

To the left, we have lots of menu items which allow us to enter the different configuration pages of our game, promotional tools, and community tools. You should explore all these pages, as we don't have much space in the book to take a look at all that great stuff.

I should also mention the help section that is accessible through the **Help** link at the top of the dashboard. There, you can find articles related to the implementation of the different OpenFeint features. You can also access the developer support forum from there, which contains lots of useful tips and news; it should be your first stop if you get stuck with something.

Integrating OpenFeint into your game

The integration process is pretty simple. We just need to add some frameworks to our project, copy the files that we just downloaded to our project, and then write a couple of lines of code. Let's get to it. You'll be using OpenFeint in no time!

Time for action – making OpenFeint work

We'll use our latest game as an example of OpenFeint integration. Have in mind that when you download the OpenFeint SDK, you get the integration instructions with it. I will summarize those instructions in here, but if at any point you feel lost or when we are done, you still get errors, try looking at the README file or at their troubleshooting guide. Having said that, let's give it a go.

1. Open the TotemBalance project where we left it last time.

2. Drag the unzipped OpenFeint folder into the project, including it as a group and not as a folder reference, as shown in the following screenshot:

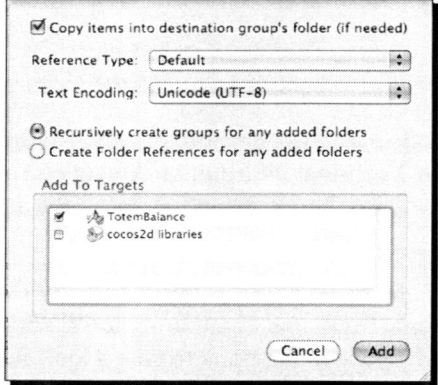

3. Delete the unused resources from the `assets` folder. For example, if your game is iPhone portrait only, remove the other two folders. I'll remove the `iPad` and `iPhone_Landscape` folders.

4. Open the project information panel by right-clicking on the project's icon in the Group and Files panel and selecting **get info**. Then do the following:

    - Select the **Build** tab and set configuration to **All configurations**.
    - Search for the **Other linker flags** setting and add ObjC to it.
    - Make sure that **Call C++ Default Ctors/Dtors** in Objective-C is checked under **GCC 4.2 – Code Generation**.

5. Add the following frameworks (if you haven't already included them) by right-clicking in your project and selecting **Add | Existing frameworks**:

    ❑ Foundation
    ❑ UIKit
    ❑ CoreGraphics
    ❑ QuartzCore
    ❑ Security
    ❑ SystemConfiguration
    ❑ Libsqlite3.0.dylib
    ❑ CFNetwork
    ❑ CoreLocation
    ❑ MapKit
    ❑ Libz.1.2.3.dylib
    ❑ AddressBook
    ❑ AddressBookUI

6. You should have a prefix header file in your project under the `Other sources` group. Add the following line to it:

    `#import "OpenFeintPrefix.pch"`

7. All the files in your project must have a `.mm` extension instead of `.m`. Select the `.m` files in your Groups & files panel and rename them to `.mm`.

8. Build and run your project. If you get no errors, then we are good to continue.

> You will notice something like 1300 + warnings when you build the project. You can eliminate them by opening the project settings and adding to Other C flags, under GCC 4.2 – Language the following: -Wno-write-strings. If you don't want to do this, it is ok, it won't affect the final product.

What just happened?

We just completed the first step of OpenFeint integration. We can't see any results, yet. Next we'll start making some changes, so we can have the player display the OpenFeint dashboard that contains information about the game, displays leaderboards, achievements, and any other OpenFeint content.

Integrating OpenFeint

Time for action – displaying the OpenFeint dashboard

1. First of all, before showing anything, we have to initialize OpenFeint. You can do that in the title screen of your game. Since our game has just one screen, I'll do that in there. Open the `GameScene.h` file.

2. At the top of the file, import the OpenFeint headers:

   ```
   #import "Openfeint.h"
   ```

3. Now we have to add the method that initializes OpenFeint and call it when our game loads. Add the following method to the `GameLayer` class:

   ```
   - (void)initializeOpenfeint
   {
     NSDictionary* settings = [NSDictionary
       dictionaryWithObjectsAndKeys:
       [NSNumber numberWithInt:UIInterfaceOrientationPortrait],
         OpenFeintSettingDashboardOrientation, @"Totem",
         OpenFeintSettingShortDisplayName,
       [NSNumber numberWithBool:YES],
         OpenFeintSettingEnablePushNotifications,
       [NSNumber numberWithBool:YES],
         OpenFeintSettingDisableUserGeneratedContent, nil];


     [OpenFeint initializeWithProductKey:@"QcXyKeEQkfvlOgzFRpSkDw"
        andSecret:@"4CHHeJHixnd6ElHgapfr5VktoLDpzSgYGYKNEM4nA"
        andDisplayName:@"Totem" andSettings:settings
        andDelegates:[OFDelegatesContainer
           containerWithOpenFeintDelegate:
           self andChallengeDelegate:nil
        andNotificationDelegate:self]];
        // see OFDelegatesContainer.h

     // You probably want to invoke this from a button instead of
        directly here.
     [OpenFeint launchDashboard];
   }
   ```

4. Since we are using the `GameLayer` class as a delegate for a couple of OpenFeint protocols, we have to make the class implement them. Change the interface of the `GameLayer` class as follows:

   ```
   @interface GameLayer : CCLayer <OpenFeintDelegate,OFNotificationDelegate>
   ```

Chapter 11

5. Now call this new method from the `init` method of the `GameLayer` class, so when the game starts, OpenFeint is configured and the dashboard launches automatically.

6. If you build and run your game now, OpenFeint will be working. However, we still have to handle some situations before moving on.

7. We have to handle what happens with OpenFeint when our application is inactive or in the background. In order to do that, we have to open the `TotemBalanceAppDelegate.mm` file and import the `Openfeint.h` file again. Then add the following calls:

    ```
    - (void)applicationWillResignActive:(UIApplication *)application
    {
      [[CCDirector sharedDirector] pause];
      [OpenFeint applicationWillResignActive];
    }
    - (void)applicationDidBecomeActive:(UIApplication *)application {
      [[CCDirector sharedDirector] resume];
      [OpenFeint applicationDidBecomeActive];
    }

    -(void) applicationDidEnterBackground:(UIApplication*)application
    {
      [[CCDirector sharedDirector] stopAnimation];
      [OpenFeint applicationDidEnterBackground];
    }
    -(void) applicationWillEnterForeground:(UIApplication*)application
    {
      [[CCDirector sharedDirector] startAnimation];
      [OpenFeint applicationWillEnterForeground];
    }
    ```

8. There is still one more thing to do. If you have already tried the application, you may notice that after you close the dashboard, the game continues playing. We have solved that by pausing the game when the dashboard is launched and resuming it when the dashboard is closed:

    ```
    - (void)dashboardWillAppear
    {
      [[CCDirector sharedDirector] pause];
    }
    - (void)dashboardDidDisappear
    {
      [[CCDirector sharedDirector] resume];
    }
    ```

Integrating OpenFeint

9. Now we are good to go. Try launching the application. See what you've got. In a real game, you would want to launch the dashboard only when the player touches some button.

The following screen will appear the first time the player plays the game, to let him confirm whether he wants to use OF or not:

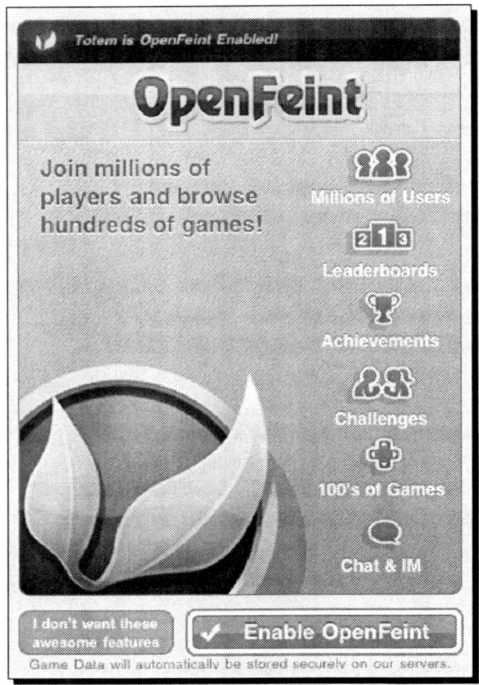

The following is the OpenFeint's main screen when set to portrait mode:

What just happened?

We just covered some necessary steps to get OpenFeint working and showing the dashboard. Let's go over them.

In the `initializeOpenfeint` method, we created a dictionary that we use as OpenFeint's settings. In there, we define things such as the orientation which OpenFeint is supposed to use, the name it should display, and if we want to enable services, such as push notifications.

Then we initialize it using the key, secret, and short name; the config dictionary we just created and we also set the delegates for it. In this case, we are using the same `GameLayer` class to handle OpenFeint events such as the dashboard opening and closing.

You may be wondering where those keys and secret strings come from. You can get that information in the main page of the OpenFeint developer site.

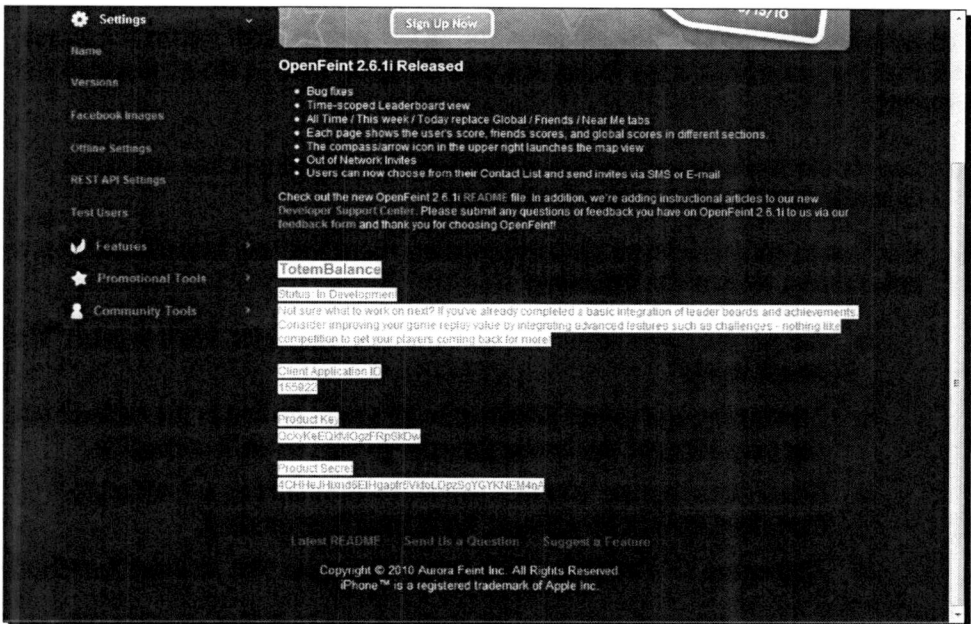

Since we set our `GameLayer` class as delegate of the OpenFeint protocol, we can have it call a few useful methods to handle situations such as the dashboard being opened or closed.

Those were the basics of getting OpenFeint set up and launching the dashboard. Next we are going to create a leaderboard, configure it, and have our game add scores to it.

Integrating OpenFeint

Adding leaderboards to your game

Leaderboards are a good way to keep your player engaged. Having them compete over a goal against their friends will keep them entertained for a while and if your game is really addictive they are not going to stop until they are in the top spot.

OpenFeint supports adding any number of leaderboards to your game where you can display scores globally or filtered by friends, filter them by time to display all of them, or just the scores submitted that week or day. It even supports adding aggregate leaderboards which summarize several leaderboards.

Let's see how to create one for our game.

Time for action – creating a leaderboard

Let´s create a leaderboard that keeps track of the fastest players. That means the player who finishes the game (makes the Totem rest over the goal) faster is the #1 player of the leaderboard.

1. Go into the leaderboards section of the OpenFeint developer site and select **Leaderboards** to create a new leaderboard.

2. We have to complete some basic information about the new leaderboard that we are creating, such as the following:

    - **Name**: The name which will appear inside Openfeint. We'll name it "Time attack mode".
    - **Descending sort order**: Whether lower scores go first in the table or last. In our case we want the lowest times to go first, so we'll uncheck it.
    - **Allow worse scores**: Whether worse scores should be submitted to Openfeint servers for a player. We'll leave it unchecked.
    - **Aggregate**: This leaderboard is not an aggregate one, so leave it unchecked.
        - **Min and max versions**: It allows you to define whether this leaderboard is visible in certain versions of your game. Leave it as it is.

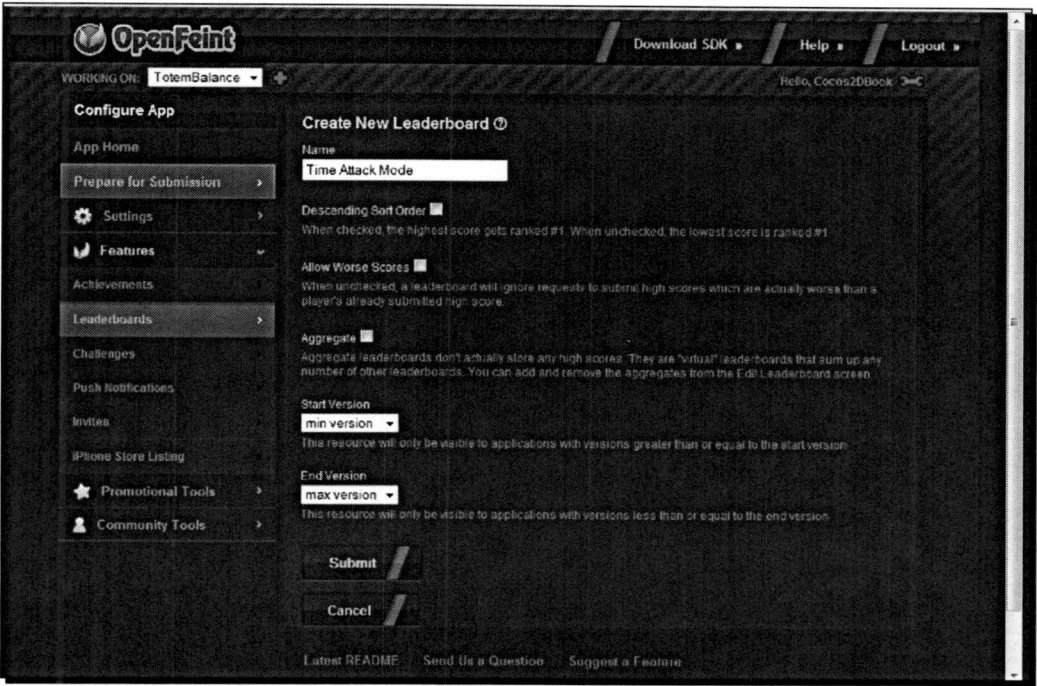

3. Now, in the leaderboards section, you can see your newly created one and edit it. Check whether an ID has been assigned to it. This ID is what we use inside our game to tell it to submit scores to that particular leaderboard.

4. Open the TotemBalance project and get ready to make some little modifications in order to support leaderboards.

5. First, we need to count the time so we know what score to submit. Add a new int property to the `GameLayer` class, and call it `timePassed`.

6. In the `init` method, add the following line to the end:

    ```
    [self schedule:@selector(countTimePassed) interval:1];
    ```

7. Add the `countTimePassed` method to the class:

    ```
    -(void)countTimePassed
    {
        timePassed ++;
    }
    ```

8. Import the following header file in your `GameScene.mm` file:

   ```
   #import OFHighScoreService.h
   ```

9. Add the following line to the `winCount` method:

   ```
   -(void)winCount
   {
     secondsForGoal++;
     NSLog(@"Seconds passed: %d",secondsForGoal);
     if(secondsForGoal >=5)
     {
       NSLog(@"WON!!!");

       [OFHighScoreService setHighScore:timePassed
         forLeaderboard:@"484243" onSuccess:OFDelegate()
         onFailure:OFDelegate()];

       [self unschedule:@selector(winCount)];
       secondsForGoal =0;
     }
   }
   ```

10. Run the game and meet the winning conditions. After a while you should see an OpenFeint notification telling you that you achieved a new high score, as shown in the following screenshot:

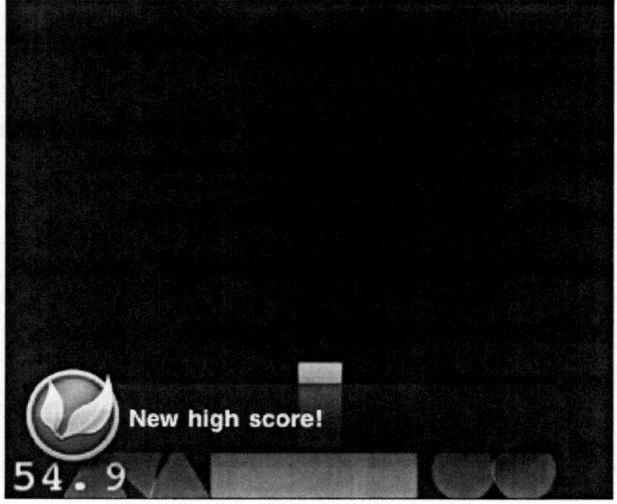

What just happened?

Yes, with just one line of code you were able to submit a highscore to the leaderboard that you created moments ago. Pretty easy, huh?

There isn't much to go over, here. After we handled how to assign points for a player by using the `timePassed` variable we used it to submit a highscore.

Have a go hero – customizing leaderboard look and feel

A nice feature of OpenFeint is allowing the developer to customize almost everything. A good Openfeint integration is the one that uses your own application's graphics to show leaderboards, achievements, and so on. So, if you don't like how these things are shown, you can retrieve the data and display it however you want.

So, what I propose to you is that you find a way to have the game show leaderboards in a customized way instead of OpenFeint's look and feel.

Hint: check the OFScoreEnumerator module, which allows an application to download a set of scores at a time. You can find more information on how to do this at the following URL:

`http://www.openfeint.com/ofdeveloper/index.php/kb/article/000079`

Adding achievements to your game

OpenFeint supports adding achievements to your game too. Achievements are another way to reward your players for doing something. Those things that the players are rewarded for can be anything, from normal behavior such as completing a level to crazy things which a player would only do to get that achievement like losing 10 times with the same enemy.

OpenFeint rewards players with Feint points which are shown in their profile allowing them to compare themselves with friends and compete with each other.

As a developer, you can create up to 100 achievements per game and assign a maximum of 1000 Feint points spread over those 100 achievements. Most games have around 15 to 20 achievements awarding around 800 Feint points. Also remember that a single achievement cannot give more than 200 Feint points.

Integrating OpenFeint

Time for action – creating an achievement

Let's see how we can add an achievement to our game. I'll guide you through the steps involved in the creation of one of them, then you can repeat the process to add as many as you want. This achievement will reward the player for removing all the touchable sprites from the screen.

1. Go into the achievements section of the OpenFeint developer site and select to create a new achievement.

2. We have to complete some basic information about the new achievement that we are creating, such as the following:

    - **Title**: The name of the achievement. It will be displayed in the list of achievements when unlocked. I'll call it `The Janitor`.
    - **Feint score**: How many Feint points you want to assign to it. I'll give it a full `200` points.
    - **Icon**: You can add an icon for the achievement or leave it blank and have OpenFeint assign a default image to it. I`ll leave it blank.
    - **Secret**: Whether it is secret or not. A secret achievement won't show its title or description until it has been unlocked.
    - **Description**: How the achievement is unlocked. I'll write: `Clean the building`.
    - **Start/end version**: The versions in which you want this achievement to appear. I'll leave their defaults values.

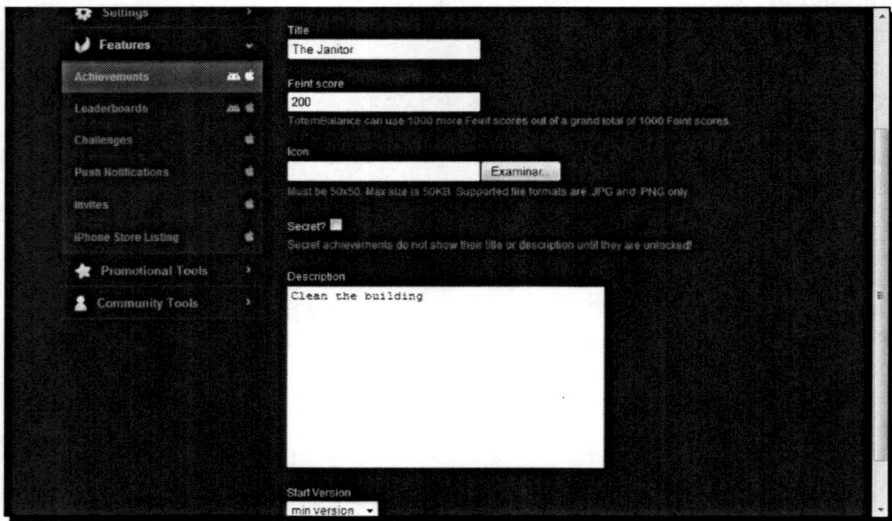

3. Once you save these changes, you can return to the achievements section. There you can see the list of achievements that you have created for the game. Take notice of the ID assigned to them since, just like with leaderboards, you will need to use it in your code.

4. Let's go back to our game's project. First we need to add the necessary code so that we know when the player meets the conditions for unlocking the achievement. That can be easily done by adding a call to a method each time we touch one of those blocks. Add the following code at the end of the TouchableBlock's ccTouchesEnded method:

```
[theGame checkRemainingBlocks];
```

5. Now, in your GameLayer class, add the checkRemainingBlocks method:

```
-(void)checkRemainingBlocks
{
  if([touchableBlocks count]==0)
  {
    [OFAchievementService unlockAchievement:@"582562"];
  }
}
```

6. In the GameScene.mm file, you have to import the necessary header file to be able to call the OpenFeint method above:

```
#import "OFAchievementService.h"
```

7. Run the game and touch all the touchable blocks in there. You should see a message pop up as shown in the following screenshot:

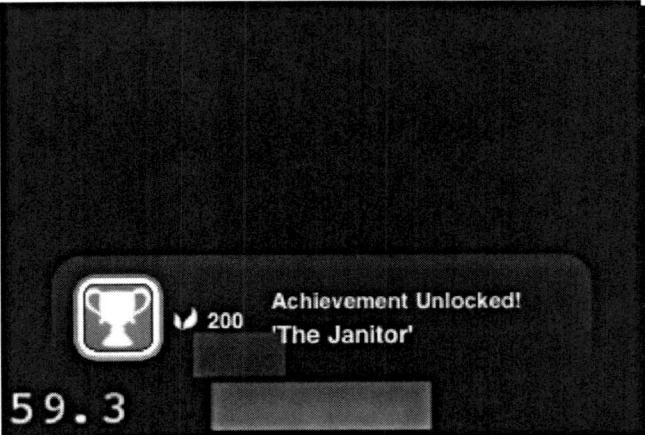

Integrating OpenFeint

 If an achievement has been unlocked and you try to unlock it again, OpenFeint won't do anything (which is good). Have that in mind if the second time you want to try this it doesn't show anything. You can only delete scores and achievements from a test user.

Creating a test user is very simple. Just click on the **Test User** tab in your OpenFeint developer dashboard, and you will need to provide them with an e-mail and password for that test account. It has to be an existing user.

What just happened?

We just saw how to add your own achievements with OpenFeint. What we did was to make our `TouchableSprite` class notify the `GameLayer` each time a block was removed. That way, when the number of blocks was 0, an achievement was unlocked.

In order to unlock an achievement, we call the OFAchievementService's `unlockAchievement` method and pass the achievement ID to it.

Pop quiz – OpenFeint

1. Which of the following services is not offered by Openfeint?
    a. Achievements
    b. Leaderboards
    c. Challenges
    d. Turn-based multiplayer
    e. All of those services are offered

2. How many achievements can you have in your game?
    a. Less than 10
    b. Any number of them
    c. Up to 100
    d. It depends on how much you pay
    e. It depends on how good your game is

3. Can you customize the look of the leaderboards?
    a. You can't. Just use what they give you.
    b. You can use some OpenFeint classes to retrieve the data from their servers and show it however you want.

Submitting your game for OpenFeint approval

Before being able to use the full service offered by OpenFeint, you must complete the submission process. It is very straightforward and doesn't take much time.

First you must complete the iPurchase information; iPurchase is a service offered by OpenFeint which adds your game to their catalogue, allowing players to browse and look for games that have OpenFeint integrated through the dashboard.

You can complete that information in the iPhone store listing tab in the developer site. Once you complete that information, you can go to the **Prepare for submission** tab and complete the process.

You'll be asked to agree to the OpenFeint Developer License Agreement. Once you do so, your game will be waiting for approval. If everything is right, in one or two days, you should receive a confirmation e-mail from the OpenFeint staff letting you know that the process has been completed successfully and all the services are online.

Summary

In this chapter, we took a quick look at OpenFeint's features and learned the steps to integrate it into our games. We learnt:

- How to sign up and download the SDK
- How to configure Openfeint and start it up
- How to show the dashboard
- How to create leaderboard
- How to create achievements
- How to submit the game for Openfeint's approval

We have reached the end of the book. I hope you found most of the content useful. I can't wait to see what games you make with Cocos2d!

A
Pop Quiz Answers

Chapter 2:

Playing with Sprites

1	2	3
b	a	e

Chapter 3:

Let's do some actions

1	2	3
c	c	e

Chapter 4:

Pasting labels

1	2	3
a	d	a

Chapter 5:

Surfing through scenes

1	2	3
c	c	c

Chapter 6:

Menu design

1	2	3
d	b	d

Chapter 7:

Implementing particle systems

1	2	3
d	c	d

Chapter 8:

Familiarizing yourself with tilemaps

1	2	3
d	c	c

Chapter 9:

Playing sounds with CocosDenshion

1	2	3
d	e	c

Chapter 10:

Using physics engine

1	2	2
e	b	d

Chapter 11:

Integrating OpenFeint

1	2	3
e	c	b

Index

Symbols

-(CCNode*) getChildByTag:(int) tag method 26
@endStone 45
-(id) addChild(CCNode *)node method 26
-(id) addChild(CCNode *)node z:(int)z method 26
-(id) addChild(CCNode *)node z:(int)z tag:(int)tag method 26
-(id) removeAllChildernWithCleanup:(BOOL) cleanup method 26
-(id) removeChildByTag* (int)tag cleanup:(BOOL) cleanup method 26
-(id) removeChild: (CCNode *)node cleanup:(BOOL)cleanup method 26
+(id)scene method 151
-(NSArray *)children method 26

A

accelerometer
  about 176
  accelX variable 179
  hardware, using 177
  hero movements, checking 177-179
achievements
  adding, to game 329
  creating 330-332
  description 330
  Feint score 330
  icon 330
  secret 330
  start/end version 330
  title 330
actions
  about 93
  animation actions 116
  basic actions 94
  composition actions 101
  ease actions 105
  effect actions 107
  special actions 111
Add button 146
addImageAsync method 89
addImage method 78
addNewSpriteX method 288
addTargetedDelegate method 54
AerialGunAppDelegate class 276
Aerial Gun game
  about 150
  bullets, reusing 171-176
  enemies behavior, enhancing 170
  enemies, creating 165
  Enemy class, creating 165-170
  game logic, implementing 159
  hero class, creating 162-164
  new scenes, creating 150
  preparation steps 160-162
  scene transitions 158
  shooting bullets, creating 171
Alignment parameter 130
allowTouch variable 57
anchorPoint property 76
Anchor point property 25
Angelcode's Bitmap Font Generator 142
Angle property 233
angleVar property 233
animation actions
  about 116
  CCAnimation class 123
  CCSpriteFrame 121
  CCSpriteFrameCache 121

stones, animating 117-120
answers
  pop quiz 335-337
AppDelegate 15, 18
applicationDidBecomeActive: method 22
applicationDidFinishLaunching method 89, 276, 280
applicationWillResignActive method 204
applicationWillTerminate: method 22

B

background
  rewindBackgroundMusic method 274
background music, handling
  isBackgroundMusicPlaying method 275
  pauseBackgroundMusic method 274
  preloadBackgroundMusic method 275
  resumeBackgroundMusic method 274
  rewindBackgroundMusic method 274
  stopBackgroundMusic method 275
basic actions
  CCFadeOut action, using 98, 99
  colour actions, using 98
  opacity actions, using 97
  position actions, using 95, 96
  rotation actions, using 97
  scale actions, using 96
  stone falling animation 94, 95
  time bar, modifying 99, 100
  visible actions, using 97
Begin 310
BitmapFontAtlas
  creating, BM Font tool used 142-147
blocks
  building 299-303
  complex shapes, creating 306
BM Font tool
  used, for creating BitmapFontAtlas 142-147
Bool parameter 66
Box2d 284
Build tab 320

C

callback method 89
CCAnimation class 123
CCBitmapFontAtlas
  texts, creating with 136-140
CCBitmapFontAtlas label 137, 140
CCCallFuncND, special actions
  example 115
CCCallFuncN method 114
CCDirector
  about 17
  AppDelegate, code 20, 21
  HelloCocos2dAppDelegate 18, 19
  scene management 21, 22
  types 18
CCDirector class 22
ccDrawPoint method 91
CCLabel 17, 23, 131
CCLabelAtlas
  scores, displaying 134
  scores, updating 134
  text, displaying with 133
CCLabelAtlas object 136
CCLabels
  about 126
  Alignment parameter 130
  Dimensions parameter 130
  FontName parameter 130
  FontSize parameter 130
  removeSpriteAndBegin method 129
  String parameter 130
  Tutorial class 130
  Tutorial class, creating 126-128
  Tutorial class, improving 133
CCLayer 23
CCLayers, adding to scenes
  Game Over screen, creating 198
  game pausing, on inactive 204
  HUD, creating 192-197
  pause menu, creating 198-204
  types 192
CCMenu 208
CCMenuItemImage 208, 212
CCMenuItemLabel 207
CCMenuItems
  about 208
  moving 211
CCMenuItemSprite 208, 212
CCMenuItemToggle 218
CCMenuItemToggle object 224
CCMenuItemToogle 208

[340]

CCNode class 45, 91
CCNodes
  about 22
  actions 93
  CCLabel, creating 24
  handling 26
  handling methods 26
  HelloWorldScene class 22-24
  HelloWorldScene.m file 23
  onEnter method 26
  onEnterTransitionDidFinish method 27
  onExit method 27
  properties 25
  subclasses 22
  subclass, features 25
Ccp 24
ccpDistance method 58
CCPointParticleSystem 234
CCQuadParticleSystem
  about 234
  bombs, exploding 235, 239
CCScheduler 34
CCSprite 131
CCSpriteBatchNode object 81
CCSprite class 37
CCSpriteFrameCache class 121
CCSprites
  creating 43
  creating, from files 44
  creating, from spritesheet 44
  creating, from textures 44
  properties, playing with 73
  sprite frames 44
  texture, changing 76
CCSprites properties
  playing with 73
  time bar, creating 74, 75
CCTargetedTouchDelegate protocol 45
CCTexture2D 78
CCTextureCache 34, 78, 89
CCTMXObjectGroup class 269
CCTouchBegan method 90
CCtouchDispatcher class 53
CCTouchEnded method 58, 90, 132
ccTouchesBegan method 180
ccTouchesCancelled method 180
ccTouchesEnded method 180, 331

ccTouchesMoved method 180
CCTouchHandler class 54
CCTransitionScene class 159
CDAudioManager
  sound effects, playing 280
CDSoundEngine
  background music, playing 279
  effects loading asynchronously 279
  setting up 276-278
  sound effects, playing 278
centerOfGravity property 233
CGPoint local variable 139
CGRectContainsPoint method 57
CGRectIntersectsRect method 184
CGRect object 57
changeDifficulty method 224
changeTime method 75
charMapFile parameter 135
checkCollisions method 186
checkGroupsAgain method 72
checkGroups method 62, 72, 75, 83, 134, 137
checkRemainingBlocks method 331
Chipmunk
  about 284
  template 286-289
classes folder 16
Cocos2d
  about 12
  Aerial Gun game 149
  downloading, for iPhone 12
  objects, retrieving in 266-269
  scenes 149
  scene transitions 158
  templates, installing 14
  tilemaps, loading in 259
  tilemaps, using 260, 261
  touches, handling on layers 179
cocos2d applications, debugging
  deallocing messages, checking 34
  debug messages, removing 35, 36
  errors, finding 35
  messages, checking 33, 34
Cocos2d, downloading for iPhone
  about 12
  folders, requiring 12
  samples project, opening 12
Cocos2d Schedulers

method call, delaying 31, 32
timers, using 27, 28
using 27
Cocos2d Sources 16
CocosDenshion
about 12, 271
sound effects adding, CDSoundEngine used 275
sound effects adding, SimpleAudioEngine used 272
using, as CDAudioManager 272
using, as CDSoundEngine 272
using, as SimpleAudioEngine 271
Cocoslive 12
collision callbacks
about 309
game, losing 310-312
game, winning 312, 313
collisions, detecting
CGRectIntersectsRect method, using 184
enemies, shooting down 184-186
collision_type 296, 309
Coloured Stones game
building 38
game board, creating 48
images, adding 41, 42
composition actions
about 101
CCRepeat 102
CCRepeat action, using 104
CCRepeatForever 102
CCSequence 102
CCSequence, using 103
CCSpawn 102
disappear effect, creating 101, 102
grid background, animating 103
configure method 280
containsTouchLocation method 57
convertToGL method 57
countTimePassed method 327
cpBody 289
cpBodyNew function 295
cpBodySetMass function 295
cpBody structure 289
cpMomentForPoly function 295
cpPolyShapeNew function 295
cpShape 289
cpSpaceAddBody function 290, 295

cpSpaceAddCollisionHandler function 309
cpSpaceAddShape function 296
cpSpaceHashEach function 290
cpSpaceRehashStatic() 315
cpSpaceStep method 290
cpSpace structure 287

D

damage method 242
dashboard, OpenFeint
displaying 323-325
data
loading 227
saving 227
dealloc method 305
debugging
debuggingCocos2d applications 33
Dimensions parameter 130
DisplayLink Director 18
drainBar method 76
drainTime method 99, 133, 134
draw method 91
drawPrimitives 91
duration property 233

E

eachShape parameter 290
ease actions
about 105, 106
animations, modifying 106, 107
effect actions
background effect, adding 108, 109
node's grid, modifying 107, 108
single action, applying to multiple CCNodes 110
Effects panel 146
endColor property 233
endColorVar property 233
endRadius property 233
endRadiusVar property 233
endSize property 233
endSizeVar property 233
endSpin property 233
endSpinVar property 233
enemyInterval variable 215
ExplosionParticle 240
ExplosionParticle class 240

External 12
Extras 12

F

fadeAndShow method 157, 158
features, CCNodes 25
fireAndDestroy method 32
fire method 30
FontName parameter 130
FontSize parameter 130
four collision functions 309
FPS 17

G

game
    achievements, adding 329
    achievements, creating 330-332
    improving, ways 148
    leaderboards, adding 326
    OpenFeint, integrating 320
    preparing 291
    submitting, for OpenFeint approval 333
game board
    creating 48
    stones, placing in grid 49, 51
GameLayer class 49, 129, 322, 325, 331
GameLayer instance 311
GameScene class 160, 305
GameScene interface 304
getChildByTag method 136
GET THE SDK button 318
Glyph cache radio button 145
gravity mode
    particle systems, implementing 234
Gravity property 233
grid
    refilling 68, 69

H

HelloCocos2d project 16
    application, running 17
    classes folder 16
    creating 16, 17
    resources folder 16
HelloWorld CCLayer 23

HelloWorld class 287, 288
HelloWorldScene class 22
Hiero Bitmap Font Tool 142

I

imageLoaded method 89
image menu items
    difficulty selection screen, adding 212-215
    using 212
images
    displaying in game, CCSprites used 41
    preloading 88, 89
initDir variable 57
initializeOpenfeint method 325
init method 42, 136, 146, 214, 215, 298, 311
initWithColor method 203
initWithDifficulty method 215, 280
iOS programming 11
iPhone
    Cocos2d, downloading 12
isBackgroundMusicPlaying method 275
itemHeight parameter 135
itemWidth parameter 135

L

Layer 15
layerNamed method 259
layer touches
    bullets, firing 180
    ccTouchesEnded method 181
    handling 180
    methods, adding to GameLayer 180
leaderboards
    adding, to game 326
    aggregate 326
    allow worse scores 326
    creating 326-329
    descending sort order 326
    editing 327
    look and feel, customizing 329
    min and max versions 326
    name 326
License files 12
Life property 233
liveVar property 233
loadBuffer method 278

logic
  analyzing 70-73
loseGame function 311
loseLife method 191

M

Mainloop Director 18
MainMenuLayer class 212
menu
  adding with texts, to main scene 210, 211
  CCMenuItemImage 208
  CCMenuItemLabel 207
  CCMenuItemSprite 208
  CCMenuItemToogle 208
  creating 207
  with texts, adding to main scene 208
menu items
  animating 216-218
  image menu items, using 212-216
  toggle menu items, using 218-224
method
  applicationDidBecomeActive: 22
  applicationWillTerminate: 22
  drainTime 99, 112
  fadeAndShow 157
  reorderChild 261
  replaceScene 157
  runWithScene 21
  setAnimation 123
  startGame 113
method call
  destroying 31
moveStonesDown method 78, 83, 119

N

newGame method 213
new project
  creating, in Xcode 38, 40
new scenes
  creating 150
  SplashScene, creating 151-157
NSMutableArray 66
NSMutableSet 66
NSSets 66
NSString object 130
NSTimer Director 18

NSUserDefaults 225
NSUserDefaults class 225

O

object layer, Tiled
  example 265, 266
  objects, retrieving in Cocos2d 266-269
  using 265
object parameter 54
OFScoreEnumerator module 329
onEnter method 54
onEnter method, CCNodes 26
onEnterTransitionDidFinish method, CCNodes 27
onExit method 54
onExit method, CCNodes 27
OpenFeint
  advantages 317
  dashboard, displaying 323-325
  downloading 318, 319
  integrating, in game 320
  making, to work 320, 321
OpenFeint SDK
  signing up 318, 319
OpenGL
  using 90, 91
OptionsLayer 219
OptionsLayer class 219
OptionsScene 219
Other linker flags setting 320
Outline effect 146

P

particle designer
  smoke trail, creating 245-248
  used, for creating particle systems 244
ParticleMeteor system
  analyzing 231, 232
particle system
  about 230
  creating, particle designer used 244
  implementing, in gravity mode 234
  moving ways, modifying 243
  ParticleMeteor system, analyzing 231
  particle test, running 231
particle system, properties

Angle property 233
angleVar property 233
centerOfGravity property 233
duration property 233
endColor property 233
endColorVar property 233
endRadius property 233
endRadiusVar property 233
endSize property 233
endSizeVar property 233
endSpin property 233
endSpinVar property 233
Gravity property 233
Life property 233
liveVar property 233
posVar property 233
radialAccel property 233
radialAccelVar property 233
rotatePerSecond property 233
rotatePerSecondVar property 233
Speed property 233
speedVar property 233
startColor property 233
startColorVar property 233
startRadius property 233
startRadiusVar property 233
startSize property 233
startSizeVar property 233
startSpin property 233
startSpinVar property 233
tangentialAccel property 233
tangentialAccelVar property 233
Texture property 233
pauseBackgroundMusic method 274
pauseGame method 205
PauseLayer class 199
pause method 22
physical game 285
physics engine
  about 284
  pop quiz 315
physics game
  Box2d 284
  Chipmunk 284
pixel formats
  about 43
  RGB5_A1 43

RGB565 43
RGBA4444 43
RGBA8888 43
placeInGrid method 47
placeStones method 50
playBackgroundMusic method 281
playEffect method 273
playSound method
  parameters 278
poly-shaped object
  creating 292-295
pop quiz
  answers 335-337
position property 25
postSolve 310
postSolve() function 310
posVar property 233
PowerVR 43
preferences
  loading 225, 226
  saving 225, 226
preloadBackgroundMusic method 275
preloadEffect method 273
preSolve 310
preSolve function 310, 311
priority parameter 54
properties, CCNodes
  Anchor point 25
  position 25
  rotation 26
  scale 25
  visible 26
  z-order 26
puzzle game
  building 38

R

radialAccel property 233
radialAccelVar property 233
radius mode
  using 239-242
rect method 57
remainingTime property 76
removal method 132
removeSpriteAndBegin method 129
removeSprite method 114

Rendering panel 145
reorderChild method 261
replaceScene method 157
Resources 12
resources folder 16
resumeBackgroundMusic method 274
resumeGame method 204
resume method 22
Resume method 201
rewindBackgroundMusic method 274
RippedHolde class 267
rotatePerSecond property 233
rotatePerSecondVar property 233
rotation property 26
runningScene method 205
runWithScene method 21

S

samples project, opening
   SpriteTest, compiling 13, 14
   SpriteTest, running 13, 14
   .xcodeproj file, opening 12, 13
Sample Text panel 144
scale property 25
scene management 21
scenes
   CCLayers, adding to 192
   layers, adding to 192
scene transitions
   from SplashScene to MainMenuScene 158, 159
selectedIndex property 224
selectMode method 214, 216
Separate 310
separate() function 310
setAnimation method 123
setIsEnabled:NO method 216
setScale method 147
setStoneColor method 48, 72, 83
setString method 136
setTexture method 77
shapes
   collision group 306
   complex shapes, creating 306
   destroying, with touch 306-308
   position 306
SimpleAudioEngine

background music, playing 274
   using 272, 273
sound effects
   handling, CDSoundEngine used 275
   handling, methods 273
   handling, SimpleAudioEngine used 272, 273
sound effects handling
   playEffect method 273
   preloadEffect method 273
   stopEffect method 273
   unloadEffect method 273
space 309
special actions
   CCCallFunc 111
   CCCallFuncN 111
   CCCallFuncND 111
   CCCallFuncND, using 114
   using 111-114
Speed property 233
speedVar property 233
SplashScene class 155
sprite
   about 37
   creating, from Spritesheet 81-83
SpriteBatchNode 83
Spritesheets
   about 79, 80
   colored stones, creating 86-88
   creating, zwoptex used 85
   sprites, creating from 81-83
sprites, interacting with
   stones, registering for receiving touches 54
   touches, handling 55, 56
Sprite texture
   CCTextureCache 78
   changing 76
spriteWithFile Class method 42
startCharMap parameter 135, 136
startColor property 233
startColorVar property 233
startCounting function 314
startGame method
   113
startRadius property 233
startRadiusVar property 233
startSize property 233
startSizeVar property 233

startSpin property 233
startSpinVar property 233
state property 45
static shapes
   placing 314, 315
step method 290
Stone class
   about 72
   creating 44-48
stones
   swapping 59-61
stones matching
   checking 62-66
stoneType property 45
stopBackgroundMusic method 275
stopCounting function 314
stopEffect method 273
String parameter 130, 135
swallowsTouches parameter 54
swap
   cancelling 58
swapStones method 58, 59

T

tangentialAccel property 233
tangentialAccelVar property 233
templates 12
templates, installing
   project, creating from 16
   steps 14
   uses 14
Test 12
texts
   creating, with CCBitmapFontAtlas 136-138
   displaying, with CCLabelAtlas 133-136
Texture property 233
ThreadMainLoop Director 18
Tiled
   object layer 265
   tile layer 265
   using, for tilemaps creation 253
tilemaps
   about 251
   creating, Tiled used 253
   loading, in Cocos2d 259
   using 251, 252

tilemaps, Cocos2d
   hexagonal 253
   isometric 253
   orthogonal 253
tilemaps creating, Tiled used
   about 253
   options, choosing 255
   steps 253-258
tilemaps, loading in Cocos2d
   actions, running on layers 261
   black gaps, fixing 263
   glitches, fixing 263
   steps 259
   tile level, maintaining 262
tilemaps, Tiled
   hexagonal 253
   isometric 253
   orthogonal 253
timePassed variable 329
toggle menu items
   using 218-221
Tools 12
Totem
   about 292
   goal platform, creating 296
   poly-shaped object, creating 292-294
TouchableBlock class 299, 306
TouchableBlock.m 300
touchableBlocks array 305
TouchableSprite class 332
tutorialBackground.png file 129
two collision_type 309
types, CCDirector
   DisplayLink Director 18
   Mainloop Director 18
   NSTimer Director 18
   ThreadMainLoop Director 18

U

unloadEffect method 273
unlockAchievement method 332
unschedule CCNode method 33

V

verts array 289
visible property 26

W

winCount method 313, 314, 328

X

Xcode
   new project, creating 38, 40

Z

Z-order 24
Z-order property 26
zwoptex
   about 85, 88
   download links 85

Thank you for buying
Cocos2d for iPhone 0.99 Beginner's Guide

About Packt Publishing

Packt, pronounced 'packed', published its first book "*Mastering phpMyAdmin for Effective MySQL Management*" in April 2004 and subsequently continued to specialize in publishing highly focused books on specific technologies and solutions.

Our books and publications share the experiences of your fellow IT professionals in adapting and customizing today's systems, applications, and frameworks. Our solution based books give you the knowledge and power to customize the software and technologies you're using to get the job done. Packt books are more specific and less general than the IT books you have seen in the past. Our unique business model allows us to bring you more focused information, giving you more of what you need to know, and less of what you don't.

Packt is a modern, yet unique publishing company, which focuses on producing quality, cutting-edge books for communities of developers, administrators, and newbies alike. For more information, please visit our website: www.packtpub.com.

About Packt Open Source

In 2010, Packt launched two new brands, Packt Open Source and Packt Enterprise, in order to continue its focus on specialization. This book is part of the Packt Open Source brand, home to books published on software built around Open Source licences, and offering information to anybody from advanced developers to budding web designers. The Open Source brand also runs Packt's Open Source Royalty Scheme, by which Packt gives a royalty to each Open Source project about whose software a book is sold.

Writing for Packt

We welcome all inquiries from people who are interested in authoring. Book proposals should be sent to author@packtpub.com. If your book idea is still at an early stage and you would like to discuss it first before writing a formal book proposal, contact us; one of our commissioning editors will get in touch with you.

We're not just looking for published authors; if you have strong technical skills but no writing experience, our experienced editors can help you develop a writing career, or simply get some additional reward for your expertise.

Unity 3D Game Development by Example Beginner's Guide

ISBN: 978-1-849690-54-6 Paperback: 384 pages

A seat-of-your-pants manual for building fun, groovy little games quickly

1. Build fun games using the free Unity 3D game engine even if you've never coded before
2. Learn how to "skin" projects to make totally different games from the same file – more games, less effort!
3. Deploy your games to the Internet so that your friends and family can play them

Flash Multiplayer Virtual Worlds

ISBN: 978-1-849690-36-2 Paperback: 412 pages

Build immersive, full-featured interactive worlds for games, online communities, and more

1. Build virtual worlds in Flash and enhance them with avatars, non player characters, quests, and by adding social network community
2. Design, present, and integrate the quests to the virtual worlds
3. Create a whiteboard that every connected user can draw on
4. A practical guide filled with real-world examples of building virtual worlds

Please check **www.PacktPub.com** for information on our titles

Blender 3D Architecture, Buildings, and Scenery

ISBN: 978-1-847193-67-4   Paperback: 332 pages

Create photorealistic 3D architectural visualizations of buildings, interiors, and environmental scenery

1. Turn your architectural plans into a model
2. Study modeling, materials, textures, and light basics in Blender
3. Create photo-realistic images in detail
4. Create realistic virtual tours of buildings and scenes

SketchUp 7.1 for Architectural Visualization: Beginner's Guide

ISBN: 978-1-847199-46-1   Paperback: 408 pages

Create stunning photo-realistic and artistic visuals for your SketchUp models

1. Create picture-perfect photo-realistic 3D architectural renders for your SketchUp models
2. Post-process SketchUp output to create digital watercolor and pencil art
3. Follow a professional visualization studio workflow
4. Make the most out of SketchUp with the best free plugins and add-on software to enhance your models

Please check www.PacktPub.com for information on our titles

Python 2.6 Graphics Cookbook

ISBN: 978-1-849513-84-5   Paperback: 260 pages

Over 100 great recipes for creating and animating graphics using Python

1. Create captivating graphics with ease and bring them to life using Python
2. Apply effects to your graphics using powerful Python methods
3. Develop vector as well as raster graphics and combine them to create wonders in the animation world
4. Create interactive GUIs to make your creation of graphics simpler

3D Game Development with Microsoft Silverlight 3: Beginner's Guide

ISBN: 978-1-847198-92-1   Paperback: 452 pages

A practical guide to creating real-time responsive online 3D games in Silverlight 3 using C#, XBAP WPF, XAML, Balder, and Farseer Physics Engine

1. Develop online interactive 3D games and scenes in Microsoft Silverlight 3 and XBAP WPF
2. Integrate Balder 3D engine 1.0, Farseer Physics Engine 2.1, and advanced object-oriented techniques to simplify the game development process
3. Enhance development with animated 3D characters, sounds, music, physics, stages, gauges, and backgrounds

Please check www.PacktPub.com for information on our titles

Blender 3D 2.49 Architecture, Buildings, and Scenery

ISBN: 978-1-849510-48-6 　　　Paperback: 376 pages

Create realistic models of building exteriors and interiors, the surrounding environment, and scenery.

1. Study modeling, materials, textures, and light basics in Blender
2. Learn special tricks and techniques to create walls, floors, roofs, and other specific architectural elements
3. Create realistic virtual tours of buildings and scenes
4. Develop a library of textures, materials, and objects that you can use over and over again

Blender 3D 2.49 Incredible Machines

ISBN: 978-1-847197-46-7 　　　Paperback: 316 pages

Modeling, rendering, and animating realistic machines with Blender 3D

1. Walk through the complete process of building amazing machines
2. Model and create mechanical models and vehicles with detailed designs
3. Add advanced global illumination options to the renders created in Blender 3D using YafaRay and LuxRender
4. Create machines such as a handgun, a steam punk spacecraft, and a transforming robot

Please check www.PacktPub.com for information on our titles

Lightning Source UK Ltd.
Milton Keynes UK
21 February 2011

167919UK00001B/57/P